Living in Cities

LIVING IN CITIES
Urbanism and society in metropolitan Australia

Edited by Ian Burnley and James Forrest

ALLEN & UNWIN   Sydney   London   Boston

GEOGRAPHICAL SOCIETY OF NEW SOUTH WALES

First published 1985
George Allen & Unwin Australia Pty Ltd
8 Napier Street, North Sydney, NSW 2060, Australia

George Allen & Unwin (Publishers) Ltd
Park Lane, Hemel Hempstead, Herts HP2 4TE, England

Allen & Unwin Inc.
Fifty Cross Street, Winchester, Mass 01890, USA

National Library of Australia
Cataloguing in publication entry:

Living in cities.

Includes index.
ISBN 0 86861 502 1.
ISBN 0 86861 494 7 (pbk.).

1. Sociology, Urban — Australia — Addresses, essays, lectures. 2. City
planning — Australia — Addresses, essays, lectures. 3. Urbanization —
Australia — Addresses, essays, lectures. 4. Sydney (N.S.W.). — City
planning — Addresses, essays, lectures. I. Burnley, I.H. (Ian Harry),
1939–   . II. Forrest, James. III. Geographical Society of New South
Wales.

307.7'6'0994

Library of Congress Catalog Card Number: 85-71648

Typeset in 10/11 Baskerville by
Graphicraft Typesetters Limited, Hong Kong
Printed in China by Bright Sun (Shenzhen)
Printing Co. Ltd.

Contents

Part III   Alternative Perspectives and Urban Conflict

Part IV   Migrant Groups in the City

Part V   Our Future Urban Condition

Tables

Figures

Contributors

Graeme Aplin is Senior Lecturer in Geography, School of Earth Sciences, Macquarie University

Mine Batiyel is an Honours graduate in Geography, University of New South Wales

Ian Burnley is Associate Professor in Geography, School of Geography, University of New South Wales

Ailsa Burns is Senior Lecturer in Psychology, School of Behavioural Sciences, Macquarie University

Richard Cardew is Senior Lecturer in the Centre for Environmental and Urban Studies, Macquarie University

Peter Curson is Senior Lecturer in Geography, School of Earth Sciences, Macquarie University

Benno Engels is a research officer in the Department of Geography, University of Sydney

James Forrest is Senior Lecturer in Geography, School of Earth Sciences, Macquarie University

Rob Freestone is Postdoctoral Fellow, Urban Research Unit, Australian National University

Ross Homel is Senior Lecturer in the School of Behavioural Sciences, Macquarie University

Ronald Horvath is Senior Lecturer in the Department of Geography, University of Sydney

Martin Pluss is an Honours graduate, Department of Geography, University of Sydney

Nigel Routh is a research officer in the Community Tenancy Scheme, Housing Commission of New South Wales

Carolyn Stone is Lecturer in the Centre for Environmental and Urban Studies, Macquarie University

Joan Vipond is Senior Research Fellow, Social Welfare Research Centre, University of New South Wales

Preface

Urban development and the business of living in cities have important economic and social dimensions. This volume of essays, written for the Geographical Society of New South Wales, addresses itself to the social dimension of urbanism, just as a companion volume, *Why cities change* (Cardew et al. 1982), also prepared for the Geographical Society, looked at processes of economic change, with particular reference to Sydney. Our aim is to provide up-to-date, specially written chapters on aspects and problems of living and the nature of society in the contemporary Australian metropolis. Although Sydney is the major empirical focus, every effort has been made to provide comparative material from other Australian metropolitan areas, to give a national perspective.

While geographers figure prominently among the authors, political scientists, urban economists and behavioural scientists also contribute to what is in essence a multi-disciplinary book. This represents in part an attempt to emphasise human geography as social science, with its own contribution to make to the broader subject area of urbanism and society. In part too it reflects those who are currently active in areas of concern to this book. The net effect, we trust, is to help improve our understanding of the human condition within Australian cities, and to increase our awareness of the nature, causes and approaches to analysis of social problems in the city.

Of the many who contributed in some way to the preparation of this book, we would like to acknowledge the assistance of the following people in particular. To Mrs Pam Gartung for her persistence in typing most of the manuscripts into the word processor, and to Mrs Jane Price for doing the same for those chapters contributed by the members of the Centre for Environmental and Urban Studies at Macquarie University, our grateful thanks. As also to Kevin Maynard, School of Geography, University of New South Wales, and to cartographic staff of the School of Earth Sciences, Macquarie University. We further acknowledge the authors themselves, and the value of their contributions as part of a co-operative venture among members of the three

Sydney metropolitan universities. We acknowledge too the assistance and support of the Geographical Society of New South Wales, without whose support this book would not have been possible.

1   Themes and issues

JAMES FORREST AND IAN BURNLEY

Urbanism is about living in cities; it represents a way of life affecting the majority of people in countries of the modernised, industrialised and urbanised western world. Such a way of life is certainly of great relevance to Australians, 70 per cent of whom in 1976 were living in cities of 100 000 or more (Burnley, 1980a). Among the three key features mentioned by Wirth (1938) in introducing his concept of urbanism as a way of life — size, density and social heterogeneity — the last, social heterogeneity, is of greatest relevance here. With increasing division of labour, separation of home from work and also separation of the economic and social roles of the family, came increasing differentiation among individuals. This gave rise to diverse occupational structures, subcultures and ideological subgroups, and social area segregation.

Urbanism was seen to represent a breakdown of community. Arguably however, communities have not entirely disappeared with metropolitan growth, as evidenced, for instance, in Pahl's (1968) concept of 'urban villages' (see also Johnston, 1979a). Urban living was also characterised as increasingly depersonalised, in response to which Wirth saw a need for the development of formal social controls, in part to control undue exploitation. In fact, new control systems are emerging, according to Bell (1973), no longer primarily economic, reflecting the heyday of *laissez-faire* industrial capitalism which so concerned Wirth, but political, manifested in the subordination of the economic order to the political in the 'post-industrial society'.

It is not the task of this volume to enter into the debate on the rural and the urban, dichotomy or continuum, but rather to investigate and highlight certain aspects of living in major urban centres in Australia. As Smith (1980:27) points out, as an entity, the metropolitan region has major implications for social control, community organisation and social planning. The perspective is broadly geographic, but within the context of social geography as social science (Johnston, 1974). It is also conceptually pluralistic, not just because the essays are written by a number of authors, but because there *are* different approaches to an understanding of urbanism and society in metropolitan Australia. In part of course this reflects the presence of major schools of thought within human geography and, more particularly, social geography.

Social geography and urban society

In recent explorations into the nature and purpose of social geography, Jackson and Smith (1984) show a clear tendency for research to follow intellectual trends within human geography (Johnston, 1983) and developments in the social sciences generally (Agnew and Duncan, (1981). Several schools of development were identified (Jackson and Smith, 1984:158–85).

1   *The positivist (or scientific) tradition* in social geography, largely deriving from the 'spatial sociology' approach of the pre–mid–1960s (Peach, 1975), and going right back to the Chicago school of human ecology of which Park's *The Urban Community* (1926) as a spatial pattern and moral order was the major precursor. This was a tradition which emphasised human geography as spatial science, employing spatial statistics to deal with a range of problems associated with the description of spatial patterns and connectivities. Within this tradition (Aplin, ch. 3), social area analysis developed as a major strand concerned generally with the social geography of the city. Early concern with links between societal structure and residential patterns through extensions of social area analysis into the considerable factorial ecology literature broadened into examination of processes underlying the patterns (Herbert and Johnston, 1976:vii–x), their basic point being that (pp. 2–3) the spatial ordering of behaviour can be explained, at least in part, in terms of its interdependence with order in the structuring of society.

2   *The behavioural tradition* which, methodologically at least, was part of the positivist tradition. As Eyles (1978) argued, behavioural geographers highlighted the nature of space as an attribute of *individual* behaviour, both overt (actual) and covert (spatial cognition and mental maps), at the expense of looking at space as a constraint that *determines* aspects of behaviour. Their major contribution lay in attempts to portray and explain elements of individual behaviour as a means to the understanding of human behaviour in the aggregate. Burnley and Routh (ch. 15) are in this tradition.

3   *The humanist tradition*, defined broadly to include phenomenological and experiential approaches to social geography. This is a perspec-

tive which seeks to provide an empathetic understanding of a particular environment from the viewpoint of the subjects themselves. This is not a field with many adherents in the contemporary Australian geographic literature (though see Johnson, 1983). Although cast partly in the behavioural mould, Homel and Burns (ch. 8) embody important elements of this experiential approach.

4   *The structuralist (radical-Marxist) tradition* in one form is the study of spatial forms as an outcome of underlying social, economic and political structures inherent in the capitalist mode of production. A feature of this mode is seen to be forever the search for surplus value, as argued by Horvath and Engels (ch. 11). Another significant feature relates to the social structure of capitalism, comprising two major classes, the capitalists who own the means of production, and the workers (employees) who own only their own labour power. While in advanced stages of capitalism such a polarisation is an oversimplification mitigated by the sheer complexity of society, the major result is a society built on inequality which is seen to operate, in particular through the housing market (cf. Berry, 1983), to produce a structurally derived ranking of socio-economic status areas within cities. But as Johnston (1979a:161) points out, not all radical contributions are overtly Marxist. Eyles (1974), for example, argues for a greater emphasis on study of conflict which is endemic to social life. This viewpoint perceives two main models of modern western society, one based on consensus, on co-operation and reciprocity and accepted norms of behaviour, the other on conflict and sectional interests as the basis of social life. Conflict and power are the basic elements of the conflict model, although much of contemporary social geography is seen to emphasise the functional at the expense of the disruptive in society. These positions are explored in part in Forrest (ch. 13).

Jackson and Smith (1984:183–84) make two points, however, about the structuralist approach. One is a general tendency to view segregation within cities as an end point of economic relations, rather than a starting point for social analysis (Peach, 1981) which is clearly the view adopted by Forrest (chs 6–7). The other is Harvey's (1982) allusion to the problem of relating abstractly formulated theory and concretely researched history, which is also treated by Horvath and Engels (ch. 11) and contributed to by Pluss (ch. 4).

But to return briefly to the concept of social geography as concerned basically only with outcome or effect (Jackson and Smith, 1984:190–92). Saunders (1981:9) asserts that the social significance of space, and hence the ability of social geography to contribute to analyses of the social organisation of space, is very limited. This is to see social geography in a similar vein to spatial sociology within the wider field of urban sociology, with an explanatory potential not only highly restricted but inconsistent with the central concerns of contemporary urban sociology itself. However, other sociologists like Lyman and Scott (1967) writing on the concept of territoriality, and Urry (1981) on interactions between space and class, argue in the opposite direction, while a geographer, Kirby (1982) provides specific examples of contexts wherein spatial concerns are essential to political and economic conflicts. And from other work by Jones and Kirby (1982) derives a central view taken in this book of a much more positive contribution of social geography: of social processes *operating through a spatial medium* to produce social outcomes. Spatial context is seen here as an integral part of factors acting to produce our urban condition, as evidenced by Homel and Burns (ch. 8).

Finally, reference must be made to the development, dating from the mid-1970s, of a growing polarisation of views among human geographers (Johnston, 1983:168). Some, advocating a greater commitment to the investigation of current social problems, looked to the provision of information and procedures for their amelioration and solution, but within the existing (capitalist) social framework (e.g. Smith, 1977; Stimson, 1982). Others advocated more radical appraisals of the role of human geography, based largely on socialist rather than capitalist ideologies (e.g. Gibson and Horvath, 1983a; 1983b).

Our urban condition

Epitomising the new geography and public policy emphasis, the liberal viewpoint among human geographers combined a belief in democratic socialism with a strong commitment to legislative action to alleviate social ills (Bullock, 1977:347). Parallelling work in the social indicators movement generally, their aim was to identify condition or levels of well-being as an input to social policy formulation (for a review of Australian work in this field see Stimson, 1982:168–95). For many of these researchers, urbanism was not only a way of life but also a system of resource allocation leading (under the capitalist mode of production according to the Marxists) to relative deprivation for some people and relative advantage for others. Thus in an edited volume looking in some detail at equity in the Australian city (Troy, 1981), a series of examples covering a variety of topic areas such as public transport, medical services and housing concluded that significant inequalities result from the way facilities and services are provided, and that most of these inequalities are inequitable (i.e. contribute to social disadvantage). The chapters by Vipond (ch. 9) and Burnley and Batiyel (ch. 10) contribute to this debate.

Of overriding concern, however, is Pahl's (1970) view that urban resources and facilities will always be scarce, and that the struggle to secure a share of that limited base makes conflict inevitable. Of critical importance, then, is the study of who controls or manipulates the resource. This is to focus attention somewhat narrowly, however, according to Jackson and Smith (1984:120), on relationships between manager and managed. Lambert et al. (1978) drew attention to the mediating role played by managers and bureaucrats as *arbiters*.

Parallel themes occur in urban sociology. Thus Szelenyi (1977, quoted in Sandercock and Berry, 1983:x) refers to the phase of social democrat concern with social inequality and the role of urban planning in the allocation of urban resources, and a current phase of concern with class analysis, the structural sources of social inequalities, and the nature and changing role of planning and state intervention in the urban system. As in social geography, part of the latter area of concern is expressed from a Marxist viewpoint; part of it is radical without being overtly Marxist, aiming to produce a political economy of space: who gets what (from the urban economy and planning system), why (Sandercock and Berry, 1983:x), to which social geographers would add the important qualification, and *where?* It is consistent with the pluralist view adopted in this volume, however, to point out that any choice among approaches or perspectives within social geography is not one among competing *theories*, but simply among competing *models* of society and circumstance, 'each containing its own built-in recommendations as to the proper way to understand and pronounce judgment upon the forms and variety of structural inequality ...' (Parkin, 1979:115). Nowhere in this volume is this point more clearly brought out than in the contrasting arguments of Horvath and Engels (ch. 11) and Cardew (ch. 12).

The role of the state

Sandercock and Berry (1983:xi) make the point that for some years past, members of the planning profession employed by planning authorities at local government level have been seen in a succession of radical texts as mere agents of capital. Like Lambert et al. (1978), they prefer the wider focus inherent in the role of the planner as bureaucrat, as arbiter between the logic of capitalism (the quest for surplus value and the ideology of private property) and the logic of socialism (social consumption and the ideology of social need). The difference between these two viewpoints involves two rather different perspectives on state actions (Johnston, 1982:22–26; for a recent review of Marxist and Weberian [liberal] traditions of social and political analysis, see Head, 1984):

1   A *pluralist* perspective adopting a state-as-arbiter position wherein (Saunders, 1980:150):

> the state is neutral in its functions and independent of any particular class interests. The state is seen as a set of political institutions standing outside civil society, and it is this position of externality and superiority which enables it to regulate and mediate the conflicts within civil society.

Hence of course the state bureaucrat or public authority planner in the arbiter role.

2   A *managerialist* perspective, focusing on decisions made by state employees. This is a perspective which involves two relevant considerations. One is the degree of freedom of action accorded to planners as bureaucrats within constraints imposed by the mode of production and political decisions at a governmental policy level. The other is an overriding constraint, an 'instrumentalist' viewpoint (Johnston, 1982:19–20) which sees the state as a body outside the capitalist mode and yet a fundamental element in a class society, 'serving the interests of the controlling class in society rather than the interests of society as a whole because it serves and supports [and gives legitimacy to] the basic capitalist institutions' (Campbell, 1981:26). So while recognising the role of the planner–bureaucrat as decision maker, it is unlikely that such a person can affect more than the detail of the control and allocation of resources. From the viewpoint of Marx's theory of political economy — historical materialism — economic forces, the capitalist mode of production, are of overwhelming importance. Any form of state action, therefore, is a manipulation of the capitalist system, a manipulation which may have an influence on the relative prosperity of certain people or places but not, ultimately, on the capitalist mode of production itself (Johnston, 1982:25–26).

In this volume, these general points are brought out in the early chapter by Freestone (ch. 2), which is concerned to identify and, largely through a physical environmental planning, 'garden city' approach, correct deficiencies in aspects of the nineteenth-century urban condition. They are highlighted again at the end of the volume in the discussions by Stone, first in terms of the development of planning policies aimed to alleviate certain elements in our later twentieth-century urban condition (ch. 16), and also in more general considerations affecting the future of large metropolitan centres like Sydney (ch. 17).

The structure of the book

The overall structure of this book is pitched at two levels, a structure within a structure. The enveloping structure involves themes and issues within social geography. Consistent with the pluralist viewpoint adopted by the editors in assembling this volume, the essays by individual authors reflect the variety of traditions of approach and interest in their subject areas. They range from the historical to the futuristic, from scientific positivist and neoclassical economic to radical-Marxist perspectives. And within that enveloping, thematic structure there is another, internal coherence developed around the sectional organisation of individual chapters. What is presented here largely reflects current work in the field of social geography by Australian geographers and other 'spatial' social scientists.

In the first section, colonial cities and their condition, Freestone looks at the garden city movement in nineteenth-century Australia as an important source of reform of more physical planning aspects of the urban condition, while Aplin, spanning the same period, looks at the socio-spatial structuring of metropolitan Australia in its pre-industrial and mercantilist or early capitalist phase. In his chapter on Strathfield, Pluss attempts to explain the evolution of one elite residential area, and uses a behavioural approach to trace its development in the western suburbs of nineteenth-century Sydney. Curson then looks at the differential area impact of the Sydney plague epidemic of 1902 as a reflection of the inequalities — the living conditions of Sydney's inner city poor — earlier brought out by Aplin.

The second section deals with contemporary social area differentiation and equity. First of all, Forrest challenges the often implicit assumptions of homogeneity of social areas in our metropolitan areas by looking at the *mix* of types of people present, and discusses the implications of his findings for area approaches to social and community planning. But not all Australians live in the metropolitan areas, and in his second contribution Forrest looks at community profiles of social areas in smaller towns, one within Sydney's commuter zone, one a mining and manufacturing centre which is functionally part of Sydney's urban field, and a third which is a market and service centre in the southwest of New South Wales. Then, focusing on a range of social areas within Sydney, Homel and Burns analyse children's experiences of their residential environments, looking especially at the impact of spatially specific as well as general (aspatial) aspects of a variety of urban environmental situations. In her chapter on unemployment, Vipond returns to the inequality theme introduced by Curson, looking particularly at relationships between unemployment rates and urban structure in Sydney, Melbourne and Adelaide. The last chapter in this section, by Burnley and Batiyel, analyses ischaemic heart disease mortality for two recent periods to see if regional and occupational differences and trends which were apparent during the 1970s occurred also at the intra-urban level.

Alternative perspectives on urban form and development, and aspects of conflict situations are examined in the next section. Adopting a radical-Marxist viewpoint, Horvath and Engels relate aspects of current social, economic and spatial restructuring of Australian cities to the broader restructuring taking place within the capitalist world as a result of the present economic crisis. Cardew, however, focusing on a reinterpretation of urban residential property market trends over the past decade, takes a neoclassical economic stance, in association with aspects of social and demographic change, to develop a 'demand pull' explanation of current trends. Forrest then takes up the overall theme of this section, looking at conflict in the city, at the range of conflict generating forces, the levels at which these forces operate, and at patterns of conflict within the city.

Returning then to the experience and location of social groups within metropolitan Australia, the next section focuses on migrant groups in the city. Burnley assesses the impacts of immigration on the social geography of our cities, casting his discussion in the context of migration processes whereby settlement took place, and also the role of state policies in fostering immigration and resettlement. Looking then at one particular and unique group within our 'migrant' structure, the Australian Aboriginal, Burnley and Routh seek to examine aspects of the urbanisation process as they affect this group: the extent of common processes at work which tend spatially to concentrate these people or to constrain opportunities and adjustment of Aboriginal newcomers to the city.

In the final section, our future urban condition, the books turns as it were full cycle, from Freestone's original discussion of planning to alleviate aspects of our urban condition in nineteenth-century Australia, to discussion of present problems and future prospects for living in metropolitan Australia. In her first contribution, Stone points to urban sprawl and the cult-of-the-quarter-acre, which till now has permeated most people's ideal of suburban living, as universally condemned by the experts as unplanned, inefficient and economically wasteful. Counter trends, towards urban consolidation, are examined against a background that rarely have attempts to contain sprawl been successful, and where they have, resultant benefits and costs have been usually regressive. Taking a broader view, Stone next points to the decline from favour of most older forms of metropolitan planning in the light of its failure to cope with economic and social change, suggesting that the form metropolitan planning takes in the future, and the functions it needs to fulfil, need to be different from those of the past. Then finally in this section, Burnley and Forrest permit themselves some crystal ball gazing into other aspects of the future of metropolitan and urban Australia.

Part I

Colonial Cities and their Condition

2 The conditions of the cities and the response: early garden city concepts and practice

ROBERT FREESTONE

This chapter looks at urbanisation, urban reform and planning in the nineteenth century and early 1900s as a background to, and significant influence upon, the garden city ideal in Australia.

The Australian city: commercial, suburban, private

Urbanisation and urban morphology

The nineteenth century was the major era of town formation. Significant levels of urbanisation in general, and metropolitanisation in particular, were evident by the 1850s. Both increased markedly in the 1880s; by 1891 half the population could be classed as urban; one third as metropolitan. The coastal capitals — Sydney (founded 1788), Hobart (1803), Brisbane (1825), Perth (1829), Melbourne (1835) and Adelaide (1837) — were unchallenged as the largest settlements (Table 2.1).

Table 2.1   Australian capital city populations, 1891–1933

	1891	1901	1911	1921	1933
Sydney	400 (35)	496 (37)	630 (38)	899 (43)	1235 (48)
Melbourne	473 (41)	478 (40)	589 (45)	766 (50)	992 (55)
Brisbane	94 (24)	119 (24)	139 (24)	210 (28)	300 (32)
Adelaide	117 (37)	141 (39)	190 (46)	255 (52)	313 (54)
Perth	16 (32)	61 (33)	100 (38)	155 (47)	207 (47)
Hobart	33 (22)	35 (20)	40 (21)	52 (25)	60 (27)
Canberra	—	—	—	3	7 (82)

Population in thousands (% of colonial, state or territory population)

13

The ground plan of urban Australia was rectilinear. The majority of government and private towns (or speculative settlements) exhibited a standard gridiron or 'chessboard' morphology. This design was quickly laid out, satisfied the military mind and aesthetic tastes of the early nineteenth century, and was a traditional framework for land speculation because it maximised the uncertainty of possible uses (Mumford, 1961; Jeans, 1965). An open space reservation surrounded most surveyed townships but, except in the case of parkland towns (see below), it was generally regarded as a holding belt for town extension. The first standard 'town planning' regulations were issued in 1829 for New South Wales. For the most part, their legacy was the same basic grid of wide streets and ten chain square blocks regardless of ridges, swamps, or other considerations. Planning was purely mechanical: Robert Hoddle laid out central Melbourne in a few hours one day in March 1837. An associate later recalled: 'I fancy there was a plan . . . cut and dried, and they just made it fit Melbourne, or any other place — simply a matter of blocks being cut out' (Russell, 1885). Melbourne, like all the capitals, soon outgrew its original shell, but the same grid was adopted with 'monotonous fidelity' in the suburbs (Bolton, 1981).

Suburbanisation, suburban development and the state

Australian settlement has characteristically straggled out over the countryside. Sydney extended further than any city in Britain or the US, with the exception of Chicago. And Melbourne was larger than Sydney (Weber, 1963:139). The most dramatic change came after 1860 with a revolution in transport progressively undoing the shackles of 'the walking city'. Railway construction became an important determinant of the timing, pace and direction of residential development. A corollary of Australian sprawl was 'primitive commercial, industrial and social equipment' (Butlin, 1964). Government investment was modest in what Szelenyi (1981:588) terms 'collectively used urban nonproductive infrastructure', i.e. parks and community facilities. Colonial political economy dictated that state expenditure be geared to productive infrastructure like railways. In fact the primary function of the first suburban railways was to link harbours and hinterlands; journey-to-work was an incidental consideration.

The state neglected the cities in other ways. No colonial legislature was especially interested in urban questions. Limited public health and building regulations were grudgingly enacted. The powers of the Commonwealth Government created in 1901 related to national issues like defence, trade and communications; there was no mandate for town planning or housing provision except to meet the direct needs of government. The minutiae of urban administration thus devolved to local authorities which arrived with the creation of a Perth Town Trust in 1838. Local government was a statutory creation of colonial authorities. It remains the weakest tier in the federal system, with fewer resources and responsibilities than anywhere in the western world (Parkin, 1982:61).

Standards of living: housing and home ownership

An outstanding feature of urban life even before the advent of the garden city was the single-storey, single family house with garden. The origin and persistence of the detached bungalow as the dominant dwelling type has several explanations. Historically, the dependent mercantile economy of the nineteenth century (Rowland, 1977) meant an absence of large-scale industrial housing. Culturally, the English country cottage was the model dwelling and if immigrants could not be yeoman farmers then they could at least tend suburban gardens. Technically, two-storey construction was inhibited by primitive building technology in the early years while the possibilities of horizontal expansion could make it superfluous. Financially, houses were an important component of private domestic investment (Boyd, 1978). In the 1870s and 1880s single-storey row houses and two-storey terraces challenged the hegemony of the detached cottage on increasingly valuable land in inner areas. However, the terrace boom had an uneven national impact. Whole suburbs were redeveloped in Melbourne and Sydney; Adelaide's transformation was more patchy; while terraces were scarcely known in Brisbane and Perth.

Most Australians desired not only to live in detached houses but to own them. The myth of home ownership, shaped partly by commercial interests and the state, was strong. 'Not to have your own home is unpatriotic', ruled the *Australian Financial Gazette* in 1890. Owner-occupation was not an unrealistic aspiration. Australian cities did not have dramatic depths of poverty except in some pockets of run-down slum housing adjacent to Sydney's and Melbourne's central business district (see Curson, ch. 5). The combination of rich natural resources, low population, productive rural industry, and organised labour, gave most Australians a relatively high standard of living. However, the cost of acquiring a house with garden was still prohibitive for many workers (Mayne, 1981).

By the 1911 census, 50 per cent of Australian householders were owners or purchasers, a figure not matched in Britain for another six decades. And to this major group of homeowners a distinctive culture was ascribed. Thus Eggleston (1932:331) cast the independent Australian as a 'self contained man', and:

... in the highly developed suburbs of an Australian city, with good accommodation, a nice garden, a back yard, vegetables in his plot and fowls in his shed, a fence against intrusion, he has probably reached a higher pitch of development than anywhere else.

Images of the garden city idea in social thought

A co-operative, decentralised society?

Many of the intellectual currents which informed Ebenezer Howard's garden city argument were replicated in Australia. *Looking Backward*, for example, enjoyed a prodigious circulation, and became a bible of the fledgling labour movement. Many of the radical and reformist works which made up Howard's reading list were available in Australia, and influenced many utopian settlements mooted, and established, in the 1880s and 1890s. In theory, two such schemes which most clearly foreshadowed elements of the garden city idea were those of Horace Tucker and, to a lesser extent, William Lane. Tucker's purpose was to settle persons of limited means in self-contained co-operative communities. Lane, a leader of the Queensland labour movement, was a utopian socialist who gradually developed the concept of a 'co-operative commune' outside conventional society, which would be a genuinely democratic and co-operating community of 1000 people.

Both schemes diverged from the garden city in basic ways, including their rural emphasis and political organisation. But there were themes later echoed in Ebenezer Howard's *To-morrow*: co-operation, decentralisation, the path to a new civilisation, democracy, *de novo* community building, belief in the force of example. And the spatial order of Tucker's system clearly foreshadows Howard's 'social cities' (Powell, 1978:158–159). Tucker's Village Settlement Association established seven settlements in Victoria, though the largest attracted only 50 families from the ranks of Melbourne's poor. By the turn of the century, most had collapsed or moved away from their original purpose. Lack of capital, limited farming expertise, poor land, management conflicts, a decline of interest in communalism, and an upturn in city employment opportunities were common reasons for failure.

A native new town movement?

Anti-metropolitanism thrived throughout the nineteenth century. But recognition of the 'centralisation curse' never boiled over into demands to build new, smaller, *urban* communities. Anti-urbanism from *within* the cities lacked virulence and innovation (Aitkin, 1972:ch. 1). The imbalance between town and country might be lamented by city-based interests, but that was all. Further, there was an influential rival culture of 'urban boosterism': by the 1880s metropolitanism was akin to nationalism (Glynn, 1970:74). And finally, there was a growing perception that, far from being an unmitigated evil, metropolitanisation was the vehicle for social and economic advancement.

In the nineteenth century new cities were discussed primarily as vehicles of urban reform. In this vein the *Australasian Builder and Contractors' News* reprinted Richardson's prospectus for 'Hygeia' as 'A model city' in February 1889. Talk of a new federal capital evoked similar sentiments. But the federal capital idea was a product of *centralisation*, a symbol of nationhood. This was a long way from the accent on voluntarism and devolution of power in the garden city. Yet there were similarities between the two. The federal capital was to be a new city beyond the Dividing Range; it was to have an agricultural backdrop; it was seen as a laboratory for social reforms; and it was to be built on land held in public ownership. There was no agitation, however, to extend these various features to other new communities.

Planned industrial decentralisation

The garden *village* was the pioneering, strand of the garden city movement. Bournville and Port Sunlight were 'garden cities in miniature' (Howard, 1911:669). Was there a nineteenth-century ancestry to the garden village in Australia in the form of planned industrial towns or suburbs? Company housing was more significant than commonly thought (Wise, 1859:92). As in other countries, it was a basic form of welfare capitalism dating from the early nineteenth century although by the late 1880s it was often becoming but one element in a broader array of welfare benefits. Most 'tied' housing schemes in the manufacturing and mining sectors were on a modest scale. Employee participation was not universal, with 'staff' ranking above 'the men'. Only one project hinted at greater possibilities.

Kooringa (1846) was developed by the South Australian Mining Association at its 'monster' copper mine at Burra Creek. By 1850 the company had erected 400 cottages and instituted various health and insurance schemes. Its most interesting attempt at civic design was Paxton Square (1852), a housing group partly enclosing an internal park. The whole exercise at Burra has been described as 'an example of enlightened community planning' comparable to Port Sunlight (Ward, 1969:669).

The Adelaide principle?

Howard dropped the reference to 'New Australia' from *Garden cities of to-morrow* but in a chapter on 'Social cities' he added an Australian scheme which he did admire. He chose Col. William Light's plan for Adelaide (1837) to illustrate the practicality of his 'correct principle of a city's growth':

> The city is built up. How does it grow? It grows by leaping over the "Park Lands" and establishing North Adelaide. And this is the principle which it is intended to follow, but improve upon in Garden City. (Howard, 1902:140)

What of the impact of the Adelaide plan elsewhere in Australia before the early 1900s? The South Australian 'parkland town' was the most direct legacy, their recurring features a central core of town lands, a surrounding belt of parkland and a circumferential zone of suburban lands. Over half the government towns in South Australia were designed with encircling parkland; the plan for Alawoona (Figure 2.1) is a typical example. The parkland town diffused into western Victoria

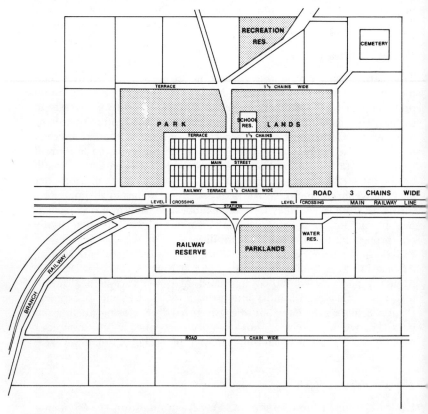

Figure 2.1   Typical parkland town: Alawoona

but had little impact elsewhere. Adelaide did begin to influence conceptions of ideal metropolitan form and growth towards the turn of the century. However, even the South Australian capital was not the model city it seemed. A combination of rapid growth and inadequate public health safeguards made the city one of the less salubrious urban environments of the 1880s (Stevenson, 1979).

Thus the garden city in its purest form stood little chance of success in Australia. Indeed, Australia began to dilute it when Howard omitted his town cluster diagram from the 1902 edition of his book and included Adelaide to illustrate his argument.

Garden city themes and planning schemata

Urban reform

The conjunction of capitalist economy, marked urbanisation, and limited development controls brought darker aspects to the cities of the 'land of promise'. *Fin-de-siecle* urban reform tended to be fragmented into relatively narrow milieux: sewerage and drainage; water supply; pollution; location of noxious trades; mass transit; overhaul of local government; civic beautification; lighting and sealing of streets; provision of playgrounds; eradication of slums. Reform activity was dominated by professionals and the middle classes. It lacked revolutionary connotations and concentrated on ameliorating symptoms rather than eradicating deeper social causes. In housing and related areas, the idea that poor surroundings *per se* were the root of ill-health, immorality and discontent, appeared repeatedly in government reports.

The complexion of most urban reform activity, like social reform generally, was that of middle-of-the-road consensus (Mayer, 1954). British ideas and legislation were also powerful precedents in many fields, although equivalent Australian initiatives usually lagged. For example, the Melbourne and Metropolitan Board of Works (1890), created after a Royal Commission found the city 'uncleanly and untidy', was modelled on the London board even after the latter 'was being contemptuously abolished' (Austin, 1965:77). Finally, improvements were effected which substantiate the years around the turn of the century as a general age of reform. Roberts (1978) estimates that thousands of lives were saved in Sydney between 1895 and 1905 by basic sanitary reforms.

Improving the residential environment

Laissez-faire in the cities was inevitably accompanied by slums. As early as 1851 the *Sydney Morning Herald* ran a series damning 'the sanitary state' of the city. In 1900, the deplorable living conditions of many Sydneysiders were once again brought to official and wider public notice by an outbreak of bubonic plague (Curson, ch. 5).

Housing reformers saw the terrace as 'an abomination, a harbinger of disease, an exercise in unbridled vulgarity, a blight on the landscape' (Kelly, 1978a:97). As an alternative, some supported 'flatted houses' for the working class, but the single family bungalow was the cherished form. In Sydney in the 1880s both the conservative *Herald*, the *Bulletin*, and later the *Daily Telegraph* (23 Jan. 1905:5) suggested that 'the wider the area upon which a city's inhabitants dwell, the better it is for their health and home comfort'.

At this stage, however, no coherent, positive policy was agreed upon whereby decent housing, and especially suburban cottages, could be brought within reach of everyone. The main consensus was the need for stricter building regulations on private enterprise and cheaper transport to the outer suburbs. The idea of public housing was too radical for most nineteenth-century reformers although municipal housing was mooted in the early 1900s, mainly because of the rise of labour as a political force. J D Fitzgerald, a future garden city advocate was lobbying for housing powers on behalf of the Sydney City Council as early as 1902 (Larcombe, 1978:18).

State governments by the early 1900s were more enthusiastic about extending home ownership than direct building intervention. Starting with the Queensland Workers' Dwellings Act 1909, they became involved in facilitating home purchase via the *credit foncier* loan system. This was the first literal expression by the state of the widely-held conviction that owner-occupation was a bulwark against social unrest (Kemeny, 1977:48–49). The need to reform the pattern and process of subdivision was the one nineteenth-century issue which led most directly to the garden city concerns of the twentieth. Economic, sanitary, and aesthetic reasons were cited by the progressive architects, surveyors and local government officials who tended to dominate discussion. Drainage considerations were frequently neglected; profit dictated provision of little or no open space and the division of land tracts into the maximum number of allotments; resubdivisions could mean even smaller plots and narrow lanes. A major theme from that time was the idea of a statutory minimum allotment size.

The legislative achievements of subdivision reformers lay in the strengthening of powers available to local government. The 1880s produced perhaps the only two pieces of special legislation in the nineteenth century. The New South Wales Width of Streets and Lanes Act 1881 stipulated 66 and 22 feet as the minimum widths of streets and lanes respectively. The Queensland Undue Subdivision of Land Prevention Act 1885 embodied similar standards and made 16 perches (about one-eighth of an acre) the minimum block size. A national wave of local government legislation early in the new century saw many new council powers over standards of street and house construction.

Emergence of modern planning thought

Recognition of the need for a more comprehensive approach to planning and development was perhaps first evident in the 1880s. Specific issues like urban landscaping, provision for public recreation, landuse zoning, model dwellings and advanced subdivision ideas were confidently integrated in generalised statements of the ideal urban environment. The 1880s also saw the formation of generalist reform bodies, prototypes of the town planning associations.

A classic paper on 'Study on unity of design in planning new towns and new suburbs' was read before the Victorian Institute of Surveyors by John Keily in September 1889. The author complained that the conventional approach to town extension lacked any conception of 'a harmonious whole'. His main premise was that development should proceed in accordance with 'some pre-existing design'. The most original suggestion was that every new community should have 'a distinct character . . . its own central features, its own open spaces, and its own public reserves'.

Attracting more interest was architect John Sulman's 'The laying out of towns', delivered at the Melbourne meeting of the Australasian Association for the Advancement of Science in January 1890. Sulman argued for a more rational, efficient, aesthetic, and closely supervised approach to design under five main headings. Proper layout, he contended, began with the location of a new settlement. He favoured the 'spider's web' model as an effective town pattern, one offering potential for decoration. Related possibilities were curved streets, tree planting, and parkland.

The Science Association set up a research committee which later endorsed Sulman's conclusions. 'The laying out of towns' can be seen as an important step in the transition of planning away from rudimentary colonial notions. It foreshadows the concerns and flavour of planning thought in the early twentieth century: pragmatic rather than utopian; preoccupied with subdivision and traffic; ready to equate town with suburban planning; and alive to the economic and career benefits of skilled design. The paper also represented an early expression of ideas later identified with the garden city.

Few definite federal city plans were produced in the early 1900s. The surveyor George Knibbs, disappointed at the rather bland outcome of the Melbourne congress on the proposed federal capital, devised his own formidable 'theory of city design' later in the year but stopped short of producing an actual sketch combining his various ideas (Knibbs, 1901). Interest in the planning of the federal capital receded from about 1903 as the 'battle of the sites' raged. It began to revive with designation of the Yass-Canberra district in 1908 and the approach of the international design competition which was officially announced in 1911.

On metropolitan form

The overall size, shape and structure of cities had received little attention before the early 1900s. The level of debate on the planning of the federal city provides one illustration. Around the turn of the century there was virtually no discussion about 'processes of city growth' and the development of 'city regions', let alone consideration of 'integrated systems of new towns'. The notion of breaking up the metropolis into separate cells by broad swathes of parkland, however, surfaced as early as 1857 in a paper on 'Sanitary reform of towns and cities' read before the Philosophical Society of New South Wales by William Bland. At the top of a hierarchy of parks and reserves, he envisaged an unbroken 'chain of open spaces' ventilating Sydney with the 'purest attainable air'. The same idea was captured in a suggestion made at the 1901 planning congress that 'farming and other open spaces should be arranged to break up the suburban quarters' (Luffman, 1901:44). Unwin's recommendations in *Town planning in Practice* were implicitly recognised in the campaign by the Melbourne-based National Parks Association (1908) for foliage 'to mitigate the heat, to limit the dust evil, and to provide beautiful and restful breaks in the mass of dwellings, warehouses and factories'.

Adelaide and the parkland towns had a significant influence on this line of thinking. The concept of a circumferential green belt was again aired in 1901, the President of the Royal Victorian Institute of Architects suggesting that the federal capital as a model twentieth-century city should be 'surrounded with woods, parks, and recreation grounds' (Inskip, 1901:31). The more advanced notion of cellular growth, implicit in the plan of Adelaide and Howard's 'correct principle' diagram of 1902, was prefigured in the seminal planning essays of Keily and Sulman. The spatial model advocated by Keily was a town centre, four square miles in area, encircled by separate suburbs, half the size. Sulman explicitly referred to the relevance of the Adelaide principle in coping with suburban sprawl.

The ideal urban environment: model suburbs

The early history of attempts to actually create ideal environments is dominated by the model suburb, or, more accurately, the model subdivision. This ultimately reflected the quantitative importance of suburbanisation: 'Australia is the small house', wrote Robin Boyd; it is the suburb, says Stretton (1970). The following discussion of model suburbs concentrates on the Sydney experience from the 1870s to the early 1900s.

The nineteenth century

The first model suburbs had several interrelated characteristics. They were a small element of the residential property market. The responsibility of 'developers' typically ended with the sale of land. They were spatial designs offering a sense of unity and amenity that conventional grids did not. The trademarks included large allotments, wide streets, open space, street trees, and recommended use zonings and building covenants. But they were also commercial enterprises and thus as much a part of the speculative subdivision process as conventional undertakings (Searle, 1971:252).

The decade from the mid-1870s saw some of the first notable attempts to break away from conventional suburban development in Sydney. The western suburbs were favoured, especially the Ashfield-Strathfield axis, because the elevation was seen to afford 'health giving airs' and the railway to Parramatta afforded accessibility (see Pluss, ch. 4). Several examples of model suburbs to the mid-1880s may be noted. The Parade (1877) at 'Burwood Heights' (now Enfield), was a small subdivision and brainchild of Richard Wynne whose previous efforts at housing reform in the inner city had been unsuccessful. Annandale (1878) was designed by F H Reuss Jr for John Young's Sydney Freehold Land, Building and Investment Co. Large lots, wide streets, a waterfront crescent, no back lanes, and small reserves were features of the original plan. The Company *Prospectus* also stated the intention of designating public building sites and preventing an 'unpleasant admixture of various and unsuitable structures' (Roberts, 1970). St John's Wood (1880) at Auburn, had small parks to preclude 'the possibility of the neighbourhood becoming overcrowded'. Campsie Park (1885) was developed by the Anglo-Australian Investment, Finance and Land Company Ltd.

Harcourt (1888), also at Campsie, was one of a number of developments given a fillip by the Width of Streets and Lanes Act, noted earlier. A project of William Phillips and Co., it has been described previously as a significant 'forerunner of the garden city concept' (Larcombe, 1979). There were features making it an important step towards the modern garden subdivision: the distinction between major and minor streets; reservation of commercial sites; primitive development controls, ensuring cash bonuses to builders of quality detached dwellings within a specified period; and an extensive landscaping program. It had 'all the elements of a complete township'. These features may have spoken 'unmistakably of health, solidity and *bona fides*' but the ground plan was the traditional rectangular grid with symmetrical vistas. Harcourt was killed by the depression of the 1890s. So too were other planned estates, including the boldest model suburb project of the nineteenth century and the most unequivocal signpost to the garden suburb: Kensington.

Inspired by 'model estates' overseas, it was the intention of the Kensington Freehold Corporation to lay out 1000 acres in the eastern suburbs 'upon the most artistic and scientific principles'. In an 'epoch making' move, it was proposed to form and metal roads, plant trees, landscape gardens, construct sewers and lay water mains prior to settlement. A design competition was held in 1889 and won by 'Rus in urbe', submitted by a team headed by Walter Vernon. The plan was exhibited at a 1917 display of the NSW Town Planning Association as 'the first Australian town planning scheme'. But the hope that Kensington would be 'a little heaven below' was not realised. The prospects for heavy land sales slumped with the economy. The area was 'cut up in the usual chessboard pattern to extract the last penny out of the estate'.

Into the twentieth century

Few model projects were launched in the 1890s, but the idea revived in the first decade after Federation. Among the model suburbs of the early Edwardian era was Appian Way precinct at Burwood (1903), created as an elite enclave by the industrialist George Hoskins. The project comprised a tree-lined and winding little street, recreation reserve, and over thirty large houses in the distinctive 'Federation' style with its touches of Queen Anne and Art Nouveau. Malvern Hill (1909) was developed adjacent to the Appian Way; buyers were assured that there would be no overcrowding and 'no fear of shops or business premises being built alongside you' (Dunlop, 1974:106).

The first, largest and best known of these early model suburbs was Haberfield (1902), about eight kilometres west of the central business district. 'Slumless, laneless, publess' Haberfield (Figure 2.2) was developed by Richard Stanton, a real-estate agent with experience in local government. He offered 'people of cultured tastes' the chance to own ready-built or custom-designed cottages. They were individually designed by J Spencer-Stanfield, decorated with nationalistic symbols like kookaburras and rising suns, and protected by special covenants which ensured no terraces or cheap, weatherboard dwellings. The wide streets were kerbed, guttered, and planted. Stanton eventually erected

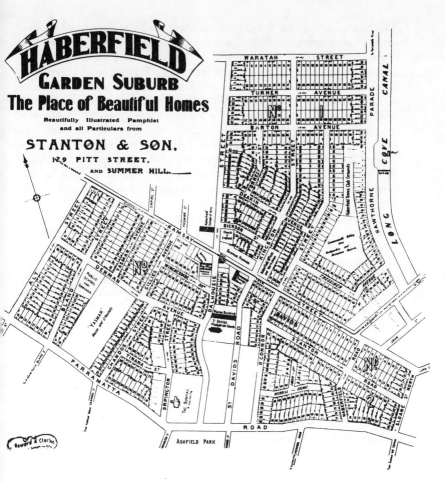

Figure 2.2 'Slumless, laneless, publess' Haberfield for 'people of cultured tastes'

some 1500 houses over a 200 acre site. The result was the most creditable attempt to create an ideal suburban environment to that time and an almost unprecedented integration of land and housing development on a large scale. The covenant idea, which gave basic control over initial development, was widely used thereafter in prestige subdivisions. Haberfield was praised as a planning experiment by many observers, including John Sulman and Sydney Jones. It was also a financial success (Taylor, 1914:103).

By 1909, Stanton was marketing his project as 'the garden suburb'.

This status, implying a direct connection with the garden city movement, has been uncritically accepted by many commentators. But Haberfield boasted features which garden city principles as they crystallised in the 1910s tried to eliminate. The layout by surveyors Howard and Clarke was strictly rectilinear, the roads were a uniform sixty-six feet wide to the letter of the law, and no parks were provided. Moreover, Stanton by his own admission was unaware of overseas developments when he set out to improve the housing and surroundings of middle-class Sydneysiders. Nevertheless, Haberfield is the crucial link between the model suburb and the garden suburb idea in the 1900s. Rosebery, a venture initiated by Stanton when he was identified with the town planning movement, was more directly influenced by overseas events.

The Sydney model suburb experience was not unique in Australia. For example, Melbourne has a similar history of exceptional suburban developments from the Georgian-style grandeur of Brighton in the 1840s to extravagant land boom products, like the 'artistic, complete and sanitary model suburb' of Hopetoun, planned on paper in 1889 by Philip Treeby (Bate, 1962:333–37). After a hiatus in the 1890s, small and select projects reappeared with restored investor and buyer confidence in the early years of this century.

Conclusion

Australian cities were not the congested, industrialised, conurbations of Britain. They did not call forth radical proposals like the garden city idea. Small-scale communal experiments recalled Howard's 'co-operative commonwealth' but most had failed by the early 1900s. Urban reformers were mainly concerned with ameliorating existing conditions. The concerns of the early twentieth century had their origins in the nineteenth, and even then many ideas had come second-hand from Britain. Only towards the end of last century was there a definite movement toward a theoretical synthesis and holistic implementation of reform ideas, marking the birth of modern planning. Metropolitan primacy was accepted as 'the normal state'. There was no native push for new towns, although the federal capital was the outstanding illustration that planned communities could be established to fulfil specialist functions. The factory village ideal, however, was only weakly developed. The best local examples of the impulse to ideal environments were in the suburbs. And the planning of new suburbs on generous lines was a far more vigorous strand of urban reform than the conceptualisation of ideal models of metropolitan growth patterns. The overall conclusion is that the nature of the Australian city and direction of reform in the early 1900s, and indeed subsequently (Freestone, 1982:32–46), were not conducive to Howard's revolutionary ideal but do indicate a general predisposition to the ideals of the garden city movement.

3 Socio-spatial structure of Australian cities 1850–1901

GRAEME APLIN

Sydney had, from the early nineteenth century, a small elite group of government officials, merchants and professional people juxtaposed against a very much larger group of labourers and unskilled workers. As the century progressed, a third identifiable group, a middle class, emerged and grew in size. These three groups, whether strictly social classes or not (Connell and Irving, 1980:1–26), tended to become concentrated in distinct districts within the city as social area differentiation occurred over time. While this chapter focuses primarily on such differentiation in Sydney in 1855 and 1901, later sections place those studies within a broader spatial and temporal context by comparing results with those of studies of other Australian cities over the period.

Cities have been classified and their socio-spatial structure modelled by many researchers. Two broad classifications divide cities into pre-industrial and industrial (Sjoberg, 1960) or pre-capitalist and capitalist (Vance, 1971). Aplin (1982) sees nineteenth-century Australian cities as pre-industrial and mercantile or early capitalist. In terms of socio-spatial structure, Sjoberg sees pre-industrial cities as characterised by an elite group living at the centre and social status declining towards the periphery. Vance, on the other hand, claims that the structure was more complex than that with mixing of social groups at the district level, but with 'upstairs, downstairs' and 'main street, back lane' differentiation within areas distinguished chiefly in terms of occupation or trade. Industrial cities on the other hand have been seen as characterised by concentric rings of increasing status and age from the core to the periphery (the Burgess model) or by sectors of differing status (the Hoyt model) (Herbert, 1972:70–78; Lawson, 1973). These models provide the broad theoretical framework for this chapter.

Sydney 1855

Mid-nineteenth-century census tabulations are not adequate for work at the detailed level required to analyse the structure of the small city of the time, particularly in the fields of income and occupation. An 1855 directory (Waugh and Cox, 1858) has therefore been used to provide addresses and occupations for those listed. But a significant section of the male workforce — those living in boarding houses, hotels, tenements, or as lodgers — were omitted, not to mention older children and women working. Labourers and unskilled workers were thus inevitably underrepresented.

Social area differentiation was evident in 1855. The merchant and professional group was concentrated in the areas of high environmental amenity such as the periphery of Hyde Park and elevated, harbourside areas to the east (Figure 3.1). The more elevated section of The Rocks was an elite area, but had been increasingly invaded over recent years by the working class (Aplin, 1982). Parts of the inner city were also beginning to experience an increase in residential densities and in the relative importance of the lower socio-economic groups as tenements were built in lanes and alleys within city blocks and formerly better-class dwellings were subdivided. The less affluent were, however, still concentrated in the lower parts of The Rocks (Kelly, 1978b), around Darling Harbour and in Chippendale on the southwestern fringe. Small shopkeepers and craftsmen-retailers, living and working in the same premises, were concentrated along George Street, Parramatta Road and Oxford Street.

Many districts were clearly mixed in socio-economic terms and sub-area boundaries were indistinct. Jevons (1858) did see clear distinctions between areas, but he was working at a much more detailed level. Using the 1855 directory data, street segments with a majority of residents falling into any one occupation group have been mapped (Figure 3.1). Most segments had no such majority, but the map does show both differentiation between areas at a district level and the complexity of the pattern at a more detailed level.

Suburban areas were beginning to emerge beyond the City of Sydney (see Figure 3.2 for municipalities). Camperdown, Glebe and Redfern, south or west of the City, were largely working class (Jevons, 1858) while the 1861 census shows that Waterloo and Randwick also had important working-class populations. The census also reveals that Paddington, Randwick and especially Woollahra municipalities, all east of the City, and St Leonards East (North Sydney) on the North Shore had above average proportions in the higher socio-economic status groups. Randwick was thus a heterogeneous area, highlighting the problems of working at this scale.

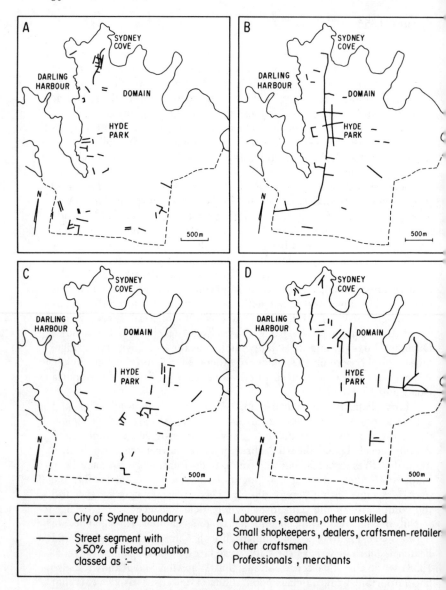

Figure 3.1   Sydney 1855: street segments with a majority of residents in one
occupational group (from Aplin, 1982: Figure 5)

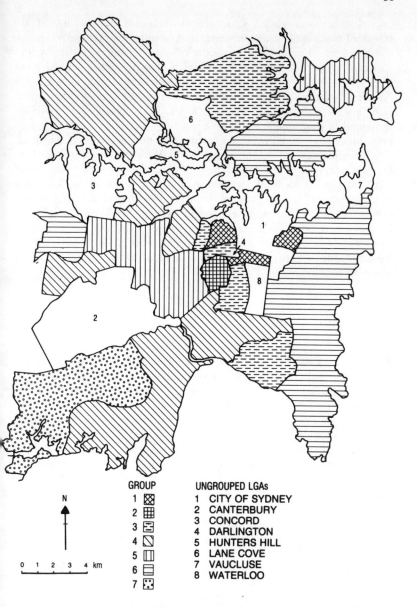

Figure 3.2   Sydney municipalities grouped on the basis of seven variables

Sydney's socio-spatial structure in 1855 did not fit any of the standard models of either pre-industrial or industrial cities. While this partly reflects the individuality of the city, it also indicates that Sydney was in a transitional phase. Accessibility was becoming a less important factor in the residential location decisions of the higher socio-economic groups. The outward movement of such people had begun, although many remained in inner areas. For labourers, accessibility remained of paramount importance as both public and private transport, other than walking, was beyond their means. In such a walking city, proximity to employment was essential for those working for long hours or dependent on daily hiring or piece-rate employment. There were no clearly defined concentric rings in Sydney's socio-spatial structure in 1855, although inner areas were becoming increasingly dominated by lower socio-economic groups, while non-residential landuses were also expanding into these areas (Edwards, 1978). Sectors were somewhat more obvious with an emerging division between the higher status eastern and northern sectors and lower status southern and western areas.

Sydney 1901

By the time of the first census of this century, Sydney's population had grown from 54 000 in 1851 to 496 000. The urban area, as defined for census purposes, had also expanded to include 42 municipalities (Figure 3.2). Data for the following analysis are from the 1901 census and from the 1899–1900 electoral rolls; the latter were used to obtain employment data not available from the census.

Local government areas (LGAs) were grouped on the basis of seven variables chosen from those available: persons per hectare; proportion in dwellings with more than two per room; proportion under fifteen years; proportion Australian born; proportion Roman Catholic; proportion of primary-school age attending state schools; and proportion of the male workforce who were labourers or unskilled. Standardised z scores were used in a simple hierarchical grouping program to derive seven groups and eight ungrouped LGAs at what was judged to be an appropriate stage to terminate the grouping process. Group profiles (Figure 3.3) show the characteristics of each group (as mapped in Figure 3.2) in relation to metropolitan mean values.

Groups may be summarised as follows. Three inner suburban LGAs forming group 1 are characterised above all else by high densities, but also by older, largely working-class populations. LGAs in group 2 are further to the southwest, have somewhat lower densities, and higher

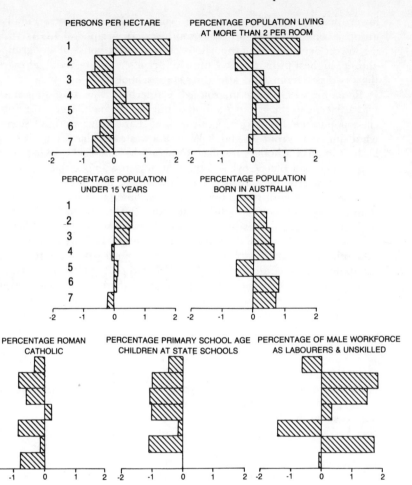

Figure 3.3 **Group profiles for Sydney municipalities, 1901**

than average proportions born in Australia and attending state schools. Both inner western and outer LGAs are included in the more geographically disparate group 3, with a younger population than the previous two. Group 4 comprises middle to outer LGAs in an arc from Marsfield in the northwest to Botany North in the south. Densities are relatively low. Manly and four contiguous western LGAs constitute group 5, a group with lower densities, older than average populations, and above average representation of the upper socio-economic groups. The ocean and harbour suburbs of group 6 are also characterised by a lower than average proportion of working-class residents. Finally, group 7 consists of two adjacent southwestern peripheral LGAs with the lowest densities and proportions of Roman Catholics of any group, and the highest proportions of those under fifteen years, living at more than two per room, and attending state schools.

Remaining LGAs are ungrouped. Canterbury was most similar to and adjacent to the group 7 suburbs, but had a much larger working-class population. Waterloo, Concord and Lane Cove were all somewhat similar to groups 3 and 4: Waterloo was most characterised by a high Roman Catholic presence; Concord by a large working-class population; and Lane Cove by apparent overcrowding and low attendance at state schools. Vaucluse was most similar to groups 5 and 6 and was contiguous with group 6 suburbs, but differed in having a larger than average Roman Catholic population. Darlington had by far the highest population density, but was otherwise somewhat similar to groups 1 and 2. Finally, Sydney and Hunters Hill were the most dissimilar from others and the last to be combined with a group as the grouping process continued. Hunters Hill had particularly low percentages under fifteen years and born in Australia; Sydney also had a large overseas-born population, as well as a large percentage of Roman Catholics.

Socio-spatial structure of Sydney, 1901

On the basis of the grouping and additional analysis of individual variables, including a number not used in this grouping, Sydney's socio-spatial structure in 1901 was complex and idiosyncratic, following no single model but exhibiting features of many. Both concentric ring and sectoral elements were evident. Inner suburbs tended to be high density areas with an older population biased towards the lower socio-economic groups. But there were also peripheral working-class suburbs. Upper socio-economic groups were most important in the eastern suburbs and the lower North Shore, along with a clear sector of development to the west, culminating in the peripheral suburb of Strathfield (see Pluss chapter 4). Between this narrow western sector of higher status areas and the much broader eastern one was a lower status sector extending from the CBD to the metropolitan periphery in a southwestern direction.

The major change between 1855 and 1901 was the sheer expansion of the metropolitan area. The high status eastern sector, the higher status lower North Shore, and the low status southwestern sector had begun to emerge by 1855, but had since extended much further outwards. Only the higher status western sector was new, beginning as it did beyond an inner, lower status ring and following the major railway line. The entire metropolitan area, apart from peripheral areas such as Marsfield, Strathfield and Hurstville as served by a dense network of tramways running directly to the CBD from the inner suburbs or, in some areas further out, to railway stations as feeder lines (Keenan, 1979). Outer areas often relied entirely on railway services. By this time it had become possible for the lower socio-economic groups to commute regularly, as fares were reduced, services improved and networks extended.

A generalised scheme of residential zones in Sydney for the 1970s and 1980s (Burnley, 1980a:171) reflects the 1901 pattern in the inner-to-middle-distance suburban areas. Major differences in recent times have been the addition of a secondary satellite CBD in North Sydney; the emergence of zones of transition around both CBDs; a change to working-class housing in the inner portions of the higher status western sector of 1901; and the evolution of areas of significant concentration of various migrant groups. In terms of the three most commonly identified factors in the factorial ecology of Australian cities — socio-economic status, family status and ethnic status (Burnley, 1980a:199) — the first two have remained of prime importance from late last century to the present. The third has only become of major importance with the great influx of non-British migrants since World War II.

Other studies of Australian cities

There have not been many studies of the socio-spatial structure of Australian cities in the nineteenth century, although there have been descriptive accounts of particular cities or particular suburban areas. Three of these, Brisbane (Lawson, 1973, especially ch. 4), Melbourne (Davison, 1979) and Perth (Stannage, 1979) are particularly relevant to the present discussion.

Brisbane in the 1890s

Lawson (1973:103–114) devotes one chapter of his very detailed work on the sociology of Brisbane in the 1890s to the socio-spatial structure of the city and suburbs. In terms of physical structure, 'the CBD ... was well developed and firmly segregated from the residential sections' (p. 102). Suburban development, as in Sydney, had not occurred evenly, 'although, in general, the density of settlement decreased with distance from the city centre, the population was not evenly spread in all quarters' (p. 103). This unevenness was attributed to two major factors: transport availability, and topography. In terms of socio-spatial structure, Brisbane, like Sydney, exhibited characteristics of various models, but conformed exactly to none. In particular, the neat concentric rings of the Burgess model were distorted by topography, the upper socio-economic groups, as in early Sydney, preferring the higher ground. Despite this, Lawson finds that the Burgess model, with Hoyt's sectoral modifications, fits 'reasonably well' if applied 'in terms of travelling time, rather than direct distance' (Lawson, 1973:104).

Marvellous Melbourne

'Marvellous Melbourne' had seen its rise and fall by the turn of the century: one of the main manifestations of the boom had been rapid suburban development. Although Davison (1979) does not treat the socio-spatial structure directly or in a clearly geographical manner, his work contains a number of relevant comments.

According to Davison, 'the suburban ideal of *rus in urbe* seems to have attracted virtually all sections of society' and 'most workingmen had little gardens attached to their homes' (Davison, 1979:140). Such development, once beyond inner suburban areas such as Collingwood, was at a particularly low average density by world standards of the day. Socio-economic status was reflected in the size and type of dwelling, ranging from the mansions of the elite, through the middle-class villas to the artisans' cottages. As in both Sydney and Brisbane, topography played a central role in the growth of distinctive sectors of development and, late last century, those sectors along the Port Phillip Bay shore, to the southeast of the CBD and east of the core towards the Dandenong Ranges were attracting the upper and middle classes (cf. Johnston, 1966). Working-class housing became concentrated on lower, flatter land immediately north and east of the CBD (Richmond, Fitzroy, Collingwood) and on lower land along the Yarra to the west (South Melbourne, Port Melbourne, Footscray), although an area of higher ground in South Melbourne — the original Emerald Hill — had long been a higher status enclave. As in Sydney, these working-class residential areas were adjacent to, or intermixed with, the main industrial concentrations. By 1891, 'the city was clearly split into two broad social areas (and) the Yarra had become the boundary ... between middle-class and working-class Melbourne' (Davison, 1979:147). Both concentric ring and sectoral elements were discernible in late nineteenth-century Melbourne.

Other factors alluded to previously were also evident in Melbourne. Transport developments played a major role in opening particular areas for suburban subdivision, in many cases preceding the development of housing estates. Despite this, many artisans and unskilled labourers still walked to work, either in their own inner suburban neighbourhoods or in the nearby CBD (Davison, 1979:151). Davison also points out that the 'highest concentrations of young married women (20–40 years), preschool children and native born were (in 1891) in the newer suburbs, especially the lower-middle and lower-class areas in the northwest' (Davison, 1979:153). These areas were clearly analogous to the outer southwestern suburbs of Sydney.

Perth

Perth also experienced rapid suburbanisation towards the end of the nineteenth century, especially after the Western Australian gold discoveries of the early 1890s. Here too, socio-economic differentiation occurred (Stannage, 1979:243):

> Perth's suburbs developed in such a way that it could be said that some were more desirable to live in than others. Differences in topography, accessibility of transport, location of industries, the cheapness of land, and people's perceptions of a hierarchy of suburbs all tended to give each suburb a fairly distinctive appearance and character.

West Perth, adjacent to the CBD, was still a prestigious area, as was East Melbourne, both being vestiges of the former inner elite neighbourhoods. Cottesloe, on the coast, was a newer upper-class area, whilst Claremont, closer to the CBD, and South Perth across the river from the CBD were middle class. On the other hand Subiaco, adjacent to West Perth but further out, was from all accounts clearly working class, as were the inner northern suburbs of North Perth and Leederville (Stannage, 1979:243–44). These broad differences were reflected in size and building materials of dwellings, as well as in their value. As in other cities, industry and working-class housing were closely associated (Stannage 1979:246). But these are only broad indications. Further detailed work is needed before an accurate geographical account of the socio-spatial structure of Perth at the turn of the century can be given.

Conclusion

All of the cities mentioned in this study had complex socio-spatial structures at the turn of the century. All showed evidence of both rings and sectors, while all were still centred on a single core CBD. Inner suburban areas, including areas immediately adjacent to the CBD, were generally districts of older and poorer people and dwellings. Lower socio-economic groups had come to increasingly dominate such areas, a process that continued into the first half of the twentieth century. There were, however, some remaining vestiges of the mid-nineteenth-century elite areas close to the CBD, usually adjacent to parklands or water frontages. Beyond this inner ring, there was some evidence of the Burgess pattern of increasing socio-economic status with distance from the centre, but with a strong sectoral component superimposed. Some sectors were thus working class from the core to the periphery, whilst others were middle or upper class. Both upper and lower socio-economic groups occupied peripheral suburban locations, though in different sectors.

Many processes were operating in the on-going urban change evident at the turn of the century, processes that had begun well before 1901 and continued long after that date. Cheap, reliable and widely available mechanised public transport made the suburbanisation of all classes possible although, in 1901, many of the working class still lived in inner areas close to industrial employment or in areas vacated by the outward migrating middle class. Transport, of course, was not the only factor involved in housing choice: the costs of suburban housing and the institutional arrangements of the market and of lending organisations placed severe contraints on the lower socio-economic groups (cf. Pooley, 1982). Environmental amenity and locational prestige greatly influenced the areal distribution of housing costs. Accessibility remained important, however, and suburban residential development was normally tied to the new railway and tramway networks.

Much more detailed analyses of a number of cities in Australia late last century are needed before more definite conclusions can be drawn. It is clear, though, that many aspects of the industrial city, as modelled in the British context by such researchers as Lawton and Pooley (1976), Carter (1978), and Dennis and Clout (1980), were evident. Only Sydney and Melbourne were, perhaps, large enough to experience the full impact of some of the changes, particularly those related to the urban transport revolution and consequent large scale urbanisation. Australian cities differed from those of industrial Britain in not having experienced widespread industrial development until well into the twentieth century; they remained basically mercantile and administrative centres. Most importantly, Australian cities lacked the long historical legacies of most British cities.

Finally, it is important to strike a balance between the idiographic and nomethetic approaches in the present context and to remember that while (Vance, 1964:2):

> ... it is fatuous to make too much of the ... 'uniqueness', it is equally dull-witted to act as if [each city were] just like all other metropolitan areas.

Comparisons and contrasts need to be made not only among Australian cities in 1901, but between those cities and their contemporaries elsewhere, and among cities at different times. Such studies have a wealth of material to draw on: contemporary descriptions, the personal memories of those still living, official statistical compilations, directories, electoral rolls, newspapers and magazines, drawings, photographs and, last but certainly not least, maps. A great deal remains to be done. .... *but not by you ! (I hope)*

Conc. on pattern of process

4 The evolution of Strathfield

MARTIN PLUSS

In 1888 Strathfield, known as Redmire Estate (or Redmyre up to 1886), was described in the *Centennial history of NSW*, as a 'purely residential suburb' with houses of the 'better class merchants and retired people' (Morrison, 1888:477). Another description in the 1890s saw Strathfield as a:

> municipality of mansions ... too far from the metropolis to permit the labouring classes seeking homes there and (with) no industries to induce such settlement.

Most urban historical geography examines segregation at an aggregate level: either studies of whole cities with a description of areas of segregation (Springett, 1982; Ward, 1975; Onokerhoraye, 1977), or the study of individual variables and how they are segregated throughout the city. Other studies focus on smaller neighbourhood communities and the social connections which bind them into segregated communities (Dennis, 1982; Boal, 1972). Some research has looked at the elements of change in an urban community; in particular whether an area maintains or loses its social identity (Dennis, 1982). Few studies explain the evolution of elite areas.

In the few studies of evolving elite areas, Cannadine recognises the possibilities of global similarities of elite areas. Referring to a statement made by Firey, Cannadine (1977:473) compares Edgebaston in Birmingham to the upper-class' district of Beacon Hill:

> If Birmingham is substituted for Boston and Edgbaston for Beacon Hill the description (made by Firey) is perfect.

If Boston has its Beacon Hill (Firey, 1947), Birmingham its Edgbaston (Cannadine, 1977), West Philadelphia its Hamiltonville (Miller and Siry, 1980), and North London its Highbury New Park (Hinchcliffe, 1981), then Sydney has its Strathfield. Using a behavioural approach, this chapter traces the evolution of this elite area in the western suburbs of nineteenth-century Sydney.

Neoclassical models explain residential segregation by examining variations in land values, and the operation of impersonal market forces like competition and choice (Timms, 1971; Pooley, 1982). In the concentric model the expansion of the city is in a succession of rings. A suburb like Strathfield emerges in the zone of better-class residences with middle-class populations. The explanation is simple. In pre-industrial Sydney, the elite lived where they worked in the core of the city, while the poor were dispersed on the periphery. As Sydney grew and transportation services improved, the city core became the centre of commerce and industry, and the poor began to cluster around the centre so they could live where they worked. The increased demand for central city locations crowded out the elite to the periphery, where they could reach their work and amenities in the core, first by means of coaches, and later by train services. The evolution of an investment-related rental housing market of terraces also attracted, and albeit forced, many of the working classes to congregate in the inner city.

Sydney's expansion in the nineteenth century was in sectors as well as in rings. There was the southern sector ending at Botany Bay; the southwestern sector along the railway line to Rockdale and Hurstville; the eastern sector serviced by ferry transport to places like Elizabeth Bay and Vaucluse, and the northern sector along the railway line to Chatswood, serviced by ferry to North Sydney. The oldest sector was along the western railway line: Strathfield's evolution is a product of the growth of this sector. The elite lived in the high-rent sectors of the city, and as they moved outwards, the 'lower classes' filtered into the houses which were frequently bought by small time investors and subdivided for renting. The elite usually were on the periphery of the sector, there were normally no houses in front of them abandoned by another group. This process of invasion and succession was evidenced in changing house values. In 1885 Burwood was at the end of the western sector. By 1895 invasion and succession had occurred, the housing values of Burwood had deteriorated and the elite had moved out, but meanwhile Strathfield on the edge retained the highest housing values for the western sector (Daly, 1982: figures 6.1 and 6.2). Neoclassical models however, have too many 'oversimplifications of a complex reality' (Pooley, 1982:201), and they fail to explain why the elite residents stayed in Strathfield, instead of moving on as the western sector expanded. The basic flaw was the failure to consider the behaviour of decision makers: the estate agents, the speculators or the residents.

Behavioural approaches study subjective decisions and actions which the neoclassical approaches fail to acknowledge (Pooley, 1982:201). There are three levels of examination needed to understand the evolution of Strathfield. First, the rental sorting mechanism which makes individuals decide to live in suburban areas. Second, the institutional developments of the property market, as with the role the estate agents played in moulding Strathfield as an ideal suburb for the elite to live in. Third, the individuals making the residential 'choice'. Though there is little evidence on why the decision to live in Strathfield was made, there is evidence that the elite made positive decisions to move to Strathfield.

The decision to live in suburban areas: evolution of suburban landuse up to the subdivision of Redmyre Estate in 1867

The changing pattern of settlement of Burwood, Redmyre, Enfield and Homebush up to 1867 was partly determined by the market forces operating in the colony in the nineteenth century. Each suburb passed through three stages of growth: rural occupation, rural-urban fringe occupation and suburban occupation. The main force leading to the growth of suburbs was improving technology; Sydney was being transformed from a walking city to a public transport city (McCarty and Shedvin, 1978:16). Sydney was becoming less rural and more urban because of the availability of money for urban development, especially in the 1880s (Daly, 1982:154). Another market force operating was the increasing population of Sydney from 30 000 in 1841 to 383 000 in 1891 (Feldheim, 1914:5). As population increased there was a horizontal expansion of the city, leading to the development of suburbs. In short, in 1841 Sydney's suburban population was 18 per cent of the total and by 1891 this had increased to 77 per cent.

There was a simple scenario for the changing settlement of the district. The present location of Strathfield is on the Liberty Plains Grant of 1793. The value of the agricultural land was soon questioned (Campbell, 1936:321). The area was destined for other uses, for when Parramatta Road was put through in 1803, 'the plains' were considered halfway to Parramatta or Liverpool. A number of inns developed, and these became known as halfway houses where horses and travellers could rest. The settlement along the highway was soon challenged by the railway, and the area was entering the stage of being on the rural-urban fringe. As settlements emerged around the railway and the area's population increased, suburbs began to evolve.

By 1867 Burwood, Redmyre, Homebush and Enfield were at different stages of settlement. Burwood with the railway passing between Parramatta and Liverpool Roads, and drawing settlement from both roads, had approached the third stage of developing into a suburb. Homebush (Underwood Estate) with the markets, highway, and the adjacent railway was on the rural-urban fringe.

Enfield (Faithful's Estate) was still mainly at the rural stage of settlement. Liverpool Road gave the village its character as a halfway place between Sydney and Liverpool, and Cooks River enhanced the rural value of the area, as well as providing timber for the colony. There were a number of rural estates in the district still in the first stage of settlement and they remained until the 1890s. These rural estates were Potts Estate, Druitt Town, Roses Estate, Meridiths Estate and the village of St Annes (Dunlop, 1974; *Echo*, 1890).

Redmyre Estate in 1867 was a 603-acre paddock between two highways (Liverpool and Parramatta Roads) and two stations (Burwood and Homebush). The rural stage had its origin in 1810, when the land was granted to Sydney's first tanner, James Wilshire (*Sydney Morning Herald*, 8 Sep. 1928). Samuel Terry, an ex-convict turned 'Botany Bay Rothschild' (Dow, 1965:128–29) purchased the land for £300 in 1824. Terry died in 1838, and the land remained in the family until 1866, when W W Billyard purchased the land for £2850. Within a year, the land was surveyed and subdivided into 77 allotments, ranging from 3 to 13 acres each. The land in 1867 was passing into the stage of being on the rural-urban fringe.

The institutional development of the Strathfield property market: estate agents mould Redmyre as a first-class suburb, 1867–90

The evolution of Strathfield as an elite suburb was due to the estate agents actively responding to the market forces and environmental conditions affecting the locality between 1867 and 1890. For the period, 430 advertisements were analysed, most of which came from the Richardson and Wrench, and Hardie and Gorman Contract Books: 50 per cent of the available advertisements were for sales in Burwood, 30 per cent Redmyre, and 20 per cent for Homebush. Clearly the unequal distribution of advertisements indicates the different stages of settlement. Burwood was already a railway suburb in 1867; eleven years later Homebush was brought into the process of suburbanisation, with the subdivision of Underwood Estate. Redmyre in the 23 years passed through two stages of subdivision: 1867–80 was a period of large country mansions and grounds, and 1880–90 was a time when these original lots were resubdivided into suburban allotments.

The estate agents involved in the 1867 subdivision of Redmyre Estate (Figure 4.1c) set out from the very beginning to give it a distinctive image. In a period when suburban land was in demand in

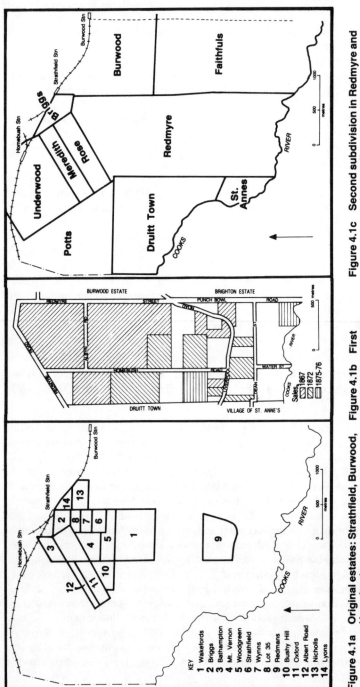

Figure 4.1a Original estates: Strathfield, Burwood, Homebush

KEY
1 Wakefords
2 Briggs
3 Bathampton
4 Mt. Vernon
5 Woodgreen
6 Strathfield
7 Wynns
8 Lot 35
9 Redmans
10 Bushy Hill
11 Oxford
12 Albert Road
13 Nicholls
14 Lyons

Figure 4.1b First subdivision of Redmyre estate

BURWOOD ESTATE

BRIGHTON ESTATE

Sales
1867
1872
1875-76

Figure 4.1c Second subdivision in Redmyre and other smaller estates

Burwood, Redmyre was created as a place offering more than a suburban block of land. The sizes of the blocks (3–13 acres) were clearly suited to large country mansions, with extensive grounds. The estate agents drew on two sets of images: the *suburban* images involved a close railway station and the fast access to the city, and the *rural* images emphasised the good soil, Cooks River, and the well-drained, elevated undulating land (*Sydney Morning Herald*, 5 Oct. 1867).

By the time the residual 200 acres were sold in 1872, Redmyre was a 'well known' property (Richardson and Wrench Contract Book 14:342–344). The estate agents advertised this part of the estate differently (Figure 4.1b). The sites near Liverpool Road were not for country residences but for suburban homesteads, a smaller version of a country mansion. These advertising differences between north and south Redmyre Estate are clearly reflected in the sales of lot 73 and lot 38. Lot 73 in 1877 was an improved homestead on 10 acres, of which 4.5 acres was a small market garden with a good water supply from Cooks River (Richardson and Wrench 20:624). Lot 38 was the residence of the Lord Mayor of Sydney — Walter Renny. Strathfield House was a 'handsome suburban villa residence' with all the luxuries of a gentleman's residence, with extensive 10-acre ornamental grounds (Richardson and Wrench 12:879–881). Clearly, the property sales to the north had a first-class character while those to the south had a rural character.

These differences in the primary subdivisions were reflected in the secondary subdivisions, most of which between 1880 and 1890 occurred on the northern side of Redmyre near the railway (Figure 4.1c). The secondary subdivisions occurred due to pressure from two sides. In the east was the growing suburb of Burwood, its commercial character and the profitable subdivision of estates near Redmyre. In the west, Underwood Estate, Homebush, was cast onto the suburban land market in the 1880s.

Ultimately, the estate agents recognised and promoted the second subdivisions of the original allotments. The resubdivisions were advertised on large 60 by 40 cm posters combined with a vigorous advertising campaign in the *Sydney Morning Herald*. The estate agents were exposing the natural and introduced features of an elite Redmyre. The estate agents were able to mould an elite Redmyre in three ways with posters showing large blocks of land; posters and advertisements highlighting the railway; and advertisements referring to the 'first class' *residents* and residences in Redmyre.

The subdivision of Wakeford's Estate in 1874 had large blocks of land (200 by 500 ft), but by the 1880 subdivision of Wakeford's Orangery, the allotments were 100 by 200 ft. On the whole, the other secondary subdivisions in Redmyre Estate were large for suburban blocks of land. As these estates in the original Redmyre subdivision

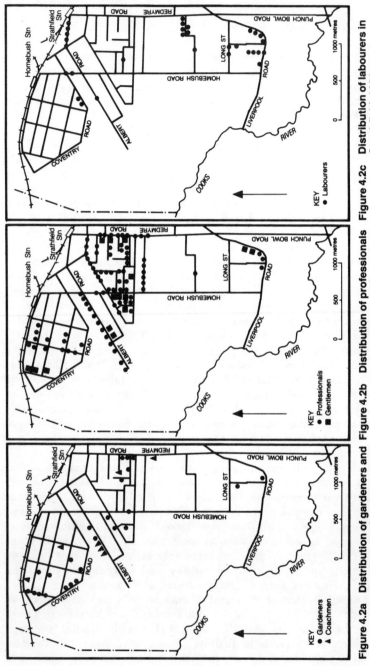

Figure 4.2a Distribution of gardeners and coachmen in Strathfield, 1894

Figure 4.2b Distribution of professionals and gentlemen in Strathfield, 1894

Figure 4.2c Distribution of labourers in Strathfield, 1894

became subdivided, the surrounding smaller estates in Redmyre began to be subdivided into suburban allotments, most of which were narrower (50 ft) and shorter (150 ft). Of all the estates examined, their block sizes were larger than those closer to the city. Good Hope Estate, Paddington, for instance had smaller frontages (33 ft) and depths (140–160 ft) (Kelly, 1978c:52). The estate agents combined the posters and the advertisements to help build up the idea that Redmyre was the ideal place for wealthy people who wanted larger than average blocks, in a growing railway suburb.

The estate agents highlighted the railway. In 60 per cent of the advertisements examined for Redmyre, the area's convenience to the station was consistently mentioned (Table 4.1). Likewise, each poster which advertised the sale of an estate had a local sketch of all the main roads near the estate, particularly those that led to the closest railway station.

Redmyre had in the 1880s a twin station catchment area (Homebush and Redmyre); which station used in the posters' local sketches depended on the location of the estate for sale, and on property developments in the area. Bushy Hill and Albert Road subdivisions were equal distances from Redmyre and Homebush Stations, but they were considered as Homebush. Underwood Estate, Homebush, had come onto the market and the estate agents were using the name to sell land in Redmyre.

Table 4.1 Mention of characteristics in real-estate advertisements

				Characteristics[a]						
	Rail	Road	1st Class Status	Other Status	Country	View	Health	Water	Facilities	No. of Adverts
Burwood	55	28	29	10	19	36	10	6	17	212
Redmyre	60	43	50	7	13	25	16	4	8	133
Homebush	61	17	13	6	13	27	25	14	5	85

[a] All figures are percentages of total number of advertisements examined for 1867–1890

Fifty per cent of the advertisements for Redmyre made reference to the 'first class' character of the area; the estate agents made reference to well known residents or 'esquires' living in the area (Table 4.1). For example, Wynn's paddock was surrounded by 'superior residences' and 'beautiful gardens of our city merchants and our professional men' (*Sydney Morning Herald*, 10 Oct. 1885). However, there were still differences: for the land sales near Liverpool Road, the advertisements were not to first-class buyers but to 'Clerks, Bank Depositors and others' (*Sydney Morning Herald*, 11 Dec. 1880). Similar advertisements were for properties near the station (Richardson and Wrench Contract Book 28:377). The 'first class' residents that the advertisements referred to were 'well-to-do', and in many cases were well known in the Sydney community. Many residents, such as Sir P S Jones, Sir E D Thompson, J Toohey, Sir J Inglis, and Dr Buchanan are listed in the *Australian Dictionary of Biography*.

The estate agents in the process of advertising and selling property in Redmyre, were actively preparing the way for an elite class of buyers. This was masterminded through impressive advertisements and posters linking together key features of the area — large blocks, good rail service and first-class residents. Other valuable features in the suburb (Table 4.1) were used by the estate agents to reinforce the growing elite character of the area, especially in relation to the surrounding suburbs.

Residential choice made: an elite area created

On the whole, most of the land sole in Strathfield was in double blocks, as with 78 per cent of Wynn's paddock and 39 per cent of Woodgreen Estate. A number of individuals purchased more than two blocks; 42 per cent of Wakeford's Estate was purchased by three individuals. Only a few land purchasers bought individual blocks (40 per cent of Wakeford's, 25 per cent of Woodgreen and 8 per cent of Wynn's subdivisions). 'Mansion villas' were built on these large individual blocks of land.

An amalgamation of similar residences and residents by 1890 had given the area a distinctive elite character. Strathfield was described as the 'beautiful and model suburb ... where so many of Sydney's most eminent professional and businessmen have made their homes' (*Freemans Journal*, 24 Apr. 1894). By using the 1894 New South Wales electoral rolls, a comparison of the social composition of Strathfield and neighbouring suburbs is possible. In the *Statistician's report on the eleventh census of NSW* (1893) the new colony was divided into a number of social classes. The occupations of the voters in seven suburbs have been classified according to this system (Table 4.2).

Strathfield had, compared to the other suburbs, the highest professional (24 per cent), commercial (34 per cent), and domestic (10 per cent) and indefinite (7 per cent) groups in its voting population. Strathfield also had the lowest number of voters employed in the industrial class (24 per cent), while the other suburbs had a much higher industrial and slightly higher agricultural voting population. There was a significant difference between the social structures of Burwood or Enfield and Strathfield. The differences are a reflection of the elite character of the area.

In the indefinite class, 70 per cent were 'gentlemen'. If Strathfield's gentlemen are added to their social counterparts, the professionals,

Table 4.2 Occupations of voters by suburb

	Auburn	Burwood	Concord	Enfield	Homebush	Rookwood	Strathfield
Professional	11.9	17.0	6.9	11.5	15.7	6.1	23.8
Commercial	15.0	30.5	17.3	18.5	18.8	17.4	34.0
Industrial	68.8	36.4	63.0	52.9	39.1	67.8	23.0
Agricultural	1.2	1.9	0.4	6.9	21.8	1.9	2.0
Domestic	2.7	8.0	7.8	6.4	3.1	5.8	10.0
Indefinite	0.4	6.0	4.5	3.8	1.5	1.0	7.2
Dependent	—	0.2	0.1	—	—	—	—
Total voters	521	1334	502	452	64	626	431

All figures are percentages, adding down

Strathfield's upper elite made up 29 per cent of the voting population. As for the domestic class, 28 per cent were coachmen and 65 per cent were gardeners for the wealthy residents in the area. They tended to live in the same streets as the professionals and gentlemen. Nearly a quarter of Strathfield's voting population was in the industrial class; quite high for an elite suburb, yet the lowest in relation to other suburbs. Labourers for housing construction comprised 37 per cent of the industrial component and they tended to live in the smaller cottages (as advertised by the estate agents) near the station and near Liverpool Road.

So far, Strathfield has been defined as an elite area without directly examining the elite who made it up: the commercial and professional occupations constituted half the voters. Clerks comprised 31 per cent of the commercial voting population, and another 25 per cent were merchants or agents. As for the professional occupations, 20 per cent were solicitors, 16 per cent accountants and 16 per cent engineers. The rest of the professionals were either doctors, dentists, or teachers, or they were high officials in government departments.

Conclusion: Strathfield today

Strathfield's individuality is a product of the forces of suburbanisation combined with skilful utilisation by the estate agents of the natural and introduced conditions of Strathfield. First, impersonal forces like increasing suburban population, the availability of urban capital and advances in Sydney's transportation system all combined to produce suburbs out of rural tracts of land. Second, when the time came for the occupation of Strathfield (1867), the estate agents emerged as the responders to the local conditions and impersonal market forces, and moulded the elite character of Strathfield's settlement. Third, in doing so, the images they moulded were responded to by an elite class of buyers who were often involved with the 'very creme de la creme of our choice society' (*Heyde Family Papers*).

Undoubtedly, Strathfield has an individuality which stands out in relation to the neighbouring suburbs: this can be derived from the social atlases compiled from the 1971 and 1976 censuses (Davis and Spearitt, 1974; Poulsen and Spearitt, 1981). Strathfield residents are still clearly upper white-collar workers and professionals. The surrounding areas are characterised by low numbers of white-collar workers and high numbers of blue-collar workers. The same contrast between Strathfield and surrounding suburbs is observed in the high proportion of employers and university students residing in Strathfield. There are other characteristics, though less distinctive than these, which highlight Strathfield's individuality. These include a large number of university graduates, a high proportion of residents with the Higher School Certificate and many residents who work in finance and public administration. Strathfield's distinctive social character is repeated in its landscape. Aerial photographs show the larger blocks of land occupied by substantial villas and mansions.

Strathfield's population has been stable since World War II: 24 260 in 1947 and 25 882 in 1981. As for the social status, according to the 1981 census, 18.6 per cent of the total population are in professional occupations. Commercial occupations (clerical and sales) involve 29 per cent of the population, while 6.9 per cent of the population are in administrative posts.

The professional and commercial occupations still dominate the social structure of the suburb. However, probably owing to the municipality's boundary expansion into Homebush and part of Enfield in 1947, 26 per cent of the population are tradesmen, production process workers and labourers. Strathfield's population is more ethnically diverse. In the nineteenth century, nearly all the population was 'Anglo-Saxon'; today 32 per cent are foreign born: 13.8 per cent of whom are from the United Kingdom, 10 per cent from Vietnam, 10 per cent from Italy, and the rest from China, Lebanon and Yugoslavia (*Sydney Morning Herald*, 12 Apr. 1983:15).

This census material can be supported by press reports concerning the suburb. Strathfield is a 'world apart from its stark industrial surroundings'. There have been a number of real-estate articles on the suburb which once again readdress the question of larger blocks of land: Strathfield's standard block of land (697 sq. m) is 'much larger than most Sydney councils' 500–550 sq. metres' (*Sydney Morning Herald*, 17 Aug. 1983). A walk in the district reveals the changing character of Strathfield; some of the older mansions are being de-molished; units are increasingly appearing around the highway and the station and the smaller individual shops are replaced by the larger Strathfield Plaza. These changes have not come easily. As early as 1890 the local elite were establishing defence mechanisms to 'resist the process of class formation' (Connell and Irving, 1980:23) or to prevent the lower classes encroaching on the elite district. Covenants prevented any dwelling under £500 from being built in the area. The council prevented the tramline extension from Enfield to Druittown, thus preventing working-class access to the suburb (*The Advertiser*, 18 Feb. 1899). The council failed in 1947 to prevent amalgamation with Homebush and Enfield, but in 1973 the council was successful in preventing amalgamation with Burwood and other councils. Even today (late 1983) the council, combined with the ever-present and vocal Strathfield Residents Against Amalgamation (SRAA), for the time being have successfully prevented amalgamation.

A possible explanation for Strathfield's present elite status lies with the council. The institutional development of the Strathfield property market was in the hands of the estate agents, but the maintenance of the Strathfield property market in the twentieth century was a product of council decisions. As long as the council keeps its present structure and function and meets the demands of those wealthy residents in large houses on large blocks of land, Strathfield's individuality in Sydney's western suburbs will continue.

5   The impact of inequality: the Sydney plague epidemic of 1902

PETER CURSON

Epidemics of infectious disease have brought death and suffering to countless millions throughout the world and at times played an important role in the social geography of western cities. The last great pandemic of bubonic plague which swept out of Asia towards the end of the nineteenth century was a case in point. It was during this pandemic that plague reached Australia. Between 1900 and 1922 at least ten major outbreaks occurred, resulting in the deaths of more than 530 persons (see Cumpston and McCallum, 1926). Overall, Sydney suffered more than any other Australian city from plague during these years, with substantial epidemics in 1900, 1902, 1907 and 1921–22. That of 1900, in terms of community disruption, human tragedy, suffering and panic, was the greatest social disaster in the city's nineteenth-century history (Curson, 1985).

By comparison, the epidemic of 1902 was a much smaller affair. It also differed from the earlier outbreak in that the city's public health authorities possessed a much greater understanding of the epidemiology of bubonic plague and, in particular, the role of the rat and flea in its dissemination. This, and the experience gained during the 1900 epidemic, undoubtedly placed the public health authorities in a much better position to fight the 1902 epidemic. Much remained unchanged from 1900, however. Large areas of the city were filthy, rat-infested and without proper means of sewerage disposal, public health laws were differentially applied and co-operation between municipalities was almost nonexistent. The 1902 epidemic focused public attention on the living conditions of Sydney's poor and on the impoverished and insanitary nature of much of the housing of central Sydney.

The data used in this paper are reconstructed from the official register of cases in 1902, the official report on the epidemic and from Sydney's contemporary newspapers.

The plague experience

The epidemiology of plague

Human plague is a flea-transmitted infection of rodents caused by the bacteria *Yersinia pestis*. The disease is ecologically very complex. Four factors are normally involved: the disease agent; an anthropod vector (flea); a vertibrate host (ground-living rodent); and man. Four types of plague are known to exist: bubonic, septicaemic, pneumonic and *pestis minor*. Among these the bubonic variety was responsible for the great majority of cases and deaths in Australia during the early twentieth century. Basically, bubonic plague is a widely circulating zoonosis maintained among a number of relatively resistant wild rodents (Poland and Barnes, 1979). Under certain circumstances the disease can reach epizootic proportions and it is only then that other species, such as commensal rats, may become infected. When the disease reduces the population of its primary host, the infected fleas may search for an alternative host and begin to infect the human population. Man is thus involved in the disease sequence only infrequently and then normally by accident.

In man, the disease is marked by an incubation period of two to six days and by the sudden onset of malaise, headaches, chills, fever and pain in the infected lymph nodes. The lymph glands become inflamed and swell to the size of a small walnut. Unless the body's natural immune system or drug therapy intervenes, death may result within a few days from heart failure. The progress of the disease is influenced by the behaviour of man, the nature of his movements and activities, by the density of population and the spatial distribution and mobility of a number of ground-living animals and their fleas.

Outbreaks of bubonic plague occurred when some ecological disruption caused the four disease factors mentioned above to come into unwanted contact. Most urban epidemics occurred where people lived crowded together in conditions of material deprivation and poverty, in close proximity to wharves, warehouses and factories. Such was the case in Sydney in 1902. For a plague epidemic to begin, however, required the infection to be introduced from overseas. This came about towards the end of 1901 when plague existed in many port-cities in regular shipping contact with Sydney.

Plague in time and space

The epidemic commenced on 4 November 1901 when an employee of J H Exton's produce store, in Hay Street, fell ill with the disease. Exton's store was located amidst a group of produce, hardware and seed stores, sharing a common yard behind which four traders kept stables and feed

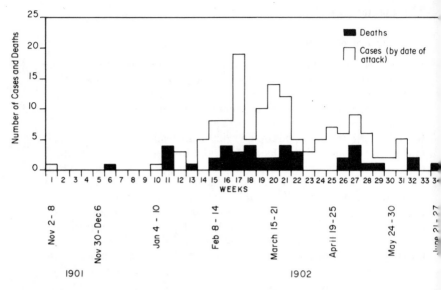

Figure 5.1   Plague cases and deaths by week of occurrence

rooms. On examination, all premises were found to be rat-infested. For 34 days this case stood alone, to be followed by another early in December. But the epidemic proper did not begin until a month later. New cases and deaths extended until the end of June. Including the two cases in 1901, 142 people are recorded as catching plague during the epidemic; 39 died. The epidemic peaked between early February and the end of March (weeks 15–21 on Figure 5.1). During this time more than 53 per cent of all cases occurred (76) and 54 per cent of all deaths (21). Then a short lull was followed almost immediately by a reprise in late April and early May. The epidemic ended abruptly in early June, although two deaths occurred somewhat later. Deaths during the epidemic were primarily concentrated in two periods, the eight weeks from 8 February and the four weeks from 26 April.

Spatial pattern of infection

Although cases of plague occurred over a widespread area of Sydney in 1902, the epidemic was primarily concentrated in the central part of the City of Sydney (Figure 5.2). In discussing epidemics of infectious disease, it is usual and often satisfactory to assign cases to the district in which the person attacked lived. In the case of plague, however, this is unsatisfactory because in most cases infection reached the patient not

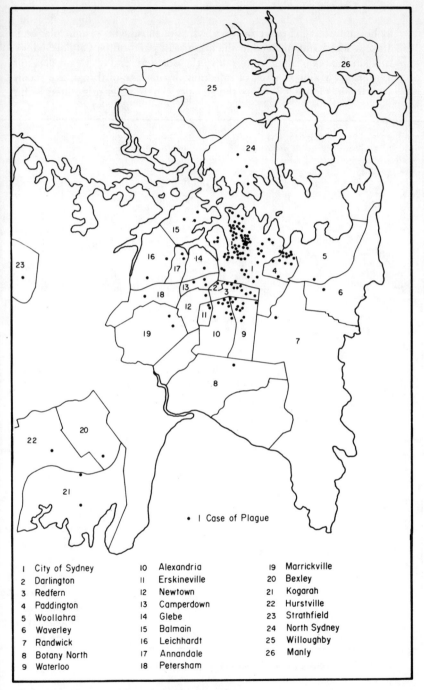

• 1 Case of Plague

1	City of Sydney	10	Alexandria	19	Marrickville
2	Darlington	11	Erskineville	20	Bexley
3	Redfern	12	Newtown	21	Kogarah
4	Paddington	13	Camperdown	22	Hurstville
5	Woollahra	14	Glebe	23	Strathfield
6	Waverley	15	Balmain	24	North Sydney
7	Randwick	16	Leichhardt	25	Willoughby
8	Botany North	17	Annandale	26	Manly
9	Waterloo	18	Petersham		

Figure 5.2   Plague cases by place of residence

at home but at his place of work. Most of those who caught plague in 1902 worked and/or lived in the innermost parts of the City of Sydney, in a small area of Paddington or in the northern end of Alexandria and Waterloo. Major sources of infection during the outbreak are reconstructed in Figure 5.3. More than 67 per cent of cases originated within

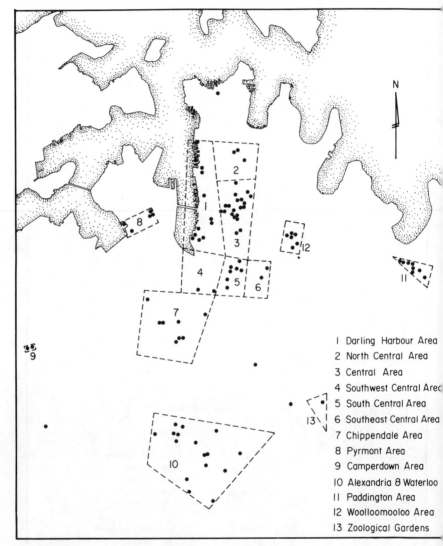

Figure 5.3   Major places of infection — plague cases

the City of Sydney, most in the area bounded by Margaret Street in the north, Castlereagh Street in the east, the Central Railway Station to the south and Darling Harbour to the west (areas 1–5 on Figure 5.3). In addition, there were notable mini-epidemics in Paddington, Alexandria and Waterloo (areas 10, 11). Together, these areas accounted for more than 87 per cent of all plague cases.

Plague does not spread directly from person to person. It requires the intervention of rat and flea. So attention must be directed towards the density and spatial behaviour of the natural born host — the rat. The general morphology and socio-economic arrangement of Sydney in many ways accounted for the distribution and diffusion of human plague in 1902. The earliest onset of the disease was occasioned by the close relationship between the Hay Street markets and produce stores, the Darling Harbour wharves to the north-west, and the densely settled and impoverished population living and working close by. Lack of proper sanitation, old dilapidated buildings, insanitary basements and yards undoubtedly helped provide a healthy environment for rats to live and breed in. Diffusion of the infection away from the wharfside and adjacent areas to other parts of the City and further afield owes much to the migratory habits of rats and the passive transport of infected rats and fleas in consignments of flour, grain, feed and other raw materials from downtown warehouses, factories and stores to suburban locations.

An overview of the geographical diffusion of plague through Sydney in 1902 is obtained by depicting the onset of cases for a series of city areas (Figure 5.4: the areas shown are those used in the official report of the epidemic. See Ashburton-Thompson, 1903). Plague first appeared in the south-central part of the city and spread to Paddington. For a month after 10 January, it raged through a series of one-storey brick cottages grouped about a central produce store. From Hay and adjacent streets the disease spread to nearby Chippendale and then to Alexandria further south. By the middle of February, plague was present in the area around Darling Harbour, the central business areas of the City of Sydney, in Chippendale, Alexandria, Paddington and Woolloomooloo. In the next six weeks, the disease spread to encompass most of central Sydney, as well as Waterloo and Pyrmont. Other cases were recorded at Camperdown, Redfern and Newtown.

Demographic and social selectivity

The 1902 plague epidemic primarily affected teen and middle-aged adult males. Fully 70 per cent of all cases and 74 per cent of all deaths were males; 82 per cent of all cases and 77 per cent of all deaths were aged between 10 and 45 years. Those most affected by the outbreak

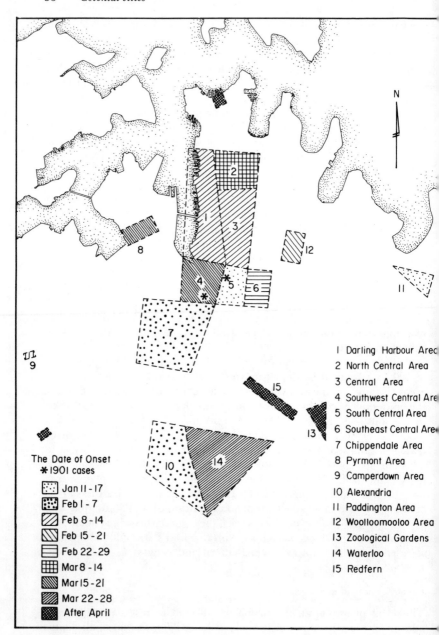

Figure 5.4   Date of onset — plague cases

were in the 15–19, 25–29 and 35–39 age groups, together comprising 42 per cent of all cases and 38 per cent of all deaths. Of the total 142 cases of plague, 39 proved fatal, a case fatality rate of just under 27 per cent. Table 5.1 shows the case fatality rate for particular age and sex groups. Although the numbers involved are small, the figures suggest both an increasing susceptibility by age, and that the full impact of the disease fell on those aged between 15 and 24 years. The small number of females affected by the epidemic largely resulted from Sydney's economic geography in 1902. Males were much more at risk of infection by dint of their virtual monopoly of jobs located in the centre of the city.

Table 5.1   Age–sex distribution and case fatality rates — plague cases and death 1901–02

Age	Cases Male	Cases Female	Deaths Male	Deaths Female	Case fatality rate Male	Case fatality rate Female
0–4	—	1	—	1	—	100.0
5–9	4	1	1	—	25.0	—
10–14	9	5	—	2	—	40.0
15–19	17	4	7	—	41.2	—
20–24	8	8	4	—	50.0	—
25–29	12	6	4	—	33.3	—
30–34	10	3	3	2	30.0	66.7
35–39	17	4	4	—	23.5	—
40–44	11	3	3	1	27.3	33.3
45–49	—	2	—	—	—	—
50–54	3	1	—	—	—	—
55–59	2	1	—	1	—	100.0
60–64	1	1	—	1	—	100.0
65–69	2	1	1	1	50.0	100.0
70–74	2	1	1	1	50.0	100.0
75+	2	—	1	—	50.0	—
Total	100	42	29	10	29.0	23.8

Source: Plague register 1902

The majority of people affected were either working class, such as labourers and factory workers, or small tradespeople or service workers (e.g. restaurant and hotel workers) (Table 5.2). Also, most of the housewives and schoolchildren recorded in this table resided close to the centre of the epidemic. Very few professional or middle-class people were touched by the outbreak. Generally speaking, seven broad social categories bore the brunt of the epidemic: labourers employed in central produce and provision stores, warehouses and factories; local tradespeople, shopkeepers and service workers dependent upon the above and the local community for their custom; people involved in

Table 5.2   Occupations of plague cases, Sydney, 1901–02

Unemployed	7	Tailor/seamstress/mercer	5
Labourer	16	Painter/cabinet maker	2
Rat catcher/cleanser	5	Other tradesmen	5
Hawker	2	Grocer/pantryman/fishmonger	5
Letter sorter/carrier	3	Hotel proprietor	1
Newsboy/fruit boy	2	Professional[a]	2
Produce store worker	4	Housewife	16
Carter	7	School child	15
Factory worker	5	Preschool child	1
Printery worker	7	Other[b]	6
Not stated	10	Total	142

Source: Plague register 1902
Notes: [a] Curate (1), dentist (1)
         [b] Actress (2), prostitute (1), groom (1), nightwatchman (1), coachman (1)

plying between central shops, warehouses and factories (e.g. carters, hawkers, etc.); members of cleansing and rat-catching teams; people who worked in or lived in close proximity to stables; workers and residents in or near to suburban produce stores; people who were unfortunate enough to work in or near (or visit) infected premises (e.g. scene shifters and actresses at the Criterion Theatre).

An unclean city

The 1902 outbreak was exacerbated by the squalor and unhygienic conditions under which many of Sydney's working-class people lived and worked. The hazardous and insanitary condition of their jobs and their generally poor nutritional status further contributed to the spread of infectious disease and premature death. A house-to-house inspection of premises in the City of Sydney carried out between May 1901, and October 1902, by the city's sanitary department, revealed the extent of Sydney's housing and public health problem (Armstrong, 1903). A high proportion of dwellings were structurally unsound, unventilated, with leaky roofs, lacking in basic sanitary facilities and with insanitary and rat-infested yards and outbuildings. More than 1200 dwellings in central Sydney were recorded as being 'so dilapidated as to be dangerous to health' and about 10 per cent of all dwellings bore visible signs of rat infestation. Only a tiny proportion of the City's 22 000 houses possessed indoor water closets and fully 37 per cent had defective sanitary fittings. Such conditions were not restricted to the City of Sydney. A survey of housing conditions in the adjacent suburbs of Alexandria and Waterloo carried out during September and October 1902, revealed conditions far worse than those prevailing in the City (Armstrong, 1903). In Alexandria, 61 per cent of the 851 dwellings surveyed were considered 'dangerous to health' and almost half of these as being unfit for human occupation. Defective lighting and ventilation were characteristic of more than two-thirds of all dwellings and almost half had defective water closets. Only 10 per cent of dwellings in Alexandria were in a satisfactory condition from a public health viewpoint.

Although most of the City of Sydney and the inner suburbs were reputed to be connected to the sewer in 1902, in fact the connection was often faulty and many residents still relied on cesspits, the pail system or on closets discharging directly into the harbour. In Balmain, one-third of all dwellings were still served by pail closets and the same system was important in suburbs such as Glebe, Randwick, Waverley and Woollahra. In the case of Annandale, Balmain and Leichhardt, the contents of these pails were tipped into the sewer through a manhole near Brennan Street, Leichhardt, while residents in Waverley and Paddington utilised the Bondi sewer near its outfall.

The administrative reaction

As in 1900, the official measures for dealing with the epidemic were in the hands of the State Department of Public Health. Day-to-day administration of preventive measures was, however, the responsibility of the local authority of each threatened and invaded area, though in practice, the only local authority to perform in any decisive manner was the City of Sydney.

Quarantine

The policy of quarantine and isolation adopted during the 1902 epidemic differed in three essential ways from that of 1900.

1   The Coast Hospital, Little Bay, was used as an isolation and treatment hospital instead of despatching patients to the Quarantine Station at North Head.
2   Only actual cases of plague were removed from their dwellings and segregated or quarantined. Contacts, such as other members of the household and/or neighbours were not formally placed in quarantine but merely kept under observation, although the general public were less than happy with this arrangement; many complaints were directed to City and health authorities. In reply, the Public Health Department simply stressed that as plague was not infectious in the same sense as smallpox or scarlet fever, there was little need to

quarantine contacts.
3   Residences and business areas of the city deemed 'infected' were
     rapidly cleaned and disinfected but were not formally quarantined
     or closed off, as in 1900. No attempt was made to confine the people
     living within the area under quarantine and everyday trade was not
     affected. Once a dwelling or business house was declared 'infected',
     people were advised to remove themselves until the property had
     been properly disinfected and cleansed. Until this operation was
     completed, only residents were permitted to approach the house.

These three measures represented a remarkable amelioration of the
controls prevailing during the 1900 epidemic, when more than 1800
people were forcibly uprooted from their homes, often at a moment's
notice, and incarcerated at North Head. Large tracts of central Sydney
had been barricaded to bar residents and other people from entry. In
1902, once a case of plague was identified, the patient was removed to
the Coast Hospital. On arrival, male and female patients were
accommodated in different wards. Acute cases of plague were placed in
the partitioned-off front section of each ward so their delirium and
ravings would not unduly upset those convalescing. Treatment largely
consisted of medicines designed to stimulate the heart's action, together
with external applications to reduce fever. Plague victims were buried
in the hospital cemetery, with both the coffin and the grave being
saturated with very strong disinfectants. Unlike the 1900 epidemic,
friends and relatives were encouraged to visit the patients, although
there is no indication of how many elected to do so. Visitors were
provided with a long, loose gown made from blue twill material, which
completely covered their clothes.

A purified city

Early in the epidemic it was decided to commence a large-scale
cleansing and disinfection program covering all infected parts of the
city. This was to coincide with a program designed to fumigate the
city's sewers and wharf areas. City officials formulated a plan to
disinfect and cleanse the heart of Sydney at relatively small cost. As
soon as plague rats or a human case of plague was detected, the
premises and surrounding block was marked off by the Health
Committee for cleansing. This operation consisted chiefly of thoroughly
disinfecting every part of the infected building, including yards and
outbuildings. Of primary concern was the discovery and destruction of
the haunts of rats within the building, ground floors and basements.
Floors of cellars and yards were dug up and saturated with acid
corrosive sublimate solution. Internal walls were sprayed and floors

flooded with the same substance. All outer walls and outbuildings were limewashed.

At the peak of the epidemic, more than 200 men were engaged in cleansing operations. About 40 blocks containing more than 8000 dwellings (about one-fifth of the City's built up area) were officially cleansed and disinfected, at a total cost to the City Council of £6053. Some of the costs of cleansing were recovered from owners and occupiers under Section 24 of the Public Health Act 1896, which empowered local authorities to cleanse and disinfect premises where such action was considered necessary to check or prevent the spread of an infectious disease. The manner of cleansing gave rise to many complaints, particularly from the City's business community. Most complaints concerned the physical damage caused by the cleansing teams, the hardship and inconvenience caused and the exorbitant charges levied by the City Council to cover the cleansing operations. As well as cleansing and disinfecting buildings, the City Council's Health Department vigorously pursued a campaign of prosecuting owners and occupiers under the Public Health Act for refusing to remove rubbish, carry out necessary structural repairs or maintain clean, hygienic, rat-free premises.

By the end of March, more than 3000 prosecutions were outstanding, with more being added every day. Finally, the Mayor of Sydney had to request a Special Health Court to sit under a magistrate. It was estimated that, as at the end of March, there was enough business to keep the court going for at least three months. By June, more than 940 cases had been heard, leaving more than 2000 outstanding. Other complaints arising from the cleansing operations concerned the impact on the distribution of Sydney's rat population. Members of the Waterloo Council, for example, complained that the Health Department was going the wrong way about stamping out the epidemic in that cleansing and fumigation was merely driving the rats further afield into the suburbs (*Daily Telegraph*, 6 May 1902:6).

'Rat Wednesday' — a grand crusade against rats!

The third measure advanced by the public health authorities to prevent plague from spreading was a planned campaign to exterminate Sydney's rat population. Rat-catching teams, initially established during 1901, were substantially enlarged and set to work in and around infected properties. In an effort to encourage the public to kill rats, a capitation bounty of threepence was placed on every rat carcass delivered to a government collection depot.

Right from the onset of the epidemic, official recognition had been given to the role of the rat and the need to do something about the city's rat population to control the spread of the disease. Throughout January and February 1902, Sydney's newspapers were full of articles describing the life history, behavioural patterns and natural haunts of rats, as well as a discussion of their important role of spreading plague. The question of a crusade against rats throughout Sydney, initially raised during the 1900 epidemic, was taken up again by the State premier in 1902. Referring to the wide publicity given to the role of the rat in spreading plague and the need to do something to control the city's rat population, the premier urged that all residents had an obligation to kill any rats on or near their properties.

Wednesday night 5 March, was set aside for the first combined crusade against Sydney's rats; all City residents were urged to engage in a co-ordinated war of extermination. To this end, 50 000 copies of a circular entitled 'Plague is Spread by Rats — It is the Duty of all to Kill Rats on their Premises' were distributed to all inner-city residents. Daily newspapers carried long articles urging participation. The City Council offered to dispense rat poison to any who required it from six carts which perambulated through City streets, or from a series of depots established at strategic points throughout the City. Heads of households were urged to oversee the laying of poison in all cellars, basements and yards and to ensure that all domestic animals were kept tied up. A number of inner suburban councils also agreed to participate in the campaign. The total number of rats collected during the first week of March was 4419 including 789 on the first Rat Wednesday. This only includes those rats formally delivered to the government depots and probably more than 7000 rats were killed in this period (*Sydney Morning Herald*, 10 Mar. 1902:7).

Overall, however, it is doubtful whether many householders, particularly those in the suburbs, heeded the government's call to participate in the campaign. Certainly there was evidence of considerable backsliding in the business areas of the City and along the wharfside. On the other hand, the crusade seems to have captured public imagination and an estimated 1000 people a day were calling at the Town Hall for supplies of rat poison during the first week of March. Despite the official failure of the first Rat Wednesday, it was resolved to repeat it the following week and at weekly intervals thereafter. The campaign also provided considerable impetus to Sydney's manufacturers and advertisers and a vast variety of rat traps (including an electric rat trap), poisons and fumigating agents were urged upon the public. On the day of the first crusade, the Balmain Council even advocated the widespread use of ferrets to help control Sydney's rat population (*Sydney Morning Herald*, 5 Mar. 1902:8). All in all, the period between 16 November 1901 and 14 July 1902 saw almost 76 000 rats killed within Sydney by the council's official rat-catching teams or during one of the rat crusades. An additional 24 000 rats were officially destroyed in the period after 14 July until the end of 1902. Probably the total was many more as often people did not bother to remove the dead rats from underneath floorboards or from backyards.

An uneasy public

As the epidemic progressed, fear and panic spread like wildfire through Sydney. Newspapers did much to encourage the growing unease by regularly publishing sensational accounts of the thousands of deaths each day from plague in India, as well as lurid details of earlier epidemics and the symptoms of the disease. The business community, as in earlier epidemics, reacted quickly to the opportunity to increase profits. Retailers of fumigants, disinfectants, rat traps and poisons, peddled their stocks with increasing enthusiasm, as did the manufacturers of patent medicines such as Bile Beans, health tonics and Life-buoy soap, while retailers of woollen socks were anxious to convince people that their goods were impervious to fleas. The manufacturers of Vidatio Health Tonic and Herr Rassmussen's Alfaline Herbal Remedy were quick to assert the efficacy of their products against plague.

Confronted by the increasing publicity linking the spread of the plague to the flea, the public was urged to adopt a variety of preventive measures to avoid flea bites, such as eating plenty of sulphur and annointing oneself every morning and evening with kerosene. Public vigilance groups sprung up all over Sydney and learned men lectured on the disease to packed audiences. Despite the official recognition of the role of the rat and flea in spreading the disease, many, including medical practitioners, tenaciously clung to the old belief that the disease was a product of miasmas generated by filth and unhygienic living conditions. Dr Sharfstein, in a letter to the *Sydney Morning Herald* (2 May 1902:6), for example, called for the erection of giant air fans in all public halls, theatres and hotels, to dispel the contaminated air.

Early in March, the public hospitals and many Sydney doctors reported a substantial increase in the numbers of people seeking medical advice for anything that vaguely resembled the symptoms of plague. Fear also spread to most of Sydney's municipalities and in late February the Redfern Council closed the local public library for fear of the infection spreading via the circulation of books. The council's librarian was pressed into service as an assistant sanitary inspector (*Sydney Morning Herald*, 28 Mar. 1902:6). Six weeks earlier the aldermen of Randwick Council had complained about plague cases being sent to the Coast Hospital rather than to the Quarantine Station.

As in earlier epidemics, Sydney's Chinese community came in for considerable physical abuse. The newspapers, City Council and public health authorities were deluged with complaints against the Chinese, accusing them of hiding their plague cases away, of living in squalor or filth and of physically spreading the disease. Where Chinese dwellings were officially cleansed, they were usually dealt with in a much more drastic manner than those of their Australian neighbours, such as the 'filthy' Chinese dwellings off Retreat Street, Alexandria, which were demolished and burned early in the epidemic. The case of Ah Won, who died of plague in the North Shore Cottage Hospital early in May, also aroused considerable public attention. It was strongly denied that he was a resident of the northern suburbs and that he really lived near Goulburn Street.

Panic spread well beyond the boundaries of New South Wales. On 14 March, the New Zealand Government invoked quarantine regulations against vessels from New South Wales and required the fumigation of all cargo and personal effects. All passengers were also required to undergo a health inspection. In Sydney, after a letter-sorter at the GPO had been attacked by plague, the postal authorities decided to spray all postal articles with a formalin solution and to insert an impregnated wad of cotton wool in every bag of mail destined for beyond Sydney. This did not satisfy the Melbourne public health authorities, however, and they pressed for more vigorous preventive measures, including the installation of ovens in all major Sydney post offices so that interstate mail could be heated to a certain temperature to destroy all germ life (*Sydney Morning Herald*, 13 Mar. 1902:8).

Conclusion

The 1902 epidemic of plague was a traumatic event in Sydney's early history. It served to expose gross social evils, including many basic shortcomings in the city's sanitation and housing situation. It also focused public attention on the material conditions of Sydney's poor. The lessons of the epidemic tell us much about prevailing social attitudes and how people reacted to social crisis. The epidemic also led to a number of changes and improvements to the human condition of people in Sydney. First, it resulted in the application of a much more humane and rational policy of quarantine and treatment of cases of infectious disease. Second, it firmly established the role of health and sanitary inspectors in monitoring the city's housing and public health situation. Third, it resulted in a large proportion of the central city

being cleansed and disinfected with the demolition of many delapi-
dated dwellings. Finally, it resulted in a number of specific measures
designed to improve sanitation and public health, such as the rat-
proofing of business houses, stables and shops and the regular removal
of business and household refuse and waste materials.

Part II

Differentiation and Equity

6 Suburbia — the myth of homogeneity

JAMES FORREST

The major focus of work on urban residential patterns over recent years has been the testing of theories about social area structure, and the analysis of social processes reflected in spatial outcomes, (i.e. social area segregation, institutional constraints affecting 'choice', and structural changes). Most social area studies tend to focus on the situation at one point in time (for a partial review of Australian work see Stimson, 1982:92–122). Very few deal with change over time, although Johnston's (1973a) work on Melbourne is an exception. Another important focus is the development and delimitation of spatial frameworks for the management of processes giving rise to spatial distributions. This provides a basis for implementation of policies aimed at the alleviation of equity problems (Logan et al., 1975).

Factorial ecologies (for a review see Davies, 1984) as the major vehicle used to examine the social area structuring of cities, have produced a wealth of information on processes leading to the 'allocation' of groups within our urban societies to particular areas. One of the major problems with the factorial ecology approach, however, lies in its inability adequately to address the question of exclusivity or heterogeneity within sub-areas (Newton and Johnston, 1976). This is because the factoring process, like all linear regression procedures, uses only modal values (usually correlation coefficients) which tend to be simply averages of characteristic associations. Some have attempted to come to grips with this problem by means of indices characterising the degree of sub-area population homogeneity or otherwise. Such indices are deficient, however, in that, while they indicate the extent to which a population is concentrated within a particular range of age, occupation or ethnic group characteristics they cannot discriminate among districts with similar levels of homogeneity/heterogeneity, but which are nevertheless concentrated in different parts of the range of characteristics in the data set (Johnston, 1979b:239; Forrest, 1980:133–134). In short, the major problem is the way in which most approaches to social area analysis contrast only the modal values of sub-areas, but give no indication of the *total* social environment (Newton and Johnston, 1976:551).

To a greater or lessser degree, therefore, descriptions of the spatial structuring of residential areas within cities are at best incomplete; at worst they are inadequate for testing theories about social area segregation, or questionable as to their validity in terms of using the output from social area analysis for planning and related purposes. The aim of this chapter is to investigate the degree of homogeneity or heterogeneity among urban sub-areas, to classify and group sub-areas in terms of the *mix profile* of population characteristics present, and to identify the importance or otherwise of each of the constituent variables within each group.

Homogeneity and heterogeneity

Using a measure of the dispersion of a population over a set of characteristics such as occupation, marital status and age, Newton and Johnston (1976:547) concluded for Christchurch, New Zealand, that homogeneity was greatest in lower socio-economic status areas, and in younger suburban areas. Heterogeneity, on the other hand, was greatest in inner-city areas and in higher socio-economic status districts. A subsequent series of analyses of several sets of homogeneity scores (one for age, one for occupations, etc.) confirmed these general finding (p. 550):

1   There was a strong suggestion of a basic dichotomy between a relatively homogeneous suburbia characterised by younger families, and a much greater variety of ages and life styles in poorer, older parts of the inner city.
2   Higher status areas are the most heterogeneous in their population characteristics, compared with middle to lower status districts. This was attributed in part to the fine ground pattern of socio-spatial differentiation in New Zealand cities generally, compared with the size of the census sub-areas, and partly to a suggestion that exclusivity was much less typical of urban sub-areas in New Zealand than, say, in Australia.

What would be more advantageous, however, would be a classification procedure which would group sub-areas both in terms of the amount of homogeneity/heterogeneity *and* overall profile similarity.

Such a classification, an entropy procedure based on information theory, has been developed by Semple et al. (1972; 1975). A recent review of the procedure, along with a FORTRAN program listing and examples of its use in a variety of research situations in human geography is provided by Johnston and Semple (1983).

No attempt is made to provide details of the classification procedure here. Its value is simply reiterated: it groups together observation units (sub-areas) with similar profiles, where profile refers to the exact shape of a data set across an ordered set of variables. In addition to giving the range or mix of characteristics present in any group-of-areas profile, comparison of group characteristic means with means for all observations (e.g. all sub-areas in a city) shows which features have an above average or below average presence, and to what extent. Comparison of group profiles also shows the degree of overlap or difference from one group profile to another.

Using the entropy method, Johnston's (1979b) classification of social areas by occupation in a southern English town clearly brought out elements of dominance, mix and overlap within and between sub-area groupings. Categorisation of sub-areas in Rockhampton, Queensland, according to their age structure brought out the heterogeneous nature of some parts of the city, compared with the relative homogeneity of others (Forrest and Johnston, 1981). Most suburban areas showed relative homogeneity of life-cycle groups: younger families with some interspersal of elderly people's home unit development towards the periphery; closer to the centre areas of broadly middle aged to elderly. Greatest diversity occurred in inner-city areas, with a mix of life styles including young working-age adults and flat development, and the elderly in aging housing areas. Using a mix of socio-economic, family and ethnic variables, Johnston and Semple's (1983) analysis of social areas in Whangarei, New Zealand similarly divided basically 'average' areas from (a) a non-familism, flatting area in the inner city; (b) high-status residential areas; and (c) low-status areas with a high proportion of Maoris. Other such community profile applications to the analysis of social areas at the local government area level similarly highlight the mix and importance of social characteristics (Forrest and Herborn, 1981; Forrest, 1982; 1984a).

Occupation structures

The 1971 Census was the last to provide a detailed breakdown of occupation characteristics at the collectors district (CD) level. Since then, it has not been possible to differentiate, within the blue-collar manual-worker group, comprising some 30 per cent of the workforce, between skilled-manual and semiskilled-manual occupations. Thus for 1971, data were derived for eleven occupational variables for males at the part-local government area (part-LGA) level for each of the main Australian metropolitan areas. Each part-LGA comprised eight to ten CDs, or an average of 6000 people. Profile results from the entropy grouping presented in Figure 6.1 represent z scores for each group of part-LGAs. These scores relate the group means for each variable to the means for all part-LGAs in each metropolitan area. The effect is to highlight those aspects of the occupation structure which most char-

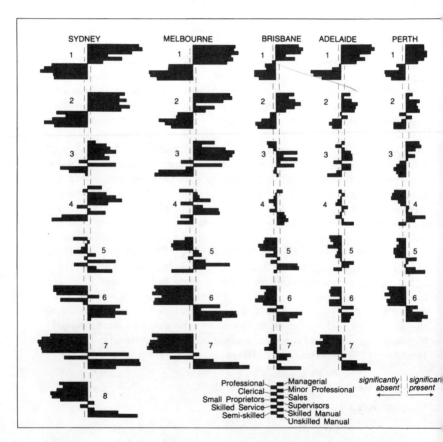

Figure 6.1. Occupation group profiles for Australian metropolitan areas, 1971 census. All profiles are drawn to the same scale, and show relative degree of presence or absence of each occupational characteristic

acterise those part-LGAs in each group (Johnston and Semple 1983:26
–27). Results for Sydney and Melbourne are directly comparable, as
are those for Brisbane, Adelaide and Perth. This is because the first two
differ markedly in size from the other three, though within-group size
differences are not all that great. Yet the part-LGAs have approximately the same population in every city. As Openshaw and Taylor (1981)
have pointed out, results collected at one scale of aggregation (relative
to city size) cannot be directly compared with those collected at a quite
different scale.

There are several findings applicable to all metropolitan areas.
There is a ranking of groups from generally high status to generally low
status. What does stand out, however, is the greater range or heterogeneity of occupations significantly present in even the highest status
group profiles; in fact all white-collar occupations are always present.
This is consistent with Newton and Johnston's (1976) findings for
Christchurch using their homogeneity index, and clearly suggests that
levels of exclusivity within higher status districts in even the largest
Australian cities may not be all that much greater than those typically
found in New Zealand cities. High-status exclusiveness in the Australian metropolitan scene, then, is something of a myth.

Lower status groups of part-LGAs are generally more homogeneously blue-collar manual in character, although the smaller the
city (e.g. Perth) the less this is so (cf. Johnston and Semple 1983 on
Whangarei). Otherwise, what is in every case different from the New
Zealand experience is the lack of any real differences in the degree
of homogeneity/heterogeneity from one group to another down the
status ranking. Within the white-collar occupations, the professional–
managerial component gradually becomes less important in favour of
clerical–sales; small proprietors, supervisors and skilled service workers
are added in; there is a gradual merging into dominantly blue-collar
manual workers. In the middle parts of the ranking, group profiles not
infrequently combine elements of both upper white-collar and lower
blue-collar elements, as in Sydney (profile 3), Brisbane (profile 4) or
Adelaide (profile 4) for example.

Occupational segregation is indeed present in Australian cities, as
the rankings of group profiles show. Examination of the detail of the
profiles as they merge one into the other shows, however, that at the
part-LGA scale at least, occupational exclusivity is much less obvious
than perhaps many of the older, factorial ecologies would have us
believe.

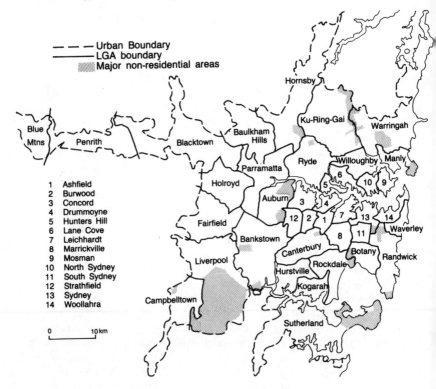

Figure 6.2   Sydney local government areas referred to in text

Income distributions

Classification of part-LGAs according to male incomes focuses attention on another of the main elements of socio-economic status, the
others being occupation and education. Using the criterion of a
diminishing increment to variation 'explained' with an increasing
number of groups, the entropy procedure was stopped at eight groups
accounting for 78 per cent of overall variation (Figures 6.2 and 6.3).
General conclusions, for Sydney, parallel those for occupation structures:

1   There is a general income-mix ranking (though with an important
no-income element probably representing full-time students) in
profile 1, to generally middle to lower incomes in profile 8, though

with a great deal of overlap from one profile to another.
2   A feature of many of the group profiles is the range of income categories present. In profile 3, for instance, while the significantly present categories are in the higher income areas, all incomes below $5000 show an at least average presence. Similarly in profile 5, nearly all income categories are present, though with an emphasis on the middle income range. What is apparent, therefore, is the considerable degree of heterogeneity of income categories present in most cases. In fact, and contrary to findings for the distribution of occupations in 1971, greatest homogeneity is to be found in the highest income areas.

Highest income areas (profiles 1 and 2) are located in some of the northern harbourside suburbs — Hunters Hill, Mosman, parts of Manly — and in upper north shore districts — notably Ku-ring-gai, northern parts of Warringah, southern parts of Hornsby and adjacent Baulkham Hills; parts of the eastern suburbs (Woollahra); and parts of Sutherland in the south. Broadly upper-middle income areas (profiles 3 and 4) are concentrated in the northern beach suburbs (Warringah), coastal parts of Waverley in the eastern suburbs, and much of the Georges River (Kogarah) and Sutherland region in the south. Parts of the inner western suburbs of Strathfield-Concord also fit into this category (cf. Pluss, ch. 4), as do most of the Blue Mountains and parts of Penrith in the outer western suburbs, much of Parramatta too, along with parts of Fairfield, Liverpool and Bankstown in what is generally considered to be Sydney's disadvantaged western suburbs.

Middle incomes, though with an important intermixture of lower incomes, (profiles 5 and 6) characterise Sydney's western, middle-distant southern and southeastern suburbs generally. Lower-income areas, though still with significant middle-income elements, are largely confined to the inner southern suburbs, notably Sydney, South Sydney, Marrickville and Botany, with another important pocket in Parramatta.

This characterisation of areas in terms of the mix of male incomes, and their location, conforms broadly to areas of need identified from a much wider range of characteristics by Stillwell and Hardwick (1973), where a clear distinction was made between inner city and western suburbs. The same broad grouping of areas also emerged from Forrest's (1977:189) characterisation of part-LGAs for Sydney in 1971, based on occupation, except that the western suburbs were generally ranked on occupation lower than inner-city areas. Part but not all of this difference can be accounted for in terms of the location of the elderly. Southern inner-city areas are also noted for their migrant population concentrations and low earning levels generally.

Figure 6.3 Male income distribution patterns for Sydney, 1976 census: outline profile shows characteristic percentages for Sydney

KEY
$000
>18
15-18
12-15
9-12
8-9
7-8
6-7
5-6
4-5
3-4
2-3
1.5-2
<1.5
none

0   20
percent

whole; the bars represent characteristic percentages present in
each group of sub-areas.

Figure 6.4　Family structure distribution patterns for Sydney, 1976 cen
nomenclature is: HSoyc — head, spouse, other adults, chil
HSWc — head, spouse, working age children; H(F)Ac and H
head (female and male), other adults, children; H(F)A and H

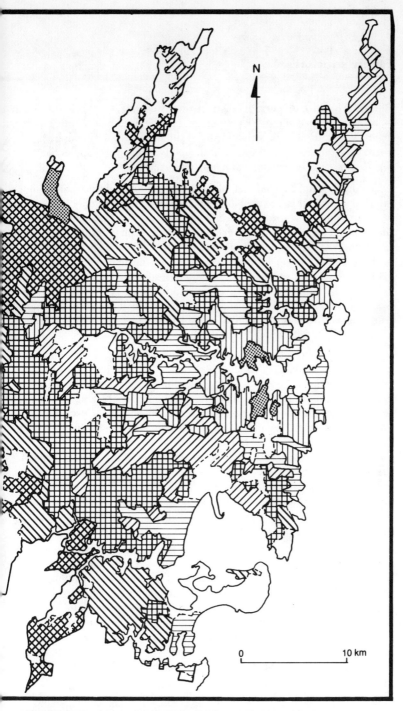

head (female and male), other adults; H(F)c and H(M)c — head
(female and male), children; H(F) and H(M) — head only (female and
male). Outline profiles represent Sydney as a whole. Bars represent
each group of sub-areas.

Family structures

Family structure mix and its distribution is part of a life style (familism – non-familism) and life-cycle stage (young families to the elderly) approach to the characterisation of residential areas. In this case, the entropy grouping procedure was stopped at seven groups accounting for 79 per cent of overall variation (Figure 6.4).

Younger families (parents plus children under sixteen) plus older families (some children of working age) dominate profile 1, together with an important single (mainly female) parent family component, merging on profile 2 into a greater emphasis on families with older children. Part-LGAs so characterised form a broad arc around the outer margins of the builtup area. One of the features of these two groups of areas, however, is the mix of older family elements. This mix is generally apparent from a close examination of the Poulsen and Spearritt (1981:30–45) age maps, but is much less obvious in more traditional family status maps from factorial ecologies of the city (cf. Forrest, 1977:189; Logan et al. 1975).

Profile 3 is close to the average for the city as a whole, with most family types present. Parts of the urban area thus identified fall into two main regions. One is a broad though discontinuous arc from the northeast (the northern beach suburbs) and northwest (Hornsby) through the middle-western (Fairfield-Liverpool) and southeastern (Botany) suburbs. The other is a major concentration southwest from the city centre focusing on Marrickville and Canterbury. Canterbury is an area of major flat and town-house development in recent years. In the case of Marrickville, the past decade or so has seen a major incursion of migrant families into this formerly elderly person, inner-city area. Hence the range of family types.

A mix of younger and older families, and the increasing importance of the single elderly, characterises profiles 4 and 5. Sub-areas form an arc of broadly middle-distant suburbs from Manly in the northeast, through Ryde and Parramatta in the northwest and west, Bankstown, then Hurstville-Rockdale in the south to Randwick in the southeast. Profiles 6 and 7 represent a mix of late life-cycle stage (the single elderly) plus non-familism groups: younger, working age adults flatting together, along with single, career (working age) oriented people. All are inner-city areas in the eastern suburbs (Woollahra-Waverley), areas undergoing rehabilitation and gentrification (Leichhardt and Drummoyne), and most particularly on the lower North Shore (North Sydney and Mosman).

Family income: spatial management implications

One of the major advantages of the entropy procedure is that it identifies the total mix of characteristics present in any group of sub-areas, a mix which, by comparison with a global mean, is further differentiated between characteristics which have an above or below average presence in the group. This is especially relevant for geographers concerned about problems of social disadvantage, translated into the considerable amount of work on territorial social indicators over recent years (cf. Stimson, 1982:168–196). Geographers at Monash University were asked by the former Department of Urban and Regional Development in 1973 for example, to advise on the delimitation and grouping of local government areas throughout Australia, and especially in the metropolitan centres, for the *areal* implementation of amended Grants Commission legislation aimed at combatting social deprivation (Logan et al. 1975:9).

In Britain, the concept of geographical imbalance among social areas was used in the Plowden Report (1967) as the basis of an *area* approach to action against deprivation. This was an attempt to solve problems of educational failure, which was associated with social deprivation principally in poorer, inner-city districts, through positive discrimination and the adoption of 'educational priority area' policies. What was not very clear, however, was how much of the problem could be accounted for in terms of an area-based approach to policy implementation, or how many of the socially deprived could effectively be reached by such an area-based policy (Berthoud, 1976:5). Little and Mabey (1972) found in practice that while the educationally deprived were in fact concentrated in certain areas, they still formed a relatively small proportion of the total population in those areas, and conversely that small pockets of deprivation in otherwise unaffected areas were overlooked. In short, an area-based approach must take account of the *mix* of people in any sub-area or group of sub-areas.

Investigation of the geographic distribution of poverty faces similar problems to those mentioned above. In the case of the last major inquiry into poverty in Australia (Poverty Report, 1975), the identification and description of poor families was facilitated by a major sample survey which allowed cross-classification of income by family structure, age, house tenure and other characteristics. Poverty was separately defined for each situation, taking account of situation and commitments (disabilities). Geographic analysis of the survey results was limited by the size and nature of the sample to relatively large areas (Manning, 1976). In the absence of any such cross-classification data

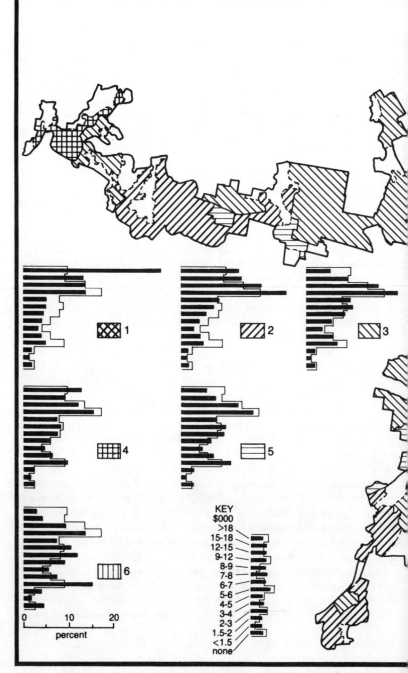

Figure 6.5 Family income distribution patterns for Sydney, 1976 census

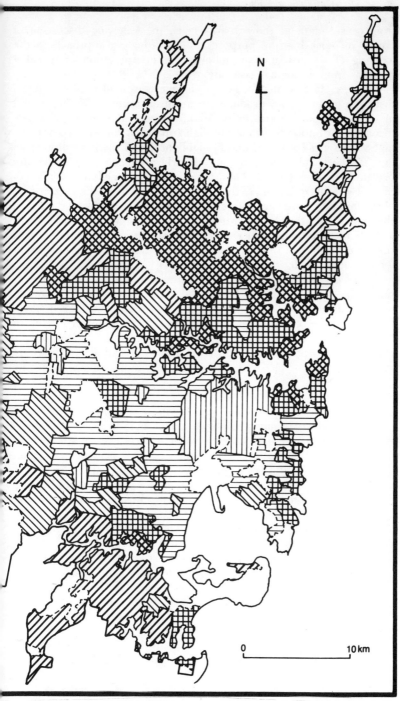

Outline profiles represent Sydney as a whole. Bars represent each
group of sub-areas.

from census data at the sub-area level, the following discussion of family incomes has the purpose of illustrating an approach to the locating of the urban poor, followed by interpretation of revealed patterns from ecological associations.

Entropy classification of family income (husband plus wife only) distributions in Sydney produced six groups accounting for 70 per cent of total variation (Figure 6.5). Within a general ranking of family income distribution from mainly high (profile 1) to lower (profile 6), highest incomes (profiles 1 and 2) highlight the northern, northwestern and southern suburbs of Sydney. Nearly all income categories are present in profiles 3 and 4. These areas include most of the lower North Shore (with the exception of the harbourside suburbs), the greater part of the middle to outer western and southwestern suburbs, and parts of the eastern suburbs. At the bottom of the mix ranking, profiles 5 and 6 identify the middle to inner western and southern suburbs and most of the eastern suburbs. In general terms this pattern largely parallels that for individual male incomes.

There are, however, a number of points of comment and interpretation. The Poverty Report (1975:17–20) associated poverty with a number of demographic characteristics, in particular the aged single (mainly females), fatherless families and the unemployed, and in near-poverty aged married couples and large families. Using cross-classified data from the Poverty Inquiry survey and adjusting for family structure, Manning (1976) described the distribution of family income poverty in Sydney:

1   A western sector, the inner west having a very high incidence of income-poverty; and a continuation of both poverty and near-poverty in middle and outer western suburbs. The main element here, as in the southwestern suburbs, is the incidence of single-parent families and the unemployed. These show up on Figure 6.5 (profile 5 and 6 areas) in the inner to mid-western suburbs, though not in the outer western suburbs apart from small pockets around Penrith.

2   A below-average incidence of poverty in the eastern, inner southern and northern suburbs (profile 4 and 5 areas on the lower North Shore and northern Warringah), taking account of family and other considerations, was associated with the elderly and single women. In fact, a number of pockets in several parts of the North Shore also represent low wage earners, the incidence of which is often overlooked in what are usually regarded as high status districts. Parts of Willoughby (Forrest, 1984a) and Warringah (Forrest, 1982) are prime cases of Holterman's (1975) point that the concentration of poverty or social deprivation on a broad area scale can overlook

smaller numbers of equally deprived people in areas of otherwise greater affluence.

3   A broad southern sector (profiles 4 and 5) including St George, Canterbury and Bankstown, continuing into Liverpool and to a lesser extent Sutherland. Here, as in some of the northern suburbs, there is a well-established pensioner population with some supplementary income sufficient to keep these elderly out of the poverty category, plus, in the southern districts but less so in the northern, an above-average proportion of low wage earners.

Conclusion

The concept of social change in metropolitan Australia includes a need to consider change for the future, in particular the implementation of policies to achieve a betterment of social conditions, and an easing of disadvantage. It also requires recognition of the reality of social area segregation in the present. In that so much planning policy is implemented on an area basis, with grants allocated, for example, to local governments areas or groupings of LGAs, there is a need for the identification and description of designated areas in overall community profile terms. One of the major problems with the social area-based work in the past has been its tendency to oversimplify, to overlook minority groups, and therefore to focus attention on *major* concentrations of advantage or disadvantage. And where deprivation is not the focus, there has been a tendency to assume a greater degree of social area segregation, of homogeneity, than really exists. The descriptive analysis discussed here has attempted to demonstrate the myth of homogeneity and the reality of an often much more heterogeneous social area structuring than has been recognised in the past.

7 Social areas, community profiles and the social geography of smaller towns

JAMES FORREST

An important aspect of the social geography of urban areas revolves around ways in which social processes, operating through a spatial medium, produce social outcomes. Not all Australians live in the metropolitan areas. Thus the purpose of this chapter is to examine the major elements of the urbanisation process associated with residential segregation in three smaller New South Wales towns: Katoomba-Wentworth Falls, which is within the Sydney urban region commuting zone; Lithgow, which is functionally part of the Sydney urban field, and Griffith, a service centre in the southwest of the State.

The mechanism of residential area segregation is largely to be found in the operation of the housing market. But the underlying social processes imply social change, especially that involved with indus-trialisation or modernisation (Moore, 1963). Thus increasing division of labour is associated with increasing specialisation, both of occupa-tions and landuses within the city. This process, often referred to as structural urbanisation, acts to produce socio-economic status dif-ferentiation among people performing different tasks requiring different levels of skill and education, hence reward through income, and from that a structuring of residential areas in terms of their socio-economic status (Johnston, 1973b:5).

Landuse specialisation, job specialisation with division of labour, and the increasing separation of place of residence and place of work are all important elements of the contemporary industrialisation-modernisation-urbanisation process. With the increasing scale of society, some would also see a decline in the cohesion of the family unit in both economic and social terms. The effect is to be found both in changes in life styles and in the spatial segregation of life-cycle stage groups — grandparents from their children's families; parents from growing-up children. The result is a separate, behavioural dimension of the urbanisation process (Johnston, 1973b:6–7) involving segregation in terms of such factors as age, marital status, house tenure (reflecting life-style differences) and the status of women in the workforce.

Migration has been an important element of urban society in postwar Australia, and hence a third, demographic dimension of urbanisation. Residential segregation of the overseas-born in Australian urban centres is associated with two major features. One concerns their economic position. Partly reflecting government immigration policy (Birrell and Birrell, 1981), many are less well qualified; most are lacking in capital. They have tended therefore to be restricted to areas of lower socio-economic status in the inner city (Johnston, 1971:47–52). Another factor relates to the manner of the migration process itself, much migration being in the form of a chain process involving a concentration of origins as well as destinations: pioneer migrants send back information, attracting their families and acquaintances to join them; the earlier arrivals help those coming later with accommodation and employment (cf. Burnley and Routh ch. 15). In many cases, migrants and more particularly their children leave the local immigrant community to become absorbed into the host society. Cultural or racial differences can, however, impede such integration, limiting job opportunities (Stokes, 1962) and imposing barriers to acceptance (Timms, 1969), often resulting in a spatial clustering of minority groups partly as a defensive mechanism.

Size, function and social area differentiation

Residential area segregation in terms of structural, behavioural and demographic processes involved in urbanisation have mostly been studied at the level of the major metropolitan areas and larger cities. There is evidence, however, that towns do not have to be very large at all to display recognisable tendencies in the same directions. A quite well-marked clustering of socio-economic groups is noted by Jones (1962) for the British towns of Hereford (population 32 501) and Peebles (pop. 6 013), for example. In New Zealand, occupational segregation is evident in Oamaru (pop. 13 350) (Forrest, 1970). A study of Timaru (pop. 27 946), using both socio-economic and life cycle–life style characteristics, brought out a fundamental division into structural and behavioural associations at the sub-area level (Forrest, 1968).

Town function may also be a significant factor leading to social area differentiation. Holding size constant, important differences in the degree of segregation among residential areas can also reflect differences in the economic base of towns (Jones, 1962). An industrial or mining town, for example, would incline towards a larger number of people in blue-collar manual occupations, towards a greater polarisation between a majority group of blue-collar workers and a minority of white-collar, clerical–managerial residents, and hence to greater segregation at the sub-area level. A service or market centre, on the other hand, with its more balanced range of socio-economic attainment, would represent much more of a continuum of change from lower to higher status sub-areas.

In a study of two small centres in southern New Zealand, however, one a service and light industrial centre of 4419 people, the other a manufacturing centre of 1861 people with more than half its workforce employed in the local textile mills, Forrest (1973) showed the importance of size rather than function as an explanation of structural segregation. Australian evidence is less conclusive. In a study of smaller cities and towns, Forrest (1977:202–204) found greater concentration (i.e. segregation) of selected family, but not socio-economic characteristics in the steel town of Whyalla, compared with the service and industrial growth centre of Albury-Wodonga and the goldmining and service centre of Kalgoorlie.

Community profile analysis

Holding size constant, each of the towns examined here has been chosen to represent different aspects of economic and/or migrant structure. Griffith (pop. 13 187 in 1981) is a market and light industrial centre in the southern New South Wales Riverina district and centre for intensive agriculture (Table 7.1) (see Davey et al. 1980:109–129). There is an important Italian component of the population associated with viniculture in the district. Katoomba-Wentworth Falls (pop. 13 942) is an important retirement, resort and service centre in the Blue Mountains some 100 km west of Sydney. It is also a commuter suburb for professional–managerial people. There are important British (UK) and 'other overseas-born' population components. Lithgow (pop. 12 793) is a coalmining and manufacturing centre with a much higher proportion of its workforce in blue-collar occupations than the other two. Information on the population characteristics of each centre was taken from the 1981 census, using collectors districts (CDs) as the basic sub-area unit. Each CD contains around 600 people on average, more in the case of Griffith, fewer in Katoomba-Wentworth Falls.

Table 7.1   Representative characteristics of study towns

Proportion who are:		Griffith	Katoomba– Wentworth Falls	Lithgow
Born in:	Australia[a]	84.3	79.9	91.4
	UK	2.8	11.6	4.8
	Italy	9.6	[d]	[d]
	Northern Europe[b]	0.5	1.7	0.1
Occupation:	Professional–managerial[c]	16.0	22.4	12.6
	Clerical–sales	27.1	23.1	18.4
	Service workers	9.0	16.3	8.9
	Skilled–semiskilled	21.4	17.6	32.4
Industry:	Agriculture	7.8	0.6	0.5
	Mining	0.2	1.1	15.0
	Wholesale/retail	25.1	16.1	12.2
	Transport/storage	4.1	6.8	9.4
	Community services	15.3	25.8	11.0
	Recreation/personal service	6.1	10.2	4.2
	Manufacturing	10.9	6.4	14.8

Notes: [a] Of total population
     [b] Germany and the Netherlands
     [c] Of total labour force
     [d] None to speak of

From experience, most people realise that their street, their suburb, contains not a single but a number of types of people: white collar, blue collar, doctors, carpenters, machinists, sales people; younger families, the elderly; people born in Australia, and people born overseas. Most areas are a mix of people, though the range, the degree of heterogeneity, may be greater in some areas, less in others. The entropy classification procedure described previously (Forrest, ch. 6) is used here to avoid the considerable loss or wastage of information associated with factorial approaches. The earlier discussion of homogeneity and heterogeneity, however, dealt with single sets of characteristics — age, income, family structure. Yet the structural and behavioural processes involved in urbanisation are not univariate. Structural aspects, the socio-economic dimension, are commonly seen as a mix of occupation –income–education characteristics, although only occupation is examined here. The behavioural or family status dimension embraces a basket of interdependent variables, notably age, sex, marital status, dwelling tenure and women in the workforce. Three of this group of characteristics are combined in this study: age, marital status and house tenure (cf. Stapleton, 1980). Variables in each of the sets were first converted to percentages of each set total so that the three summed to 300 per cent (Johnston and Semple, 1983:24), and were then subjected to entropy classification.

Community profiles

Structural characteristics

Classification of CDs according to occupational structure by sex follows
the trend of most classifications which identify a person's socio-
economic status simply in terms of position within a job occupation
ranking (Runciman, 1967). The entropy classification procedure
selected here for discussion divided the CDs in each town into a
number of groups accounting for between 63 (Katoomba) and 71
(Griffith) per cent of overall variation across all CDs. Turning first to
distinctive features of the groupings for Griffith (Figure 7.1), the
profiles show a general status ranking from more white collar (managerial–professional–clerical–sales) (profiles 1, 2) to more blue collar
(skilled–semiskilled–unskilled) in profile 6, although an important
feature within that ranking is the general *mix* of people by occupation in
all profile groupings. There is a significant (though below average)
blue-collar element in the 'best' areas, just as there is a significant
(though again below the town average) white-collar component in the
'lower' profile groupings. No areas are homogeneously white or blue
collar. Bearing this point in mind, attention can now be focused on
those aspects of each grouping where the occupational characteristics
show an above average presence.
    The first entropy-derived group profile comprises mainly profes-
sional–managerial and clerical–sales occupations for both males and
females, with a less important service and transport–communications
component. Profile 2 comprises more important male managerial–
professional and clerical–sales components, but also a significant
skilled–semiskilled element, both male and female. Profiles 3 and 4
overlap to a considerable degree, and are close to the average for
Griffith as a whole. Main differences are an emphasis in profile 3 on the
white collar and, especially for females, on the skilled–semiskilled;
changing in degree to profile 4's slightly less emphasis on the white-
collar groups in favour of the unskilled and unemployed. This tendency
towards a blue-collar emphasis is maintained in profiles 5 and 6, the
former emphasising all blue-collar groups plus the unemployed
(though note the female white-collar component), the latter placing
more emphasis on the unskilled and unemployed (though again, note
the service and transport–communications components). Mapped distributions for the six entropy groups for Griffith bring out the town's
general social topography. Broadly higher status districts (1 and 2) are
located in both northern and east-central parts of the town. Broadly
middle status areas (3 and 4) are concentrated to the northwest and

northeast. Generally lower status areas (groups 5 and 6) are a feature of the southern parts of Griffith.

Distinctive features of the classification for Katoomba-Wentworth Falls are first, and allowing for differences in the occupational profile for the urban area as a whole, the similarity with Griffith group profiles at least near the top and bottom of the range; second, and again like Griffith, a general ranking from higher to lower status though with considerable overlap from one group profile to the next; and third, the occupational heterogeneity of all group profiles (Figure 7.1). Profile 1 highlights a dominantly white-collar emphasis, overlapping to include a skilled−semiskilled component in profile 2. Profile 3 is close to the average for the district as a whole, while profile 4 represents a single CD of mainly female professional and skilled−semiskilled employment. Profiles 5 to 7 place gradually less emphasis on white-collar occupations and more on blue-collar (especially females in profiles 5 and 7), with a gradually increasing importance placed on the unskilled and unemployed. Mapped distributions show the basically higher status area (1 and 2) in southeastern and southwestern Katoomba and eastern Wentworth Falls. The full range of occupations (profile 3 areas) occupies the balance of Wentworth Falls and much of central Katoomba. Profile 4 is adjacent to the hospital. Profile 5, mainly middle-status areas, dominates northern Katoomba. Generally lower-status areas, though with important white-collar components still present (6, 7) characterise much of western Katoomba.

Allowing for the greater proportion of skilled and unskilled in Lithgow, the major difference between that town and the other two is the lower degree of residential segregation by occupation. Lithgow shows relatively small differences between group and city-wide profiles, and a consequence of this is the need for seven groups to account for basically the same level of variation accounted for here, compared with six for the other two centres (Figure 7.1). Profile 1 is basically white collar with a professional-managerial emphasis. It overlaps into a still basically white-collar profile 2, though with more clerical–sales (especially for females). Profile 3 is a mix of (male) professional–managerial plus clerical–sales and skilled−semiskilled.

Middle-status elements dominate profiles 4 and 5, the main difference being the change from a white and blue-collar mix on the former to a more blue-collar emphasis on the latter. Two final profiles, 6 and 7, are increasingly blue collar and unskilled−unemployed in character but still, as with the other two towns, with other occupations present. Higher-status areas (1 and 2), with an admixture of skilled−semiskilled elements, occur to the southwest of Lithgow, and to a lesser extent to the southeast. Broadly middle-status areas (4, 5) predominate in central parts of the city north (5) and south (4) of the railway line.

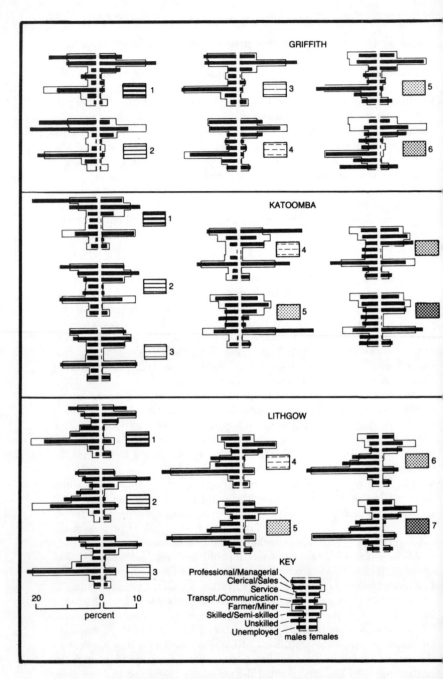

Figure 7.1 Occupation mix group distributions. Outline profiles represent each town as a whole. Bars represent each group of sub-areas.

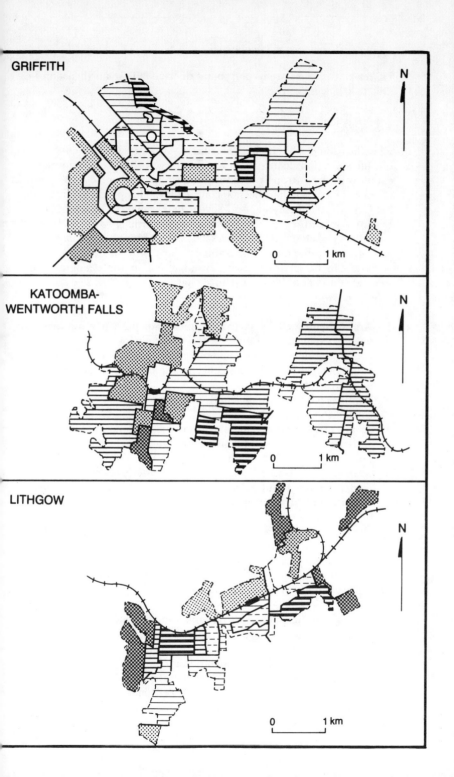

GRIFFITH

KATOOMBA-
WENTWORTH FALLS

LITHGOW

Lower-status areas are in peripheral districts, to the northeast and east and to the west of the town.

Behavioural characteristics

Classification of CDs by age, marital status and dwelling tenure brings out life-style (familism − non-familism) and life-cycle distributions for each town; the entropy procedure was stopped when 80 to 83 per cent of overall variation had been accounted for. This produced five groups for Griffith and Lithgow, and seven for Katoomba-Wentworth Falls. Distinctive features of the profiles for Griffith (Figure 7.2) are the overall mix of characteristics present in most groups of areas, such that each group profile merges into and overlaps with the next, and also the variation in life styles present, brought out in the changing mix of marital status and dwelling tenure characteristics. The five social area types, in profile order, are:

1 Areas dominated by young families with both parents in mainly owner-occupied dwellings, to the northeast of the town.
2 A mix of younger families and older folk spanning a range of marital situations, with significant concentrations of public housing mainly in southwestern areas.
3 Families with school-age children, older folk, and owner occupance, to the north and northeast.
4 A mix of age and marital status groups, but dominated by young, working-age adults and single-parent families in private-rental housing areas in central and southern parts of Griffith.
5 Mainly older families, emphasising the elderly widowed in a mix of owner-occupied and private-rental housing in central western and eastern rural-urban fringe districts.

The family status characterisation of Katoomba-Wentworth Falls is in some ways more complex than that for Griffith (Figure 7.2B), but this is at least partly a consequence of the dispersed nature of the built-up area and the smaller CDs, which provide a finer sieve for social area segregation. Main profile types are:

1 Young families, married parents though with some solo-parent families, and owner occupance in northern parts of Katoomba and Wentworth Falls.
2 Average areas with few outstanding characteristics relative to the urban area as a whole: an older version of profile 1 with most social types present, and typical of much of Wentworth Falls as well as eastern and western parts of Katoomba.

3 Families with school-age children and both parents, though again, as in profile 1, an important single-parent family element in dominantly public-housing areas in northern and southern parts of Katoomba.

4 Mainly middle-aged areas of owner occupance and some rental housing in southeastern Katoomba and northeastern Wentworth Falls.

5 An above average number of single, working adults and solo-parent, young families in rental accommodation in central and southern parts of Katoomba.

6 A single CD in central Katoomba of dominantly private rental housing and single or widowed people of young working age to elderly.

7 Middle-aged to elderly single and widowed, mainly owner occupance, around the southwestern parts of Wentworth Falls and north-central Katoomba.

Lithgow has a lower degree of segregation of young families than either of the other two centres (Figure 7.2), and like Griffith a lower level of segregation of the elderly than Katoomba. Tenure characteristics show much the same structure in all three centres. For Lithgow the five profile types are:

1 Mainly families with dependent children, a mix of marital status characteristics though with a strong solo-parent component, reflecting the importance of public housing, on the western outskirts of the town.

2 Most age groups apart from young working-age adults, though an emphasis on young to primary-school-age children, some elderly widowed, mainly owner occupance, in southwestern suburbs.

3 Average areas for Lithgow, perhaps more middle aged and older, and a range of marital status characteristics in central and much of the eastern half of the town.

4 A mix of younger families and the elderly, single-parent families and widowers, in a mix of private and public rental housing plus some owner occupance, mainly in south-central Lithgow.

5 A single CD, non-familism oriented, mainly private rentals and young working-age adults, single people and solo-parent households, in the central part of Lithgow.

Demographic structure

The demographic structure of the three towns varies markedly. Griffith has a strong Italian component, while Katoomba-Wentworth Falls has

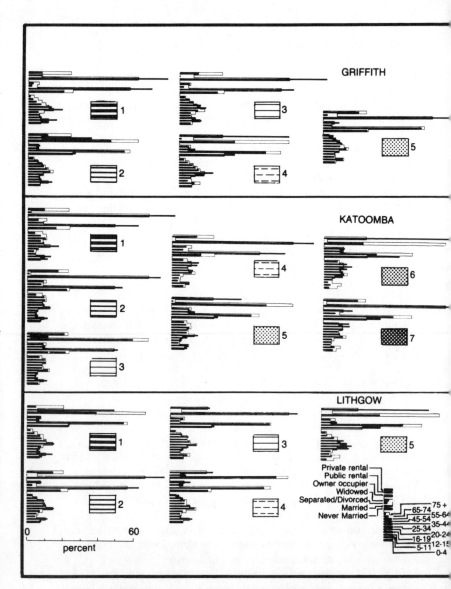

Figure 7.2 Family structure patterns: age, marital status and tenure. Outline profiles represent each town as a whole. Bars represent each group of sub-areas.

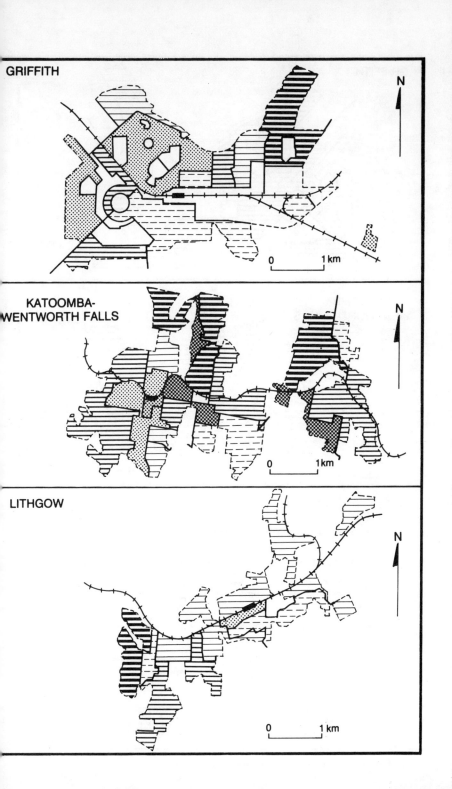

GRIFFITH

N

0   1 km

KATOOMBA-
WENTWORTH FALLS

N

0   1km

LITHGOW

N

0   1 km

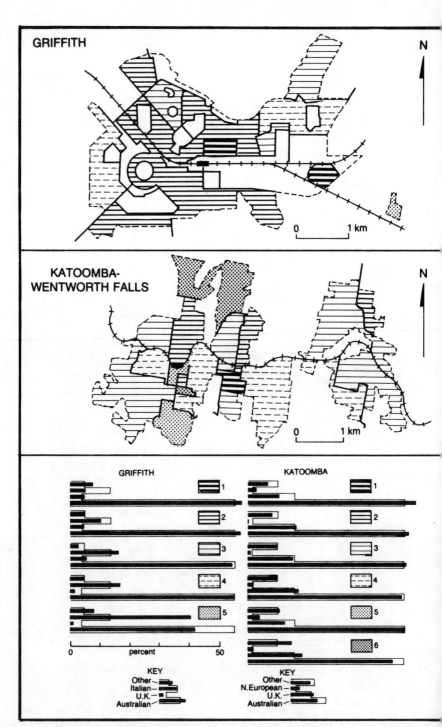

Figure 7.3 Ethnic mix group distributions

a more important UK, northern European and 'other' (mainly other European) element, a much greater mix of birthplace backgrounds than Griffith. Lithgow, with only a minor overseas-born component, is not included in this part of the study. The entropy grouping procedure was stopped when 80 to 84 per cent of explanation was achieved.

Migrant groups, though in most cases spatially separated from the Australian born to a greater or lesser extent, are much less segregated than in most overseas countries (Burnley, 1976). Of all migrant groups in Australia, however, the Italians are among the most segregated in our cities (Forrest, 1977:188–197), and this is borne out in Griffith. Profiles bring out a basic separation of the two main birthplace elements, the Australian born and the Italian born (Figure 7.3). Profiles 1 and 2 are dominantly Australian born, with important minority elements of people from the UK and other European (non-Italian) origins, located in central and southern parts of Griffith. Fewer Australian born and more from Italy characterise profiles 3 and 4, on the northwestern and western margins of the town. Greatest emphasis on the Italians, together with other European groups, occurs on profile 5, representing the largely rural-urban fringe area east of Griffith.

Katoomba-Wentworth Falls has a much more heterogeneous inter-mixture of birthplace groups than Griffith. Thus profiles 1 to 3, mainly Australian born but with near-average northern European and 'other' (mainly European) components, dominate Wentworth Falls and mainly north-central parts of Katoomba (Figure 7.3). Profiles 2 and 3 merge somewhat imperceptibly into group 4 areas, the main difference being the more UK-born emphasis, in CDs mainly located on the eastern margins of Katoomba and southwestern margins of Wentworth Falls. A dominance of northern and other Europeans, brought out in profile 5, is a feature of several central and southern parts of Katoomba, while profile 6, highlighting other overseas born plus those from the UK, are largely a feature of the northern districts of Katoomba.

Conclusion

In that the ability of community profile analysis to highlight both the separateness and the mix of characteristics present in an area provides a more accurate and true-to-life characterisation of urban sub-areas, it provides also a better basis for a social geography of towns. Results have shown, first, that all those aspects of the urbanisation process — structural, behavioural and demographic — are present even for the small towns examined here. They also show that major differences in town function do not make any appreciable difference to the degree or nature of subarea segregation, at least in terms of the main structural and behavioural dimensions. Only on the demographic dimension are there important differences involving the Italian born. But even here, the segregation of this birthplace group compared with that of other non-Australian born is consistent with findings for Australian cities generally.

8 Through a child's eyes: quality of neighbourhood and quality of life

ROSS HOMEL AND AILSA BURNS

Several other chapters in this book have compared different areas of Sydney in terms of their history and present populations. In this chapter we ask the question: how does life differ for children living in different parts of the city? Do children today growing up in, say, an inner-city industrial suburb feel notably less happy about their lives and their surroundings than do those living in more privileged environments? Or does each adapt to what they know?

In considering this question we draw on data from our Sydney Area Family Study (SAFS) which involved interviews with nine to eleven-year-old children and their parents living in eighteen Sydney suburbs. These were selected to cover the spectrum from poor to prosperous, and to include both inner and outer regions of the city. To rank suburbs in terms of their relative 'quality' or advantage level, we used the social risk index developed by Vinson and Homel (1976). This risk score is derived from a basket of measures, including average income and education of the area, and also local unemployment, health, welfare, divorce/separation and crime figures. It thus constitutes a good summary measure of the advantage or disadvantage level of an area. The eighteen suburbs selected for the SAFS had risk scores ranging from very high to low risk, (high quality).

The SAFS interviews with parents and children covered a wide range of topics, but the present discussion concentrates on two areas: children's feelings about their neighbourhood, and their evaluation of it; and children's friendship patterns and sense of well-being. The fundamental question being asked is — is the objectively measured quality of a neighbourhood paralleled by the quality of life experienced by the children who live there?

103

People or places?

People with money buy houses in desirable areas. People without money find cheap accommodation where they can. As a result, area of residence is correlated with income. And since better jobs are better paid, and better education increases the likelihood of obtaining a better job, people of different occupations and education cluster in different suburbs. So when we look at what children living in particular neighbourhoods have to say about their lives, we need to know whether their feelings derive from where they live, or from their membership of a particular kind of family which prefers (or is forced) to live in a certain type of area. This can be done by using appropriate statistical controls. So if, for example, children in higher and lower risk areas evaluate the quality of their lives rather differently, we can investigate whether this is largely due to qualities of the parents and family or qualities of the area, or indeed to both.

The families interviewed

The sample comprised 321 nine to eleven-year-olds and their parents. The children were randomly selected from the eighteen state schools and seventeen Roman Catholic parochial schools that served our eighteen suburbs. There were 157 boys and 164 girls. A rather complex three-stage sampling procedure was used which allowed us to represent the full range of risk scores across the city, but which allowed for the sample to be weighted so as to represent the total Sydney population. Children were interviewed at school, parents some six weeks later at home. No child was included in the sample unless parental permission had been obtained.

Children's evaluations of their neighbourhood

How do children feel about their neighbourhood? We asked them to nominate the good points, the not-so-good points, the things they would like to change, and to give an overall rating of the area as 'a place for children to grow up in' (Homel and Burns, 1983b). The ratings were very positive. Only 10 per cent of all children regarded their suburb as 'not so good'. The statistically significant relationship between these ratings and the risk scores of the eighteen suburbs, shows that children living in the two highest risk areas (Q and R) were notably less happy than all others with their surroundings (Figure 8.1). The much higher degree of dissatisfaction in Area R than in Area Q

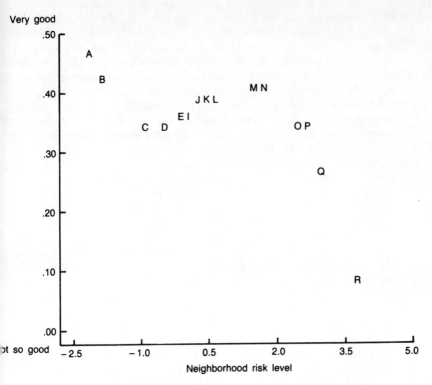

Figure 8.1 Proportion of children rating their neighbourhood as 'very good', by risk level (predicted probabilities from regression analysis)

parallels the substantial risk differential between the two; Q and R are both inner-city industrial suburbs, but R is older and more closely built up. Areas A and B, which are prosperous semi-rural suburbs on the north-west fringes of the city, also stand out, but otherwise children's satisfaction levels vary very little across the fourteen middling suburbs which range through the southern, eastern, northern and western regions of Sydney.

Children seem equally happy with quite a wide range of suburbs, but much prefer bushland neighbourhoods and do not consider industrial suburbs as good places for them. It is possible of course that children of more prosperous, or better-educated families, like their neighbourhoods better than other children regardless of the nature of the neighbourhood, and this was checked. Not so. The risk score was the only significant predictor of the children's ratings.

What did the children like and dislike about their neighbourhoods?

Parks, other playspaces, friendly children and adults comprised virtually all the 'likes'. Conversely, lack of playmates, lack of parks and
playspace, and traffic, noise, pollution and unfriendly adults accounted
for most of the 'dislikes'. To see whether children living in different
suburbs had different good or bad things to say about their surroundings, the frequency of mention of various characteristics against
neighbourhood risk scores was plotted. This showed a very strong
inverse relationship between appreciation of publicly provided playspace (parks) and space privately available although not necessarily
privately owned (gardens, backyards and nearby bushland). In the
higher risk areas, many residences had little or nothing in the way of
garden or backyard. As a result, the higher the risk level of the
neighbourhood, the more likely the children were to mention parks,
playgrounds and ovals, and also playmates. The lower the risk, the
more likely they were to mention private gardens, backyards and
bushland. In addition, two groups of children stood out, those in the
two highest risk areas and those in the two lowest. Children in the
highest risk areas were generally unable to nominate any positive
environmental features other than parks, but compensated to some
extent by concentrating on the availability of playmates within the
area. Those in the two lowest risk areas by contrast were distinguished
by their appreciation of the open bushland of these two fairly recently
developed suburbs.

A plotting of 'not-so-good' features separated out Areas R, A and B
from the others for complaints about traffic, noise, dirt and lack of
playspace, with R in each case receiving many more complaints, A and
B far fewer. Complaints about unfriendly people by contrast showed a
strong positive linear relationship with risk, whereas complaints about
lack of playmates were greatest in Areas C to L (comfortable, quiet
suburbs). Area A and B children also found it hard to nominate
anything bad about their suburb. Children's replies to the question 'If
you could change one thing, what would it be?' virtually duplicated the
answers noted above.

A canonical correlation analysis which included all the items
discussed above showed that two major dimensions underlay the
children's answers. The first, and much more important, was a
good–bad dimension, which showed a strong incremental relationship
with risk. The second dimension contrasted open playspaces (parks,
bushland) and no complaints about playmates with a somewhat lonely
peace and quiet (quiet streets, big backyards and gardens, but a lack of
playmates). On this dimension Areas A, B, R and Q (and to a
lesser extent O and P) are grouped together as offering children a less
privatised way of life than the middling suburbs. This distribution
indicates that to some extent children's appraisals appear to agree with

the adult view of 'suburbia' as quiet, spacious and secure, but somewhat lacking in social life.

What conclusions can be drawn? It is important to bear in mind that the items from which the risk index was derived were, with one exception (pedestrian injuries), unrelated to the questions asked of the children. The 24 variables which made up the risk index were all social or medical in nature — health, employment, income, education, welfare and crime statistics. No direct measures of traffic levels or environmental quality were included. Nevertheless, risk scores and children's ratings were highly concordant. It can be concluded that children are very sensitive to the advantages and deficiencies of their local environment; they do *not* simply accept whatever it is that is provided.

How do risk scores compare with those of the real-estate market? Cunningham (1984) has provided a status ranking of Sydney suburbs made by real-estate agents. This had a 0.77 rank order correlation with risk scores of the eighteen suburbs. The main reason for the discrepancy between the two measures was the high-status ranking accorded by estate agents to two (and particularly one) high-density mixed population suburbs (our neighbourhoods J and L) which included smart apartment blocks, cheap rental accommodation and major traffic routes. The children did not share their elders' appreciation of the charms of these areas.

The questions asked of children — 'What's good and what's not so good about your neighbourhood?' — meant that regardless of the global evaluation they had just given, they were required to nominate something good (or bad). Some children who had given very high or low ratings dealt with these questions by replying that there was nothing good (or bad) to report. In other cases however, the children responded by nominating the best and worst features irrespective of the global rating. The results are particularly interesting for highest risk areas, where the children most commonly nominate parks, and to a lesser extent playmates. These nominations contradict Jacobs' (1961) classic criticism of urban planners' enthusiasm for providing parks and playgrounds in poor city areas. Jacobs pointed out that most assaults on children occurred in parks and playgrounds, where adult supervision was minimal, and argued strongly for the play and social experience offered by 'lively city sidewalks', where children are protected by the casual but nevertheless effective surveillance of adults going about their business. The high-risk area children in the present sample however criticised the street life available to them as dirty, dangerous and unsuitable for play. Rather than appreciating their 'lively city sidewalks', they complained about the unfriendly behaviour of local adults, and considered parks to be the best feature of their

changed?
times?

environment. Jacobs may have been romanticising children's experience of city life. Alternatively, differences between Australian and American cities may be relevant. Even the highest risk areas of Sydney are probably much less hazardous environments than their counterparts in great American cities like New York and Chicago.

The attitudes of children in the lowest risk areas, A and B, deserve comment. Both suburbs have recently been developed on what was previously market garden land on the outskirts of the city. They have been settled primarily by young families of above average socio-economic status and a preference for a semirural lifestyle; there is little local employment, and many parents commute long distances to work. Because of their low incidence of social problems, these areas earned risk scores lower than more expensive and more fashionable mixed-population suburbs closer to the city. Although they are thus dormitory suburbs lacking well-developed community amenities, these suburbs were very positively regarded by their child residents; indeed the evaluations proved even more positive than their risk scores would have predicted. The availability of large amounts of playspace, both private and parkland, emerged as the crucial factor. This echoes Zill's (1984) finding in a United States national sample that the children best pleased with their environment were those living in prosperous suburbs and those living in extreme rural environments.

It is important to recall that children's evaluations were independent of those factors that might be expected to influence their attitudes — for example, the family's socio-economic status and ethnic and cultural background, the type or quality of housing in which the child lived, and his or her age and sex. Regression analyses showed that none of these variables made a significant contribution to neighbourhood ratings. It can be concluded therefore that what the children were expressing was a set of preferences which are a 'natural' response to the physical and social environment, and that their preferences are not an artefact of geographic variations in the socio-economic, housing or ethnic status of families.

Children's well-being and social life

Children have very clear ideas about what constitutes a good and a bad environment. But does living in a better or worse neighbourhood influence how they feel about their world? From our child interviews we derived information on three topics: children's satisfaction with different areas of their lives; the amount of negative emotions they experience; and their friendship patterns (Homel and Burns, 1983a).

To measure *life areas satisfaction*, the children were presented with a set of five line-drawn faces with expressions ranging from very happy to sad. Once it was established that the children understood this to be a scale, they were asked to choose the face which best represented their feelings about themselves. The procedure was then repeated for feelings about friends, schoolwork and family. The children were then presented with a set of faces representing various *emotions* and asked to choose that which displayed worry. Once the correct choice had been made, the question was asked: 'What about you? Do you worry about things: often, sometimes, hardly ever, or never?' A list of common sources of worry was read to the children who were then asked to nominate which if any was true for them. The same procedure was repeated for anger and fear ('being scared'), and in the latter case the question was also asked: 'Who is the person you are most afraid of?' Finally, the children were asked to select one of five faces (smiling to sad) to 'show how things are going in your life'.

For *friendship patterns*, the children were asked: 'How many children do you play with, at school and at weekends, etc? Do most of your friends know each other? Do you have a best friend, or a number of friends you like about the same? When children choose sides for a game, are you usually: one of the first children picked, one of the last, or in the middle? Do you ever feel lonely and wish you had more friends? Do you like most of the children in your class? Not counting your family, are there any grown-ups around where you live with whom you like to talk and spend time?': Asked of parent 'Compared with other children the same age, how well does your child get along with other children?' Most of these measures come from the schedules developed by the New York based Foundation for Child Development (Lash and Sigal, 1976) and have now been extensively normed (Zill, 1984).

Life areas satisfaction

A preliminary analysis showed satisfaction with the various life areas to be rather high overall, that with family being greatest, followed by friends, self and schoolwork. Mean satisfaction scores for areas of different risk levels showed dissatisfaction rose steadily with neighbourhood risk, the effect being most marked in respect of family and friends. The analysis also highlighted the importance of another aspect of the environment, namely whether the family lived in a street consisting solely of dwellings, or in a street consisting of a mixture of residential and industrial or commercial buildings. Twelve per cent of our sample were resident in such 'mixed' streets, and these children consistently showed higher levels of dissatisfaction. A multivariate analysis with these and other environmental and family variables showed that the effects of risk and street type were statistically significant. Several housing measures were also significantly associated with satisfaction scores, with our interviewers' rating of housing quality and upkeep the strongest predictor. Living above ground floor, living in rental accommodation, low income, and belonging to a single-parent household were also associated with lower happiness, particularly in respect of one's family. Boys and children from larger families were less happy about their schoolwork. Children of highly educated (particularly university educated) parents and from families who were Orthodox in religion (Greeks and Cypriots in the main) were less happy about themselves, perhaps reflecting pressure on the child to achieve high standards as well as an emphasis on self-improvement (Marjoribanks, 1979).

In summary, results show that environmental variables retain their predictive power after the influence of family background variables has been controlled. Indeed, the negative effects of low social class are to a considerable degree captured by the environmental predictors. For example: factors involved in negative feelings about friends are residence in a high risk area, living above ground level in a block of flats, and being of Orthodox or minority religion. Another example: the child most likely to express unhappy feelings about his or her family lives in a non-residential street, comes from a single parent and/or low-income family, lives in rental accommodation in a high risk area and has parents who are *not* Orthodox or committed Protestant in religion (children from these religious groups stand out as particularly happy about their families).

A word of warning about the 'happiness with family' scores. This should not be interpreted to mean that these children were necessarily dissatisfied with their families. As we shall see, one reason that some children were less happy about their families was because they were worried or anxious about their welfare, health and safety.

Negative emotions

Only a minority of children indicated they were frequently worried (19 per cent), afraid (13 per cent), angry (17 per cent) or unhappy with life (20 per cent). Children living in commercial or industrial streets consistently reported more worry, anger, fear and unhappiness. Those in the highest risk areas also expressed more negative emotions, especially compared with those living in the 'best' neighbourhoods. Again, poor housing was also associated with negative outcomes, particularly higher levels of worry. Children from single-parent families also worried more, as did those from families of very low occupational status. Multivariate analysis confirmed the significance of these findings, and also showed that the interaction between street type and neighbourhood risk level was significant for all emotions (except anger) and for summed scores of all four emotions. What this means is that children living in non-residential streets were at risk on all four types of emotion, but particularly if they lived in a high risk area. Occupational status had a pervasive influence, and a number of traditional indicators of social standing — income, education and lone parenthood — made a contribution, as did religion (Orthodoxy), large family size and sex (girls more fearful and angry). Overall, the environment variables (including housing) were responsible for a substantial proportion of the variance in the effects found. Thus, for example, the most fearful children lived in nonresidential streets in high risk neighbourhoods, had fathers of unskilled status and poor education receiving a low income — and they were more often girls. The only exception to this general pattern was, once again, that the children of the most highly educated parents tended to have above average fears and anxiety.

Sources of worry, anger and fear

Girls did not report any higher overall frequency of worry than boys, but they did worry more about friends ceasing to like them (67 per cent *vs* 49 per cent). Girls reported feeling scared much more frequently and were up to three times more likely to refer to specific fears such as burglars, thunder and lightning, spiders and insects, violent television programs and horror movies. Fear levels did not vary across neighbourhoods, but girls in the high risk areas were especially prey to fears of being hurt by someone or something dangerous when they went outside. Girls were also almost twice as likely as boys to report that the person they were most afraid of was their father. Girls in highest risk neighbourhoods were three times more likely to fear fathers than those in lower risk areas, although this effect does not reach statistical significance (cell frequencies were small).

Girls also reported more sources of anger than boys and a higher frequency of angry feelings. Teasing by boys was a major source of anger and much more commonly reported by girls in the highest risk neighbourhoods (84 per cent *vs* an average of 47 per cent). High-risk neighbourhood girls were also more likely to harbour resentments and jealousies against other children receiving more attention and rewards than themselves, being left out of things, and losing in games, although these trends did not reach statistical significance. However, by far the most frequent cause of anger — conflict with brothers and sisters — tormented boys and girls equally. Living in a commercial/industrial street was significantly associated with fears of not being liked by other children and fear of father. Anger at cross-sex teasing was significantly greater among the nonresidential-street girls.

Friendship patterns

Multivariate analysis showed four predictors to be significant over and above the contribution of all others. These were: street type, neighbourhood risk, outside playspace and occupational status. The higher the neighbourhood risk level, the less likely children were to like most of their classmates, and the more likely they were to have one best friend rather than to like a number of friends equally. Plotting these two items against the risk scores of the eighteen neighbourhoods showed that the two lowest and the four highest stood out from all others. Children in the highest risk areas differed markedly from those in the second highest, and there was a further gap between this and the next two highest. In the highest risk neighbourhood barely half (53 per cent) of the children liked most of their classmates, compared with an average of 88 per cent over all other areas. Best friends were reported by 47 per cent of children in the three highest risk areas, compared to only 21 per cent in the three lowest risk areas. Children in the higher risk areas were also somewhat more likely to play with friends after school and during weekends (85 per cent in the three highest risk areas compared with 58 per cent in the three lowest), but were less likely to be described by their parents as getting along with other children.

Children living in non-residential streets were more likely than others to describe themselves as often feeling lonely (24 per cent compared with 6 per cent). Almost one quarter (24 per cent) of children living in industrial streets but only 9 per cent in residential streets reported that they were 'one of the last picked' for games. Children from industrial streets were also less likely to like most of their classmates (11 per cent *vs* 24 per cent), an understandable reaction to what appears to be a pattern of rejection by peers.

Children who lived in homes without outside playspace were less likely to play with friends out of school (47 per cent compared with 71 per cent of other children) and were considered by parents to get along less well with other children. Absence of playspace was slightly correlated with risk ($r = 0.2$) but had an opposite effect on play to the latter (which as noted above was significantly associated with more out-of-school peer play). This apparent contradiction probably arises from the fact that only a small minority of children (5.6 per cent) had no access to outside playspace.

Occupational status was associated with the number of friends that the child reported playing with regularly and with the child being friendly with adults outside the family. Mean values indicate that it is the children in the highest occupational category who stand out on these items, nominating an average of 9.2 regular playmates (compared with a range of 5.2 to 6.7 among the children of other occupational groups) and being more likely to be friendly with non-family adults.

Children's well-being: a summary and interpretation

The analysis suggested that residence in a pocket of disadvantage, either in a commercial or industrial street, or in an enclave of poor housing, or in housing that deviates from the standard of the neighbourhood, is the best predictor of children's social and emotional well-being. The minority of such children, especially those living in inner-city areas, stood out from all others in their feelings of loneliness, dislike of other children, feelings of rejection, worry, fear, anger and unhappiness with various aspects of their lives, their families in particular.

What interpretation can be placed on these findings? Is it something about the families that come to reside in such areas, or the effect of the neighbourhood itself that affects how children feel about their lives? A detailed look at individual families shows that the two influences are entwined in complex ways. An example is the daughter of a family that lived above a drapery shop in which both parents worked long hours. The parents were working hard to provide their children with a better future, but because of the nature of the area insisted that the children stay close to home at all times. The ten-year-old daughter had few playmates, felt very lonely and isolated and often angry, especially about 'always staying home and never going out'. Shopkeepers were in fact well represented among the nonresidential-street families, often lived above the shop, worked long hours, and experienced considerable stress. They were often of limited education and a number were immigrants, some with limited command of English. Other low-income families lived nearby in run-down premises available at relatively low rents.

Not all of the children involved of course fitted the picture we have been describing. Commercial-street children in the very lowest risk areas were no different from others on our various measures, and even in the highest risk industrial streets some children were as happy and sociable as any in the sample, though virtually all disliked the traffic, the noise and dirt, and the lack of suitable play space. For significant numbers however, family and neighbourhood disadvantages combined to restrict their social life, alienate them from school and classmates, and burden them with worries about the welfare of their often vulnerable families. These children constitute the most disadvantaged group in our sample. They are a modest minority but remember that this was a semi-volunteer sample which only included those who accepted the invitation to take part (70 per cent). There was evidence from teachers and other sources that the least coping families were overrepresented among the nonrespondents.

Neighbourhood risk also had an impact on children's social and emotional well-being, but in a different way. Those children living in high risk areas, but not necessarily in industrial or commercial streets, showed a pattern of social constriction rather than maladjustment. They were less likely to like most of their classmates, more likely to concentrate their affections on one best friend, less happy than average with their friends and less likely to be regarded by their parents as getting along well with other children. The association with neighbourhood risk is, however, nonlinear. In the twelve 'middling' neighbourhoods, there were no differences in the children's self-reports. It was only in the highest risk areas, and in particular in the very highest, a run-down inner-city suburb, that liking for other children faltered. Similarly it was only in the two lowest risk areas, semirural newer outer suburbs where the children had access to a wide range of out-of-school activities (several for example had their own horses) that the incidence of 'best friends' declined. It seems then that 'ordinary' suburban life in today's western cities promotes a generally positive attitude towards other children, with a little over one-third of children at any one time having a 'best friendship'; but that growing up in a rough neighbourhood constricts these positive attitudes, and increases the likelihood that a single person will be selected as an intimate. It also suggests that growing up in a privileged semirural environment dilutes the need for such close exclusive friendships, perhaps by providing alternative affective ties (one child commented that 'because I've been brought up with animals I love them as well as my friends').

It came as no surprise that girls reported different kinds of fears and worries than boys; this sex difference has been noted by researchers since the 1920s (McCandless and Evans, 1973). More central to our aim here was the finding that some of the more socially-inspired fears (for instance of staying home without adults as protection, of being attacked on the streets, and of father) were more common among girls in high risk areas and those living in industrial/commercial streets. While not all these areal effects reached statistical significance, in part due to small cell frequencies, it seems clear that environmental disadvantage is especially noxious to girls. Angry feelings, too, were more commonly reported by girls, and anger at teasing from boys was particularly common among high risk and nonresidential-street girls. This suggests that early sexual hostility and hazing is a feature of high risk environments.

Conclusion

The material presented here contains many gaps. We have hardly mentioned the influence of environmental factors on parents' evaluations of the neighbourhood and on their social life and well-being, although we do have data on these topics. Our analyses indicate that all these aspects of parents' lives differ in different environments, although they are also of course influenced by other factors. Moreover, we have not emphasised the roles of a number of nonenvironmental variables as influences on the well-being of children, except where they shed additional light on the effects of residential status. In particular, much more could be said about differences between boys and girls, between immigrant and Australian-born families, and between those of high and low social status. Nonetheless the SAFS data clearly demonstrate the importance of environmental variables for understanding the emotional and social well-being of children. Sociologists and psychologists have tended to underrate the importance of locality and to claim that social class and parental characteristics are the crucial variables determining life style and development (Pahl, 1973; Bronfenbrenner, 1979). In the light of our evidence, this seems too limited a perspective.

9 Unemployment — a current issue in intra-urban inequalities

JOAN VIPOND

This chapter reviews research that has been undertaken on unemployment differentials within large cities. Its concern is with the relationship between unemployment rates and urban structure. Its focus is unemployment in Sydney, Melbourne and Adelaide.

Variations in employment opportunities within cities are similar to variations in other urban services, such as medical facilities. Both affect people's living standards if, in the areas of scarcity, too little is provided to satisfy minimum requirements. When there is general over-supply, there may be cost and efficiency problems but distributional issues are less important. That is why the unemployment issue in cities became important in the 1970s. From May 1974 to May 1975 the national unemployment rate rose from 1.6 per cent to 4.7 per cent. In May 1984 it was 8.9 per cent. In between, unemployment fluctuated but never fell to its May 1975 level. In such circumstances the performance of large cities as labour markets becomes a matter of social concern.

High unemployment rates are clear indicators of labour market failure. In fact unemployment may be a minimum measure of failure since an absence of jobs may lead other workers to leave the labour market despite desiring to work. These are discouraged workers, the 'hidden unemployed'.

Macroeconomists have analysed the cause of fluctuations in national unemployment rates. Their unresolved debates need not concern us here. To urban specialists, interest centres on why unemployment rates differ within cities. Their skills are relevant to analysing where unemployment occurs rather than why it has reached its current levels.

Reasons for variations in unemployment within cities

The literature on unemployment within cities contains three different arguments on causation. They may be called the non-spatial model, the 'trapped' hypothesis and the spatial model. These explanations are different but not necessarily contradictory. Controversy centres on their relative importance: some writers, for example Evans (1984), argue that only the first matters.

The non-spatial model

The non-spatial model suggests that unemployment variations in cities have nothing to do with location. They merely reflect variations in the characteristics of resident workforces and the fact that unemployment is higher among some types of workers than others. Generally, the less skilled and less educated have a greater probability of being unemployed than the skilled and the educated. Workers at the extremes of the age range have higher unemployment rates than prime age workers. Females tend to have higher unemployment rates than males. Married workers seem to be less likely to be unemployed than the unmarried. Race or ethnicity may be another factor determining unemployment rates.

In the United States and the United Kingdom, the non-spatial model has been used to explain why unemployment rates are high among men who live in inner-city areas. Such men often lack skills and education. A high proportion are older workers. In the US especially, many are black. The inner city also provides cheap housing that suits the single and the newcomer to the city. It contains cheap boarding houses and hostels and rented accommodation of all price levels.

The non-spatial model is not, however, confined to explaining inner-city unemployment. It can be generalised to state that unemployment variations reflect the heterogeneity of workers' characteristics. Thus, high unemployment in the outer, working class suburbs may be attributed to the youthfulness of their workforces and the lack of education, experience and skills among teenage workers.

The 'trapped' hypothesis

The second approach, called the 'trapped' hypothesis is about structural changes in large cities. It suggests that in the general suburbanisation of jobs and people some workers have been 'trapped', that is, stranded without access to jobs. The hypothesis is essentially about the inner-city unemployed as it suggests that it is inner-city residents who have been left behind. It is not an argument about numbers of jobs and numbers of workers in the inner city since it is well known that people moved to suburban homes before jobs decentralised (Moses and Williamson, 1967). Rather it is an argument that some types of jobs moved (particularly factory jobs in manufacturing industry) while some types of worker (the low-skilled) were unable to follow because they could not afford suburban housing (Harvey, 1973:60–64). There are many spatial elements in the hypothesis but it concerns more than just space. The model is dynamic and concerns 'differential disequilibrium in the spatial form of the city'. It also has implications for equity since 'the rich and relatively resourceful can reap benefits while the poor and necessarily immobile have only restricted opportunities' (Harvey, 1973:64).

The 'trapped' hypothesis is relevant to the UK where much low cost housing is provided by the public sector and much of it is located in inner-city areas. It does not, however, receive universal support there. Evans (1980:457) rejected the view that a city can be seen as a set of separate labour markets and argued that factory closures in one area would set up a chain of worker movements that would eventually return the labour market of the entire city to equilibrium.

In the US it is racial discrimination in access to good housing that traps blacks in inner-city ghettoes and prevents them moving to the suburbs which have the growing employment opportunities (Kain, 1968). Harrison (1972:116) however, has argued that 'in no part of the American city does the labour market "work" for non-whites'. The author has shown that in Sydney there may be some evidence to support the 'trapped' hypothesis though it is not totally convincing. It is true that male unemployment was a problem in inner-city areas in 1947 before recent suburbanisation. The supporting evidence is that the spatial differentials in unemployment rates seem to have increased since then (Vipond, 1981). In general, however, Australian studies have not paid much attention to the 'trapped' hypothesis. Instead, they have developed a spatial model: a static analysis of the labour markets of large cities. It suggests that spatial frictions contribute to unemployment differentials. The emphasis has been so different from that in the UK and US that Evans (1984) has labelled it 'Inside out down under? Outer city unemployment in Australia'.

Evans (1980:446–447) has described the different theoretical assumptions used in the 'trapped' hypothesis and in the non-spatial model in the following way:

> On one view, the urban area is a set of labour markets between which movement is for most people difficult and expensive. On the other, it is a single labour market in which changes in one part of the area lead to equilibrating movements as people commute to jobs in other areas, in the

process possibly changing the occupation or industry in which they are employed.

The spatial model

The third explanation of intra-urban unemployment, the spatial model, introduces an intermediate view. It does not assume that the city can be divided into discrete, separate, labour markets. On the other hand it denies that the equilibrating movements described by Evans can ever be complete. It suggests that equilibrium is prevented by the spatial frictions within the labour markets of very large cities. As a result, some differentials in unemployment rates are longlasting.

The spatial model cannot be tested by simply looking at actual unemployment rates because these reflect not only the influence of spatial frictions but also the effects of the non-spatial influence, the heterogeneity of the city's workforce. To understand the spatial model we have to begin by imagining that all workers are the same. We maintain some realism, however, by assuming that employment opportunities in the city are highly centralised. This is the case in Sydney. In 1981 the outer ring of suburbs contained 50 per cent of Sydney's population, 48 per cent of the workforce but only 29 per cent of jobs. The middle ring contained approximately 30 per cent of people, workers and jobs; an even balance. Jobs were concentrated in the inner ring (41 per cent) where only 22 per cent of workers and 20 per cent of the population lived.

The spatial model of the labour market incorporates, from residential location theory, the assumption that workers prefer to work near their homes. Doing so saves on transport costs. The model also assumes that wages are the same throughout the metropolis. As a consequence labour markets in the outer ring will be more competitive than those in the middle ring while the inner-city labour market will be the least competitive. By competitive we refer to the number of applicants for each vacancy. These will be highest in outer suburban areas since the local unemployed will not be the only ones competing for vacancies. In addition, local residents who currently commute may also try to obtain work nearer home. Furthermore, house prices are cheaper in outer areas. This observation is reinforced in Horvath and Engels' chapter and it is a reversal of the classical models of urban residential structure. The outer suburban house prices are an incentive to the residents of the inner and middle areas to try to obtain outer suburban jobs.

Differences in the competitiveness of labour markets alone are not enough to explain differences in unemployment rates. All that has been shown so far is that even if all workers and all jobs were alike, all workers in the outer suburbs would be unable to find *local* employment. To explain differences in unemployment rates it must be shown that these workers are disadvantaged *relative to those from other locations* when they move out of their highly competitive local labour markets to search for jobs in the rest of the city.

One disadvantage concerns the distance of their homes from available jobs. For low-income workers, particularly part-time workers, reasonable commuting times may be quite short. Possible commuting distances are also affected by transport availability; many low-income workers cannot afford cars. Here the structure of outer-suburban areas is important, especially the fact that new suburbs are a product of the automobile age. Trains exist, but they provide radial routes to city centre, and new housing estates are not located close to stations. There are buses, but they are privately owned and government regulated. In Sydney they are regulated to protect the railways rather than provide customers with the services they need. The result is that public transport access to modern factories, which have not been built along railway routes, from modern housing estates is expensive and slow. This is a friction of distance which affects workers too poor or too young to own cars. If they live in the inner city they have much better access to local jobs than do outer suburban residents.

Another disadvantage in the outer areas concerns information flows. Vipond (1982) has shown that the formal information networks in the Sydney labour market concentrate on inner-city vacancies. Possibly this is because the organisations which disseminate information have not yet adjusted to the process of suburbanisation of jobs. Another reason may be that formal information networks are only used as a last resort, and that informal communication is preferred. The latter may be adequate for employers in outer suburban areas where, as we have argued, labour markets are more competitive.

These disadvantages of access to jobs and access to information about vacancies will be greater, the greater is the distance of a locality from the centre of jobs, the CBD. As a result, area unemployment rates will increase directly as the distance of an area from the CBD increases. This prediction is the essence of the spatial model. It emphasises that the model is not an explanation of observed spatial patterns of unemployment rates within cities, rather it is an analysis of how space operates to restrict the smooth functioning of the intra-urban labour markets. The frictions of distance in large modern cities disadvantage the suburban worker compared with workers who live closer to the city centre. To explain the actual concentration of unemployed within the centres of large cities, one must combine the spatial and non-spatial models. Because it is static, the spatial model is not a contradiction of the 'trapped' hypothesis. Whether the frictions of distance have been reduced or increased by the suburbanisation of jobs is an open question.

Australian studies

In Australia, political economists, geographers, sociologists and economists have analysed urban labour markets, yet despite differences in their disciplines, aspects of all three models of intra-urban variations in unemployment can be detected.

The political economy perspective

Stilwell's work reflects the key characteristics of the political economist. Issues are analysed within the context of the wider changes that are occurring in society, particularly the current economic crisis in capitalism. Unemployment is said to be a problem *in* cities rather than *of* cities (Jones and Stilwell, 1983). Its spatial concentration simply reflects 'that our cities intensify the distributional inequality in the impact of the current economic depression' (Stilwell, 1979a:15). The solution to the problem is to change the capitalist system. This requires 'demands for redistribution of power and wealth, for more democratic control over the allocation of resources and the nature of technology' (Stilwell, 1979b:31).

On unemployment rates in Sydney, Stilwell (1980; 1979a:ch. 7; 1979b) commented on the high unemployment rates found both in the inner city *and* in the western suburbs. The former he ascribed to the decline of manufacturing in developed countries and to the rationalisation of production to reduce costs. An additional factor is technological change. In pointing to the decline of inner-city manufacturing Stilwell used arguments similar to those of the 'trapped' hypothesis, though in the specific context of the condition of capitalism after the mid-1970s. Horvath and Engels (ch. 11) also discuss the decline in inner-city manufacturing as part and parcel of urban restructuring, with disinvestment in inner-city wholesaling and manufacturing zones, and in consequence deindustrialisation of inner Sydney (and Melbourne).

In discussing suburban unemployment, Stilwell cited demographic and locational factors. The former refers to the concentration of young workers in the outer suburbs. Two specific locational factors are access to jobs and employer discrimination against workers from outer areas. Stilwell's comments on demography and location are easy to fit into the non-spatial and spatial models, respectively. It is, however, difficult to see how they fit into his own analytical framework. Indeed, they seem to be *ad hoc* comments borrowed from more orthodox approaches which he criticised for their 'spatial ideology', that is, attributing causes to spatial rather than more fundamental, aspatial factors. Given his emphasis on the global factors affecting urban society, it is scarcely surprising that Stilwell did not try to evaluate the relative importance of the various mechanisms by which unemployment becomes concentrated in some parts of the city.

Geographic perspectives

The work of Australian geographers provides valuable comparisons in intra-urban unemployment among cities. Forster (1983), for example, suggested that the 'trapped' hypothesis is not relevant to Adelaide as that city has little inheritance of nineteenth-century manufacturing. Nevertheless, Adelaide has a similar pattern of unemployment to Sydney. It has high inner-city unemployment among men and a concentration of unemployed women and juniors in the outer suburbs (northern in Adelaide as compared with western in Sydney). Forster cited residential segregation of different types of worker as a major, causal factor. In addition, he noted the problems that women and young workers from the outer suburbs have in reaching jobs which are still centralised.

Forster noted the way that bureaucratic processes can unintentionally compound problems so that the non-spatial and spatial causes of unemployment are only conceptually separate. The South Australian Housing Trust is, by Australian standards, a large-scale landlord but to meet crisis needs for accommodation it must offer whatever it has available. Consequently, families in financial crisis, perhaps because of unemployment, will often be offered houses in an area where they are least likely to find employment. Forster (1983:45) also tackled the policy problem that spatial change may redistribute jobs but is unlikely to create new vacancies.

> It *does* matter if a given level of unemployment is shared less equitably and borne with more hardship because it is spatially concentrated in outer-suburban public-authority housing estates that have few facilities for people with low mobility and little money, and offer a poor chance to compete for the jobs that do become available in the metropolitan area.

In contrast to Stilwell, he argued that reforms of the urban system may achieve greater intra-urban equality in employment opportunities.

In Melbourne, unemployment rates are similar to those in Sydney and Adelaide. High unemployment is found in the outer suburban areas of Frankston, Dandenong, Preston, Broadmeadows and Sunshine and in the two inner-city areas, St Kilda and Collingwood-Fitzroy (Maher, O'Connor and Logan, 1981). The authors attributed the patterns to both location and workers' characteristics but emphasised that in considering the geographical distribution of job opportunities one must consider not just the location of jobs and houses but also workers' access to transport.

Case studies

It is perhaps ironical that it is in an analysis of unemployment in Sydney by geographers that we can find the most detailed exposition of the non-spatial model (Burnley and Walker, 1982). The authors used data from interviews of inner-city residents to isolate the main characteristics of the unemployed. They were found to have low skills, low education levels and poor health. In addition, the unemployed were likely to be foreign born (from Greece, Yugoslavia and Lebanon), not to have resided long in Australia and to speak English poorly. The authors referred to elements of the 'trapped' hypothesis in noting the type of jobs recently lost from inner-city areas: in heavy industry, textile, clothing and footwear industries. Since the authors concentrated on inner-city unemployment, they were not interested in locational factors and the spatial model. Their finding that age was not a relevant factor in inner-city unemployment may, however, have indirect relevance to that model. Much outer suburban unemployment is attributed to the youthfulness of workers from these areas. Perhaps their problem is not age but the concentration of a large number of workers of the *same* age in areas which are disadvantaged.

Interview surveys of outer-suburban unemployed workers in Blacktown, Sydney and Frankston, Melbourne by Cass and Garde (1984) and Brewer (1984) respectively, provided support for both the non-spatial and spatial models. The writers found that the unemployed lacked skills and education. Cass and Garde emphasised transport problems as an aspect of disadvantage to the Blacktown unemployed. In both studies it was found that the unemployed often had to rely on public transport which is poorly provided in all outer suburban areas. In searching for jobs, the unemployed often depended on informal methods such as visiting factories and asking friends and relatives. Interestingly, however, Brewer noted that outer metropolitan residents were more reliant on newspaper advertisements than either the inner-city unemployed or rural workers.

While some geographers and sociologists have used interview methods for the analysis of urban unemployment, other geographers and some economists have used multiple regression techniques. Their works apply to Sydney and Melbourne a combination of non-spatial and spatial approaches (Vipond, 1980a; 1980b; 1981; 1982; 1984; Faulkner and Nelson, 1983).

Early work established that while spatial patterns of male unemployment in Sydney conformed with those found in the UK and the US there were differences in male and female unemployment rates in Australian cities that had not been previously analysed. While male unemployment in local government areas declined with the distance of an area from the CBD, there was no statistically significant relationship between the location of an area and female unemployment rates (Vipond, 1980a; 1980b; 1981). Male unemployment in Melbourne does seem to decline as distance from the centre increases but patterns of female unemployment are not as predictable (Beed, Singell and Wyatt, 1983).

Vipond (1982) was stimulated by the differences in the unemployment rates of males and females to further explore suburban unemployment problems. A survey of vacancies in the Liverpool (western Sydney) CES office showed that not all vacancies from neighbouring CES offices reached the Liverpool office despite there being a telex network between the various CES offices. Many of the vacancies listed in the Liverpool CES offices were located in the City of Sydney. In 1983, the introduction of the Job Bank system, the computerisation of vacancies and the installation of visual display units in CES offices, improved the means of transmitting vacancies. However, the study also found that the alternative means of information on vacancies, advertisements in the *Sydney Morning Herald*, also concentrated on inner-city jobs. It is thus probable that news about outer-suburban vacancies is still less likely to reach the formal information networks of the labour market than is news of inner-city vacancies.

Perhaps suburban jobs are filled by word-of-mouth. This would be likely since, as we have noted, jobs in these areas are highly desirable because they involve lower transport costs. However, unemployed workers often have poor access to informal information networks. If all unemployed had to rely on formal networks, those in the outer suburbs would have less chance of hearing of local jobs than workers in the inner suburbs.

Possibly more important than information networks are transport networks. Vipond's 1982 findings on Liverpool are very similar to those of Faulkner and Nelson (1983) on Frankston. Both research reports commented on the poor public transport links from housing estates to industrial estates. In both cities, public transport routes radiate out from the CBD. Peripheral, cross-country routes involve many interchanges thus increasing the time, cost and risk of delay in the use of public transport.

Faulkner and Nelson calculated complex measures of accessibility to jobs throughout the Melbourne Statistical Division in cumulative opportunity indices. These indices measured, for various occupations, the percentage of Melbourne Statistical Division jobs that could be contacted within a given travel time by workers residing in each local government area. Different indices were constructed for public and private transport and the dispartiy between the two was measured. The indices showed that access to jobs was much better in central areas than in the outer suburbs. Moreover the disparity in access to jobs by use of public and private transport was much less in inner than outer areas. The second finding was attributed to the more dense public transport network in inner areas, the radial nature of public transport networks and the fact that suburban employment centres are not located on major public transport routes.

In addition to exploring in some detail how transport and information networks are less adequate in suburban than inner-city areas, some used multiple regression techniques to test whether spatial factors were significantly associated with unemployment patterns (Faulkner and Nelson, 1983; Vipond, 1984). The technique was used to analyse the variation in unemployment rates among local government areas in Melbourne and Sydney, separately. The authors, acknowledging the non-spatial model, noted that some of this variation is due to the characteristics of the resident workers, for example, their age and skill levels. The purpose of their tests was to measure whether the location of the local government areas was also a significant factor.

There were some differences in the statistical test adopted for Melbourne and Sydney. Perhaps the most important was that in Sydney the location factor was measured simply by the road distance of each local government area from the Sydney GPO. In Melbourne the location factor was measured by the cumulative opportunity indices described above.

The results from Sydney and Melbourne were very similar. They suggest that within large Australian cities, the more inaccessible an area to jobs, then other things being equal, the higher will be the unemployment rates of residents. Of course, high unemployment rates are found in the centres of cities which are the areas of the highest accessibility of jobs. That is because many people who have a high probability of becoming unemployed live in the inner cities. If we control for that factor, there is another relationship to be found: among homogeneous workers it is likely that unemployment will rise the more distant the worker's home is from the city centre. In Sydney it seemed this location factor affected males and females equally. In Melbourne, lack of transport to jobs seemed more likely to be linked to female than male unemployment rates. The difference may, however, have been due to the difference in testing methods.

Conclusion

From the many analyses of unemployment in major Australian cities it appears that two of the three models described in the second section of this chapter are relevant, the spatial and non-spatial models. The third, the 'trapped' hypothesis has not really been tested. No one, however, has been able to measure the relative importance of the spatial and non-spatial factors associated with unemployment differentials. Nevertheless, various authors have drawn conclusions for policy. Jones and Stilwell's (1983) dismissal of spatial factors, that unemployment is a problem *in* cities not *of* cities, has been noted. Evans (1984) called spatial factors 'a relatively minor problem'. On the other hand Forster's (1983) views on the importance of the *distribution* of unemployment rates as an equity issue have also been reported. Faulkner and Nelson (1983:xii) echo his comments in their conclusion: 'While transport is not likely to be involved in determining the overall *level* of unemployment, it does have some influence on the distribution of unemployment'. In agreement with the latter view, it can be accepted that urban policy is unlikely to be able to create jobs. Nevertheless in the making of urban policy (and more important in neglecting to make changes in it) the implications for the incidence of unemployment should be recognised.

Acceptance that the spatial aspect of unemployment is important does not however, lead to simple solutions. Probably different approaches must be adopted in the short run and the long run. In the short run, the existing urban structure is fixed and unemployment continues to be a major problem. Increasing the spatial equality of its incidence must lie in making access to work more equal, especially through changes in the transport system. The work of Faulkner and Nelson, Cass and Garde and Brewer suggests that public transport is the issue though private transport may also be important. It is possible that the structure of urban areas built since the car era cannot be serviced by public transport. If so, the prospects of improvement are dim. Current research, however, suggests that our existing transport networks are far from being as good as they could be. Morris (1981), for example, has demonstrated the spatial inequality of government-funded transport. McDonnell's (1982) description of the organisation of public transport in western Sydney shows it to be burdened by out-of-date legal restrictions. The difficulties of change are likely to be political. It may be as difficult to redistribute transport systems as it has been to relocate hospitals. On the other hand, the rewards may be greater. A reduction in the disparities in access to jobs created by a better transport system will also create a reduction in the disparities in access to the many other amenities of the metropolis.

Between 1976 and 1981 about three-quarters of the net growth of Sydney was absorbed in the eight local government areas with centres more than 50 km from the CBD. In 1981 those areas contained only 9 per cent of jobs but 15 per cent of the Sydney population. The problem of suburban unemployment is therefore likely to be a continuing one in our newly emerging urban structure. In Sydney there has been little change in town-planning procedures for outer suburban growth since the rise in unemployment in the mid 1970s, as Carolyn Stone's chapter indicates. Ten years later, it would appear that there is a need for more attention to be paid to issues concerned with access to jobs. There is a need to integrate new suburban areas with all the services of the existing city, not just those of physical land development, the traditional concern of town-planning processes.

10 Indicators of changing mortality in Sydney and Adelaide: inequalities in well-being

IAN BURNLEY AND MINE BATIYEL

Work at the national level has shown that heart disease mortality fell significantly during the 1970s, with downwards trends in most statistical divisions and major occupational groups (Gibberd et al., 1982). However, regional differences and occupational differentials were sustained throughout this period. In this chapter, mortality from ischaemic heart disease is analysed for the 1975–77 and 1980–82 periods to see if such differences persisted or diminished at the intra-metropolitan (LGA) level.

There are many problems associated with the interpretation of the spatial incidence of mortality or morbidity, even after age standardisation. In a modern society there are high levels of population mobility with comparatively few people spending all their lives in the locality in which they were born. Thus, any local incidence of high mortality may not reflect environmental conditions operating at the time but the conditions in existence early in a person's life, and in a different location. Similarly, mortality or illness associated with specific occupations (occupational health being a long-recognised field of medicine) may be reflected in the mortality by usual residence of the deceased, even though the risk factors occurred in another locality, such as where they worked. Further, it is difficult to determine which environmental factors may be operating with a local population having, for instance, a high incidence of lung cancer: contaminants in a factory, carcinogens in a local environment, or cigarette smoking, or all of these. Nevertheless, it is possible to demonstrate distinct differences in mortality and morbidity among areas of cities (Burnley, 1980b) and a real persistence of higher-than-average mortality over time in some cases.

Explanatory approaches have sometimes been used to account statistically for variations in mortality between areas, within that subdiscipline of medical geography termed 'spatial epidemiology'. Despite the often sophisticated multivariate statistical procedures which have been employed, the problem of 'ecological fallacy' and spurious correlation have not been eliminated. This is because of the difficulty of making inferences about subgroups or individuals of a population of given areas from the aggregate (census) populations of those areas. Even when indicators measure what they purport to measure, rather than acting as surrogate indicators, the populations of those areas are often heterogeneous in makeup. Forrest (ch. 6) on heterogeneity shows that many inner and outer residential areas of Australia's large cities are mixed in socio-economic status and demographic composition in a way which cannot be characterised by the single indices commonly used in linear regression procedures. Frequently social indicators measuring an apparent trend may mask the real character of a population, and yet these indicators have been used as independent variables in correlation and regression-based explanations of variations in mortalities or social pathologies.

Percentage population in manual occupations, for example, has frequently been taken as an independent variable influencing the occurrence of higher mortality, yet in the same LGA, a not insignificant proportion of the population will be in more highly skilled and paid work. Similarly, the proportion of adults who are single, separated or divorced has been taken as being indicative of socially isolated populations, yet many single and divorced persons are well-adjusted individuals, and in any case the majority of adults in the LGA may be married, even if the proportion is lower than in most other LGAs.

Nevertheless, studies have found spatial associations between social isolation, social class, and crowding indicators and a range of social pathologies and mortalities (Myers and Manton, 1977; Burnley, 1977; 1978; 1980a and b). This was found in Sydney, Melbourne and Adelaide for ischaemic heart disease and for cancer mortality in the period 1969–73. Social isolation was the most important variable in statistical explanation of the quite acute spatial variation in mortality across cities by LGA, with status second, and crowding last.

Myers and Manton's (1977) study of Hanover, Germany, after statistically controlling for status, age, social isolation and related variables found, however, that crowding accounted for a significant amount of the variation in mortality from most medical causes among urban sub-areas. It was hypothesised that crowding generated increased stress which was reflected in higher mortality from heart disease and from cancers of certain types. A relationship between stress affecting the endocrine system which increased susceptibility to cancer was hypothesised. This rigorous study nevertheless illustrates the problems of inference about causality in ill health and mortality in this type of analysis. Accordingly, while some possible relationships are tentatively suggested in the present chapter, the focus is on high and low incidence after demographic controls are introduced.

Intra-metropolitan spatial variation in mortality

Methodology

In the following analysis standardised mortality ratios (SMRs) are used to assess levels of mortality for LGAs within Sydney and Adelaide, with particular reference to mortality from heart disease. The formula for the standardised mortality ratio for a given region is:

$$\frac{\Sigma \, p_x^i \cdot M_x^i}{\Sigma \, p_x^i \cdot M_x^s}$$

where p_x^i = the population of region i in age group x
    M_x^i = the mortality rate in region i for age group x
    M_x^s = the mortality rate in New South Wales for age group x.
Testing for statistical significance is undertaken using Poisson probabilities and comparing the sum of the actual deaths over the given three-year period to the sum of the 'expected' deaths obtained by applying State age-specific mortality rates to the local population.

The task now is to test for significant variation among urban sub-areas, and the persistence or otherwise of any such variation, after controlling for age, over a considerable period of time. Variations between areas of metropolitan Sydney are examined, based on findings from recent research by the author and honours students, and on work undertaken by the New South Wales Department of Health. A review of the findings of an atlas published by CSIRO on disease mortality in South Australia, with particular reference to LGAs within Adelaide (Keig, 1984), is also included. Reference is further made to earlier studies by the present author on mortality from heart disease and cancer in Sydney, which help illumine the persistence of variation. These illnesses between them account for over 55 per cent of deaths. The emphasis in the Sydney case is on premature mortality, particularly that of persons between the ages of 50 and 64.

The case of Sydney

Work here is at different geographical levels: the former four (now three) Health Commission health regions; the statistical subdivision level; and the local government area level. Mortality in the old Inner Metropolitan Health Region remained significantly high for both sexes over the period 1975–77 to 1980–82. This area included the older inner LGAs of Sydney, South Sydney, Leichhardt, Marrickville, Ashfield and Drummoyne which had experienced higher mortality during 1969–73 (Burnley, 1977; Vinson and Homel, 1976), the first three particularly. Mortality also became significantly high in the Western Metropolitan Health Region. The data suggest that the relative variation between broad regions of Sydney in mortality persisted (Figure 10.1).

The standardised mortality ratios shown in Table 10.1 are calculated from expected values applied to State mortality as in 1975–77 and 1980–82. It is known that much of the overall mortality decline in Australia during the 1970s resulted from declines in heart disease and stroke mortality. Tables 10.2 and 10.3 show SMRs from heart disease mortality among males in 1975–77 and 1980–82, relative to State mortality at each time, for metropolitan Sydney statistical divisions,

Table 10.1   Total standardised mortality ratios for health regions of New South Wales, 1975–77 and 1980–82

Region	1975–77		1980–82	
	Males	Females	Males	Females
Inland Country				
New England	102	98	102	99
Orana and Far West	n.a.	n.a.	117[a]	105
Orana	102	103	114[b]	105
Far West	131[b]	109	129[b]	105
Central West	113[a]	111[a]	107[a]	111[a]
Southwestern	n.a.	n.a.	104	98
Riverina	104	89	104	104
Murray	97	97	104	89[c]
North and South Coastal				
North Coast	87[c]	86[c]	89[c]	88[c]
Southeastern	197	106	105	104
Secondary Conurbations				
Hunter	103[b]	101	104[a]	108
Illawarra	97	96	96	98
Sydney Metropolitan Regions				
Southern Metropolitan	n.a.	n.a.	104[b]	105[a]
Old Inner	115[b]	108[b]	116[b]	109[b]
Old Southern	97	100	95	102
Northern Metropolitan	89[c]	93[c]	90[c]	93[c]
Western Metropolitan	101	106	104[b]	104

Source: Mortality data by age, cause and sex for periods cited
Notes: [a] Significantly high at 1 per cent level
         [b] Significantly high at 5 per cent level
         [c] Significantly low at the 0.025 level

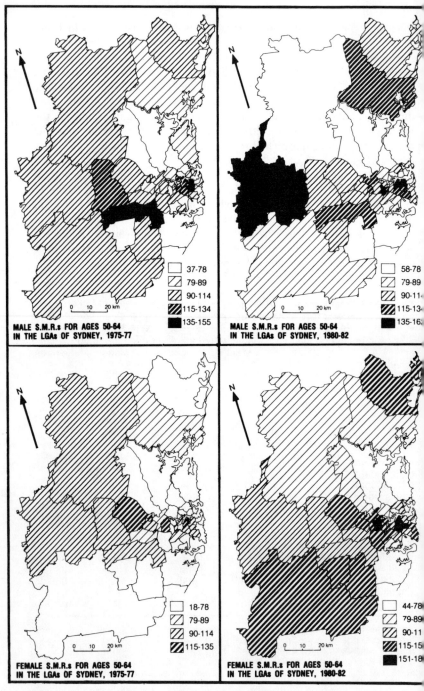

Figure 10.1   Ischaemic heart disease mortality in Sydney, 1975–77 and 1980–82

Table 10.2   (A)   Total male heart disease mortality age 35–49 in Sydney statistical subdivisions, 1975–77 and 1980–82

Statistical Subdivision	Standardised Mortality Ratios		1980–82 Relative to 1975–77	
	1975–77	1980–82	Level	Change (%)
Gosford-Wyong	81.1[d]	73.7	82.4	1.6
Western Sydney	111.9[b]	101.9	83.9	−25.0
Southwestern	139.4[b]	113.3[b]	103.5	−25.9
Inner Western	93.5	93.3	89.7	−4.1
Central	138.2[a]	147.4[a]	134.3	−2.8
Southern	83.8[d]	84.3[d]	75.7	−9.7
Northern .	70.2[d]	67.6[d]	51.9	−26.1

(B) For age 50–64				
Gosford-Wyong	104.2	126.3[b]	109.9	5.5
Western Sydney	101.1	91.2	90.8	−10.2
Southwestern	118.6	101.2	98.7	−16.7
Central	109.0[b]	128.8[a]	105.1	−3.6
Southern	84.3[d]	89.3[d]	82.6	−2.0
Northern	74.9[c]	76.3[c]	62.9	−16.0

Source: Censuses, 1976 and 1981
           Age-specific mortality data for statistical subdivisions
           Column 3 of the table is the 1980–82 SMRs relative to 1975–77 age specific mortality
Notes: [a]   Mortality significantly high at the 0.01 level
         [b]   Mortality significantly high at the 0.05 level
         [c]   Mortality significantly low at the 0.01 level
         [d]   Mortality significantly low at the 0.05 level

Table 10.3   Observed and expected deaths from total heart disease in the age group 50–64 (males) and limits for *p* and Poisson Significance at the 99 per cent level, 1975–77, for selected LGAs, Sydney

	Observed deaths	Expected deaths	Limits for $p < 0.01$		Standardised mortality ratio
			λ1	λr	
South Sydney	81[a]	56.7	38.6 −	78.9	142.9
Sydney	210[a]	37.5	108.7 −	170.1	152.7
Hornsby	115[b]	156.9	126.1 −	191.4	73.3
Ku-ring-gai	127[b]	182.5	149.5 −	220.2	69.6

Source: Column 1 from census, 1976
           Column 2 from age-specific death statistic by medical cause of death, ABS, Sydney, NSW, and by LGA
           Column 3 from Geigy Scientific Tables, p. 154
Notes: South Sydney and Sydney, and Hornsby and Ku-ring-gai are respectively contiguous LGAs
         [a]   Significantly high at 99 per cent level, $p = 0.01$
         [b]   Significantly low at 99 per cent level, $p = 0.01$

and declines in mortality as in 1980–82 compared with standard rates (and expected values) for 1975–77. The tables show that while mortality fell in the central subdivision where mortality traditionally had been relatively high, it fell by only 4 per cent for the 35–49 age group, compared with a State decline of almost 20 per cent. Meanwhile in the 50–64 age group, with more deaths but many still clearly premature, the decline in central Sydney was less than 4 per cent, compared with almost 16 per cent for the State of New South Wales. Mortality actually increased in Gosford-Wyong, but there was a distinct decline in the southwestern SSD. While analysis at the SSD level masks many variations evident at the LGA level, it is evident that with heart disease the declines have been uneven among major regions of Sydney, and inequalities have increased relatively.

Observed and expected mortality for men from total heart disease in LGAs of high and low mortality during 1976–78, standardised around the 1976 census as the midpoint (30 June) of the three years 1975–77 is shown in Table 10.4. The Poisson probabilities show that in South Sydney and Sydney, premature mortality (to age group 50–64) was significantly high with mortality 43–53 per cent higher than expected. Over the three-year period, there were 97 more deaths to males in this age group that there would have been, had the mortality level been the same as that of New South Wales. Conversely, in Hornsby and Ku-ring-gai, two outer northern, low density, mixed or higher rent shires, there were 48 fewer deaths than expected.

For the 1980–82 period, the SMR for Sydney LGA is 162, with 78

Table 10.4   Observed and expected deaths from total heart disease, males aged 50–64, and limits for p and Poisson Significance at 99 per cent level, 1980–82, selected LGAs, Sydney

LGA	Observed Deaths	Expected Deaths	Limits for $p < 0.01$ $\lambda 1$	λr	Standardised mortality ratio
Inner Areas					
South Sydney	65[a]	52.2	35.3 –	73.6	124.4
Sydney	203[b]	125.3	98.1 –	156.8	162.0
Leichhardt	134[b]	98.1	74.4 –	126.5	136.6
Marrickville	158[a]	128.9	100.7 –	160.1	122.5
Hornsby	123[c]	167.1	135.6 –	203.2	73.6
Ku-ring-gai	114[c]	175.9	146.4 –	216.4	64.8
Warringah	200[c]	264.0	220.4 –	304.5	75.8

Source: 1981 census and age-specific death statistics by sex by LGA and for NSW
Notes: The inner areas are contiguous
         Hornsby and Ku-ring-gai are contiguous
         [a] Significantly high at 97 per cent level, $p = 0.03$
         [b] Significantly high at 99 per cent level, $p = 0.01$
         [c] Significantly low at 99 per cent level, $p = 0.01$

more male deaths from heart disease to persons aged 50–64 than expected (Table 10.4); in Ku-ring-gai, the difference was 62 deaths fewer. The number of deaths in Sydney LGA was fewer mainly because of falling population numbers. As indicated at the LGA level, spatial variability in mortality increased between 1975–77 and 1980–82 for both the inner core and relatively privileged outer northern LGAs.

Space precludes detailed analysis here but equivalent female mortality variation among areas was greater than for men, although the overall female mortality level was lower. Statistically significant high and low incidence occurred, and in broadly comparable areas, although it was not particularly high in Sydney LGA. Taking the 50–64 age group, there were 68 female deaths from heart disease in Marrickville during 1978–81 compared with 42 expected deaths (an SMR of 161); in Leichhardt there were 52 deaths compared with 33 expected deaths (an SMR of 159). The high incidence in Randwick LGA was unexpected (107 deaths compared with 77 expected) (an SMR of 139). In the central Sydney statistical subdivision, there were 371 female heart-disease deaths in the 50–64 age group, compared with 281 expected deaths (an SMR of 132).

In Sutherland, on the southern fringe of Sydney, there were 69 deaths compared with an expected number of 91 (SMR = 75.6). In Ku-ring-gai, there were only 30 deaths to women from heart disease in this age group compared with an expected 67 (SMR only 44.8); in Hornsby there were 40 deaths compared with an expected 61. In contrast to the males, female mortality from heart disease (ages 50–64) was significantly high in outer western Blacktown (79 deaths compared with 57 expected). Such differences have persisted over time, and indicate that more 'at risk' populations experiencing higher premature mortality from heart disease live in particular areas, notably the inner city, but not exclusively so, since Blacktown in the west has persistently higher mortality. Likewise there has been a persistence of lower than average mortality in northern and southern outer areas of Sydney.

The case of Adelaide

In earlier work, Burnley (1980b) found statistically significant variations across Adelaide in the incidence of ischaemic heart disease mortality. It must be borne in mind, however, that while distinct variations occurred among areas, the overall level of mortality, and heart disease in particular, was up to 10 per cent lower in South Australia, than in the eastern states of Victoria and New South Wales (National Population Inquiry 1975). While it is tempting to suggest that the lower densities in Adelaide would generate less stress and premature mortality, it is equally plausible that long-term selective internal migration of healthier persons from the eastern States up to the 1970s might have contributed.

Keig (1984) found 'high to very high' mortality levels (total mortality) during 1969–73 for both sexes in the inner suburban LGAs of Port Adelaide, Hindmarsh, Thebarton, Unley, Kensington and Norwood, all predominantly low-income neighbourhoods. In addition, 'very high' male mortality was found in Enfield and Adelaide City, while 'very high' female mortality was recorded in Henley and Grange, and St Peters. Low to very low mortality was found in many of the LGAs outside the inner suburban ring. A similar pattern was found in the subsequent five-year period 1974–78. Areas of high mortality for both sexes included Port Adelaide, Hindmarsh, Unley, Adelaide City, Kensington and Norwood, St Peters, and Thebarton. Again, many areas outside the inner ring LGAs were 'low to very low' in mortality levels, as tested by application of Poisson probabilities. Keig notes the decline of ischaemic heart disease (ICD 410–414) in Australia since the 1960s. There are suggestions that parallel trends in Australia and America include changes in dietary patterns, increased exercise and higher fitness levels, reduction in cigarette smoking and improvements in medical treatment for both hypertension and acute myocardial infarction (Hetzel, 1981; Dobson et al., 1981).

Male mortality from ischaemic heart disease in 1969–73 was high in inner LGAs including Port Adelaide, St Peters, Kensington and Norwood, and Unley. In a number of these inner LGAs, particularly those mentioned, male mortality levels were high (relatively) when compared with the State levels in 1974–78. The pattern of female mortality in Adelaide shows some similarity with that of males in that generally inner LGAs had the highest mortality levels. Mortality was high in 1969–73 in St Peters, Unley and Willunga, with Port Adelaide and West Torrens approaching significantly high levels. In 1974–78 mortality was even higher compared with the whole State in Hindmarsh, Unley, Kensington and Norwood, and Henley and Grange, and remained high in St Peters. There was less consistency in areas of low mortality over the two periods in Adelaide, whereas ischaemic heart disease in the inner areas of the city appears to have become even higher.

Conclusion

There are certain parallels in mortality trends between Sydney and Adelaide. There was, first, the relatively high mortality in the inner city and certain outer LGAs; second the higher heart disease mortality in the inner city; third the relatively low mortality in outer LGAs, especially the lower density or higher income districts; fourth, the persistence of high mortality in the inner LGAs over time; and fifth, the failure of mortality from ischaemic heart disease to make other than minimal decline in the inner city, although declines commensurate with the decline at the national level have been evident in many outer areas of the cities. Thus spatial contrasts in the incidence of statistically significant high and low mortality increased over time.

Mortality variation from heart disease could be accounted for by the notion that occupational-specific mortality may be spatially represented 'on the ground' since occupational groups tend to have particular residential patterns, i.e. there is a relationship between social and spatial distance. Indeed there have been occupational differentials in mortality in Australia as elsewhere (Dasvarma, 1977) and, while decline has occurred in most occupational groups (Gibberd, 1982), differentials among groups have been sustained.

While some traditionally low income-occupation status LGAs in the inner city had relatively high mortality incidence, working class LGAs in outer suburban areas, however, had statistically significant both high and low mortality. This suggests that social isolation and local community structure have an influence on mortality through intervening variables. Specifically, those persons who are detached from community life may experience more stress, may drink or smoke to excess, may have poorly balanced diets, and thus may be much more at risk of dying prematurely from heart disease.

At the national level, mortality has been found to be higher among single persons and separated and divorced people, particularly men (Young, 1976). Such persons tend to be overrepresented in inner-city areas, commonly in rental accommodation. Aspects of marital status, in addition to occupation are clearly involved through the operation of the housing market, since cheap private sector residential accommodation, particularly flatettes and boarding houses are mainly concentrated in the inner city. With separation or divorce, less affluent individuals may find rental accommodation; in the past this normally meant the former husband if the wife was allowed to occupy the family home while the children were still dependent. This is not to suggest that all such persons were at risk.

These considerations give rise to two theoretical perspectives: the 'breeder' and 'drift' hypotheses. The 'breeder' notion suggests that certain neighbourhoods are breeding grounds for conditions of social disorganisation, social isolation and associated states of crime, violence and ill health. This relates to the 'born on the wrong side of the tracks' syndrome, as well as to physical and social environmental characteristics. The local community, by virtue of inadequate social supports, poverty and poor social cohesion, generates much of the pathology and risk of ill health.

The 'drift' hypothesis states that persons more at risk drift, by intra-urban migration, to neighbourhoods where social isolation and anomie (Durkheim, 1924) are reinforced. There may have been family breakdown, job retrenchment or both, or persons downwardly socially mobile moving into the insecure tenure of cheap rental accommodation. Whereas upwardly mobile persons move out of the inner city, those downwardly mobile, or those detached from communal life, drift into the inner city. At the extreme end are the homeless, predominantly older men in the past, but recently augmented by younger people. The homeless men's institutions in Sydney could no longer cope by 1984, with an estimated 7000 sleeping out or squatting in derelict housing in sections of Woolloomooloo, Darlinghurst and Pyrmont. Despite gentrification and residential revitalisation in parts of the inner city, more 'at risk' populations remain, or drift into particular neighbourhoods, where self neglect, and the absence of visits to the doctor for regular checks increase the risk of heart attacks.

Probably both breeder and drift processes are involved in the Australian metropolis, with the drift form of explanation being more plausible, given the high mobility of the overall population. However these explanations need to be integrated with a class analysis which would include the issue of access to decent housing with security of occupancy.

The increase in spatial variability in ischaemic heart disease mortality gives cause for concern. It would appear that fewer persons in the inner city, especially men, have availed themselves of preventative approaches, such as balanced diets and exercise, or have had access to sympathetic medical care. There is a theoretical oversupply of medical practitioners in the inner city, but much of this is accounted for by concentrations of practitioners and specialists in the CBD to service city office workers, or in professional offices near the major teaching hospitals. A number of the rental housing blocks and remnant tenement districts in Sydney are poorly serviced either with direct medical care or community health centres. The latter in New South Wales have been officially prevented from providing primary medical care other than counselling services. Further, since the period under study, hospitals have been required to charge for their outpatient (accident and emergency) services; in the past, many poorer persons obtained medical care from outpatient departments, as most were not medically insured.

Finally, while there was considerable community change in the inner city in the 1970s and early 1980s, the residential revitalisation and associated in-movement of middle-class households, mortality, both total and ischaemic, remained relatively high. This suggests that in a time of rising unemployment and growing disadvantage, 'at risk' populations vulnerable to such misfortune are still present in strength in the inner city.

Part III

Alternative Perspectives and Urban Conflict

11 The residential restructuring of inner Sydney

RONALD HORVATH AND BENNO ENGELS

Australian cities are presently undergoing major social, economic and spatial changes (Daly, 1982; Cardew et al. 1982; Maher, 1982; Logan et al. 1981; Stilwell, 1980). Increasingly the source of this change is seen to be located primarily in the international capitalist economy, with local factors playing an important though secondary role. There is, however, less agreement about the nature and magnitude of the change and the specific social and economic aspects of the built environment that are being affected. Focusing on Sydney, this essay offers the hypothesis that the current social, economic and spatial restructuring of the city is a consequence of a broader restructuring taking place within capitalism and originating in the present economic crisis.

The contemporary restructuring of capitalism and urbanism: an hypothesis

Since the 1960s international capitalism has been in a restructuring crisis involving qualitative change within the capitalist mode of production (Gibson and Horvath, 1983a), in particular within the variant form of monopoly capitalism which has been economically dominant within international capitalism during the twentieth century (Gibson and Horvath, 1983b). At the root of the crisis is the inability of monopoly capital to extract sufficient profit to maintain a regime of expanded capital accumulation. The response has been to institute a program of rationalisation and restructuring of the mode of production in a manner such that the initial emergence of a new type of capitalism, global capitalism, is now evident. As global capital becomes established within a particular sector of an economy, such as banking or manufacturing, a competitive struggle between firms organised along monopoly and those organised along global lines ensues. The consequence is a further decline in the profitability of firms still organised along monopoly lines and the further dominance of global capital.

Ascertaining the geographical dimensions of restructuring requires an understanding of space as socially produced (Harvey, 1982; Soja, 1980.) According to this perspective, each mode of production creates its own specific spatial forms and locational rationale. The spatial organisation of international relations under monopoly capitalism is characterised by developed 'centres' and underdeveloped 'peripheries'. The restructuring resulting from the emergence of global capitalism is to create a new international spatial order with new centres of investment and new peripheries of 'redundant spaces' (Anderson et al. 1983) which are experiencing disinvestment and a downturn in economic activity. The same spatial locations that had once facilitated capital accumulation have now become a barrier to further profitability (Soja et al. 1983:199). An important result of the current global spatial restructuring is the emergence of a world hierarchy of cities, and with it a corresponding restructuring of the internal organisation of such cities, including Sydney (Cohen, 1981; Hymer, 1975; Friedmann and Wolff, 1982; Ross and Trachte, 1983).

The familiar spatial models of the capitalist city that have acted as the basis of urban geography for many years are to some degree dated, because they were designed to describe cities which were the product of older variants of capitalism. Urban geographers using these models have long recognised that cities change but have often located that change within technology, especially transport technology. By contrast, within an urban restructuring framework, the dynamics of the built environment are seen as resulting fundamentally from the investment/disinvestment process and from class struggles which are in turn brought about by the structural changes resulting from economic crisis. Most work on urban restructuring to date has emphasised these general economic dynamics in largely theoretical terms (Gordon, 1978; Harvey, 1978; 1982; Walker, 1978; 1982; Smith, 1982), although some recent empirical work has specifically used an urban restructuring framework (Soja et al. 1983; Ross and Trachte, 1983).

The last major phase of urban restructuring within advanced capitalist cities saw a massive investment of capital into the fringe of metropolitan areas, giving rise to the suburbanisation process (Harvey, 1978; Walker, 1978; 1982). However, the past decade and a half has marked the beginnings of major changes in the inner cities of advanced capitalist nations, as well as among the metropolitan areas in different nations. The magnitude of this change warrants the term 'inner-city restructuring'. The economic dimensions of this restructuring appear to involve a substantially new pattern of revalorisation and devalorisation of the inner-city built environment with a tendency towards disinvestment in inner-city wholesaling and manufacturing zones and a reinvestment in residential and office landuses.

Accompanying economic restructuring of inner cities is a process of social restructuring. This process is contradictory in nature, involving simultaneously a tendency toward impoverishment of some fractions of the working class, while possibly improving or at least maintaining the standard of living of other fractions. The term 'peripheralisation of labour' has been used to identify the effects of the first tendency (Gibson and Horvath, 1983a; Ross and Trachte, 1983; Soja et al., 1983). The second tendency suggests the possible formation of a 'new labour aristocracy'.

In summary, the general hypothesis which directs our empirical research in Sydney is that inner cities in advanced capitalist nations are currently being economically and socially restructured as a consequence of the current crisis of capitalism.

The restructuring of inner Sydney

The current phase of social and economic restructuring of inner Sydney can be traced back to the processes which set off the 'boom' in Sydney's property market between 1968 and 1974. According to Harvey (1978; 1982), a switching of investment capital into the built environment takes place immediately preceding a profitability crisis in other sectors of a capitalist economy. In fact not only was 'investment attracted away from other sectors of the economy' in Sydney, it was also a short-lived phenomenon that 'involved a frenzy of buying, selling and building' which was followed by an economic crisis (Daly, 1982:1–2).

Any attempt to explain the important changes occurring within inner Sydney (Daly, 1982; Kendig, 1979; Maher, 1982; Cardew et al. 1982) must take account of the increasing interdependence of the Australian economy with the international capitalist system (Fox, 1981; Crough et al. 1980; Crough and Wheelwright, 1982; Daly, 1984). As the Australian economy becomes further locked into the sphere of international capitalism, its major cities are drawn into an 'emerging hierarchial network of global cities' which act as corporate headquarters and banking and stock market centres. The resulting restructuring of the CBD, with growth in office space as a prominent feature, is documented for Sydney by Daly (1982).

While it is true that 'office jobs are primarily concerned with the collection, processing and exchange of information' (Alexander, 1982:75), a more satisfactory interpretation of the function of offices under global capitalism is in terms of their role in the 'internationalisa-tion and concentration of industrial and financial control' (Soja et al. 1983:222–226) within certain major cities in the world. Within Syd-ney's CBD one activity, banking, which accounted for 9 per cent of the total office space in 1976 (City of Sydney, CBD Study, 1978:42), is clearly being restructured and is moving increasingly into the orbit of global capitalism.

Banking in Sydney operated within a state-regulated monopoly capital environment from the depression of the 1930s. Toward the end of the 1960s, global banks from abroad began setting up representative offices and merchant-bank subsidiary offices. These grew from six in 1968 to 101 in 1981 (Bell, 1983:40). The response from Australian bankers was to begin restructuring. This involved a decline in the importance of transactions which supported their existence as mono-poly bankers and an increased involvement with international capital markets (Daly, 1984). Since 1980, this has produced in Sydney what could be described as a global banking district covering some four hectares in the CBD and bounded by Bridge, York, Macquarie and King Streets (Bell, 1983:62–3).

If banking is an example of an economic activity in inner Sydney which has succeeded in restructuring the inner-city built environment, manufacturing generally offers a marked contrast. At a national level, Australian manufacturing is generally rationalising or deindustrialising (Crough and Wheelwright, 1982; Gibson and Horvath, 1983; Linge and McKay, 1981). Although no comparable study of inner Sydney manufacturing is available, data on employment in manufacturing and the number of establishments suggests that deindustrialisation of inner Sydney has been going on since at least the early 1970s (Cardew and Rich, 1982; Kendig, 1979).

The inability of non-residential activities such as manufacturing to compete with other landuses within the current climate of economic restructuring has necessitated, in some instances, plant closure and relocation to the suburbs or even outside Australia. Consequently, the balance has tipped in favour of other landuses which can more effectively bid for the limited space available within inner Sydney. The result is that residential landuse has retained its once threatened space and even begun to invade non-residential areas. The conversion of warehouses and light manufacturing structures into 'loft-style' resi-dences, a massive phenomenon in New York City (Zukin, 1982a; 1982b), appeared in Sydney in at least the early 1980s. The recent construction of luxury apartments in the City of Sydney, the building of flats and high rises throughout inner Sydney (Horvath and Tait, 1984: map 34) together with the rehabilitation of housing, has involved a dramatic turnabout.

The class struggle, manifest through the social mobilisation of residents and unionists within the building industry between 1971 and 1974 also significantly affected inner Sydney's restructuring. Had it not been for the social mobilisation of residents in resident action groups (Nittim, 1980) and the informal alliance of these groups with certain unionists, who imposed green bans on construction sites, the commercial redevelopment of many inner-city neighbourhoods would have taken place. No less significant was the halting of expressway development which together with proposed commercial development would have continued a zone-in-transition landuse pattern and social ensemble which has typified metropolitan inner cities since the advent of industrial capitalism. The linking of resident action groups who mobilised in the sphere of consumption, and the radicalised building unionists who mobilised in the sphere of production produced, for a short time, an urban social movement (Castells, 1977). Its timing coincided with the beginning of the restructuring crises of capitalism being examined here.

Significant changes in the type of residents who live in inner Sydney have been associated with the capital reinvestment process. Thus gentrification, generally involving a decline in traditional working-class residents and a simultaneous increase in professional–white-collar residents, has been occurring in inner Sydney since 1966 (Table 11.1). This increase of professional, technical, administrative and clerical workers corresponds to changes in the employment structure of the inner city.

Deciding whether or not the increased presence of white-collar workers means that a new and relatively affluent group is moving into inner Sydney requires better data than are presently available. By contrast, the 1981 census provides unambiguous data which reveal the peripheralisation of another segment of inner Sydney's population. One of the two major concentrations of unemployment in metropolitan Sydney is located in a belt from Marrickville and extending continuously to Kings Cross and Woolloomooloo (Horvath and Tait, 1984: map 28). The explanation of this inner-city island of unemployed is, arguably, to be found within the current restructuring crisis of monopoly capitalism.

The restructuring crisis has made a profound impact upon inner Sydney. Portions of the built environment have been reshaped through a process of reinvestment/disinvestment. Social restructuring has also been initiated. The inner city is a relatively large area, however, and a general overview can obscure the diversity taken by this social and spatial restructuring process within them. We turn now to examine the residential restructuring taking place within a single inner-city suburb.

Table 11.1 Selected occupational types as percentage of total workforce for inner-city LGAs, 1966–81

	Professional and administrative				Clerical				Working class			
	1966	1971	1976	1981	1966	1971	1976	1981	1966	1971	1976	1981
Leichhardt	7.8	5.9	17.3	24.1	12.9	14.5	14.9	17.7	53.0	40.1	30.6	23.9
North Sydney	26.4	29.1	30.5	34.0	27.2	29.2	27.9	27.4	22.0	16.0	11.7	10.2
Randwick	17.2	18.3	18.9	19.8	21.5	22.6	22.1	22.9	33.1	27.3	23.3	21.2
South Sydney	n.a.	5.4	7.0	12.6	n.a.	10.2	10.7	14.0	n.a.	51.2	40.4	32.0
Sydney City	12.5	18.8	20.1	22.6	12.0	14.0	12.5	14.4	45.1	26.4	18.9	15.9
Waverley	18.9	19.4	20.3	20.3	22.4	23.3	21.4	21.9	28.5	23.2	18.6	17.7
Woollahra	37.9	34.3	36.0	37.0	22.2	21.4	19.9	20.0	12.9	13.7	9.2	8.1

Source: ABS Censuses of 1966, 1971, 1976 and 1981

The residential restructuring of Glebe

Originally, Glebe was given to the Church of England in 1790 as a land grant from the Crown. In the late 1820s Glebe was subdivided into privately owned estates. It became a 'semi-rural retreat' for Sydney's gentry (Solling, 1972:23). Further subdivisions took place in the 1840s for upper and middle-income homebuyers. From 1861, subdivision of land continued, to produce social differentiation in the built environment of Glebe by the end of the nineteenth century (Solling, 1972). The northern parts — Toxteth, Eglington, Boissier and Betts Estates — were developed with large houses on larger parcels of land for upper and middle-income residents, (there are parallels here with Pluss' chapter 4 findings in Strathfield); Forest Lodge, Bishopthorpe, St Phillips, Bishopgate and Hughes were developed as lower-middle and working-class housing.

After World War I, there was a noticeable deterioration in the housing stock, especially in the upper-middle class areas. The expansion of industry on the margins of Glebe and improvements in urban transportation made fringe suburbs an attractive alternative to a Glebe that had become a densely populated suburb, characterised now by row upon row of terrace houses. The consequence was an exodus of Glebe's wealthier residents and the conversion of their larger houses into boarding houses for the working classes.

A deterioration in the housing stock also took place in the original working-class portions of Glebe and by the 1930s parts of Glebe 'were considered as one of the most unsavoury parts of Sydney' (Painter, 1980:3). During World War II, the legislative enforcement of rent control appears to have played a significant role in reinforcing the deterioration and disinvestment process within Glebe and other inner-city housing areas (Kendig, 1979:112). The rational outcome was the formation of a 'rent-gap' between inner city and suburban ground rent levels (Smith, 1979:545). Not until the rent-gap has sufficiently developed, argues Smith, will it be possible to witness a reinvestment into inner-city areas because the ground rent which could be realised through housing reinvestment (i.e. potential ground rent) must exceed the ground rent which is currently being acquired under existing landuse.

The historical formation of a rent-gap signalled that Glebe was ready for another round of reinvestment but before any residential restructuring could begin, some sort of qualitative change in the form of 'collective social action' was necessary (Smith, 1979:545). A number of such changes took place between 1960 and 1974, which at first arrested and then reversed the process of decline in Glebe. The enforcement of rent control impinged upon the operation of the housing market and represented a barrier to the residential restructuring process. The dismantling of the rent control legislation was a gradual process which initially began in 1954 but did not accelerate until the State Liberal Party regained office in the mid-1960s (Nelson, 1980:145–53). This trend was clearly visible in Glebe with an increased number of properties removed from rent control during the 1960s. By 1968, the process was well under way and the protection once offered by the legislation had almost been nullified by an increased number of amendments. Between 1956 and 1983, 1206 properties were decontrolled.

The removal of rent control literally gave the green light for residential restructuring, particularly gentrification, but it also destroyed the only flimsy hold that lower-income groups possessed over cheap inner-city housing. Decontrol of a property involved a restoration of all powers of property disposal to the owner, which permitted its return to the open market for sale or rental at market levels. The consequence of decontrol was the removal or 'displacement' of lower-income groups from the inner city.

The removal of rent control increased the potential for home-ownership in inner Sydney and the late 1960s marked the return of the middle class to Glebe. The discovery of Glebe by a more affluent social class is attributed to 'a rejection of the suburban lifestyle' and a change in attitude towards inner-city living which possessed 'an architectural and historical appeal' for the new occupants (Kendig, 1979:126; Logan, 1982a:91). Consequently, in 1969, the Glebe Historical Society was established as the institutional expression of the mobilisation of Glebe residents, a mobilisation which must be partially credited for securing Glebe for residential restructuring.

Dissatisfied with the amount of flat redevelopments taking place in Glebe and after a number of confrontations with the local council over this and other environmental issues (Painter, 1980:28), the Glebe Society mobilised local residents to directly influence planning policy through lobbying and municipal electoral politics. In August 1971, Leichhardt went to the polls and like many other local resident groups in Leichhardt (Johnston, 1975), the Glebe Society supported its candidates in the municipal elections under the broader platform of a 'Campaign for a better council'. The outcome was a new council (1971–1974) led by middle-class residents that implemented more stringent zoning restrictions for Glebe, prohibiting uncontrolled flat redevelopment and incursions of nonresidential landuses, such as industry.

Like many of Sydney's inner areas, Glebe's survival was threatened by a proposed network of expressways. Construction for the North

Western Expressway was planned to commence in 1972 and the Western Expressway, some ten years later (Cain, 1975:65). The Glebe Society alerted the public to this threat and some of its members helped form the Glebe Anti-Expressway Action Group (GAEAG) which organised public opposition to the proposed expressways. In 1971, the historic Lyndhurst mansion and housing in the Dargham Street area of Glebe were threatened with demolition. In response, GAEAG called upon the New South Wales Builders Labourers Federation (NSWBLF) to intervene. Their response was to impose a 'green ban' upon the North Western Expressway in 1972 (Cain, 1975:71–72). The alliance between GAEAG and the NSWBLF was another instance of collective social action which brought about an important change within Glebe because their united action impinged upon the operation of the housing market, very much in the same manner as the restrictions imposed upon the market through rent control, forty years earlier. It altered the power relationship between residents, developers and a variety of State apparatuses which controlled Sydney's built environment.

The next important change to take place in Glebe was the purchase of the Glebe Estates by the federal Labour Government in 1974 from the Church of England. The provision of cheap-rental housing through rehabilitation rather than redevelopment would have generated further confidence in residential restructuring of Glebe through the 'neighbourhood effect' and contributed to the shelving of expressway plans. Once a qualitative change had taken place, the revalorisation of Glebe's built environment was assured, and it took a number of residential forms.

Types of residential restructuring

The following typology is designed to discriminate between the main types of residential restructuring that are taking place within Glebe. Four types of residential restructuring are discernible.

1 *State-managed redevelopment*: The clearance of previously developed land and the construction of multi-storied rental accommodation in Glebe by the Housing Commission during the 1960s and 1970s was designed to 'meet the long waiting list for cheap inner-area public housing' for low-income groups (Kendig, 1979:137–8). State funded and managed redevelopment was primarily restricted to the less desirable fringe areas of Glebe that possessed a mixture of landuses, including wholesaling and manufacturing (Figure 11.1).

2 *Private redevelopment*: This made a more significant contribution to

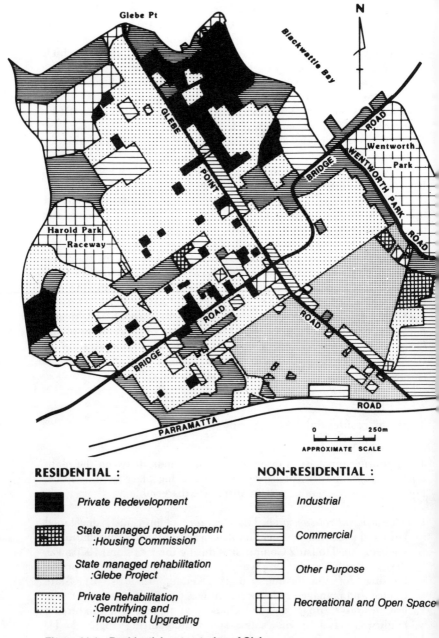

Figure 11.1 Residential restructuring of Glebe

RESIDENTIAL :

- Private Redevelopment
- State managed redevelopment :Housing Commission
- State managed rehabilitation :Glebe Project
- Private Rehabilitation :Gentrifying and Incumbent Upgrading

NON-RESIDENTIAL :

- Industrial
- Commercial
- Other Purpose
- Recreational and Open Space

residential restructuring. Investment in flat redevelopment by developers increased dramatically during the 1960s and 1970s. As an indication of the impact of this submarket within the redevelopment process, between 1965 and 1980, 939 strata titles were registered for residences in Glebe (Sydney University, Sample Survey Centre's Strata Titles Files). The largest amount of redevelopment took place north of Bridge Road and east of Glebe Point Road (Figure 11.1). Here developers could assemble large parcels of land necessary for flat construction. This was an area of previously industrial landuse, the redevelopment of which displaced industry in favour of residential landuse. Further horizontal expansion has been contained by zoning restrictions and rising land prices.

3   *State-managed rehabilitation*: This involved federal government purchase of the Glebe Estates containing 700 dwellings and 60 commercial sites on 19 hectares of land (Figure 11.1). The intention behind the purchase was to provide welfare housing through the rehabilitation of an entire neighbourhood. The Glebe Project is distinguished as state-managed rehabilitation from the more common private forms because this type of residential restructuring is state funded and does not involve the removal of the original occupants, the working class.

4   *Private rehabilitation*: When examining the private rehabilitation process, it is necessary to distinguish between gentrification and incumbent-upgrading. Gentrification is defined as 'the process by which working-class neighbourhoods are rehabilitated by middle-class homebuyers, landlords and professional developers' (Smith, 1983:139). By contrast, incumbent-upgrading involves the rehabilitation of housing 'with no significant changes in the socio-economic status of the population' (Clay, 1979:7). Unlike the other residential restructuring processes examined, private rehabilitation is an uneven spatial process within the designated areas on the landuse map, which also contains unaltered pockets of housing. Despite these limitations, available data indicates that gentrification is the dominant form of private rehabilitation in Glebe.

Characteristic of a neighbourhood that is being gentrified is a rise in house and land values (Lang, 1982; Hamnett and Williams, 1979). Movements in house and land values for Glebe and other inner-city suburbs from 1950 to 1983 are shown in Table 11.2. In each case, the period 1970–76 marked a dramatic increase in values corresponding to Sydney's property boom of the same period. Certain suburbs, such as Paddington, Glebe and Balmain have witnessed more dramatic rises, accompanied by an equally high turnover rate of houses sold (Figure 11.2). Research conducted in Melbourne's inner suburbs has docu-

Table 11.2 Average house plus land prices for selected inner Sydney suburbs, 1950–83

	1950	1960	1970	1976	1977	1978	1979	1980	1981	1982	1983
							All figures are in dollars ($)				
Balmain	750	5000	9500	38000	42000	47000	58000	80000	100000	90000	85000
Glebe	2200	9000	20000	43000	47000	52000	65000	90000	115000	100000	100000
Leichhardt	1600	7000	15000	26500	28000	31000	38000	54000	70000	63000	65000
Marrickville	3000	7000	16000	37000	40000	44000	52000	63000	80000	70000	70000
Newtown	800	5400	10000	25000	25000	27000	32000	47500	65000	65000	67500
Paddington	1600	7500	25000	40000	45000	55000	65000	90000	120000	135000	125000
Redfern	1050	7000	15000	35000	37000	40000	50000	60000	75000	65000	75000
Ultimo	1050	3800	8000	25000	25000	27000	32000	50000	70000	70000	67500

Source: Valuer-Generals Department

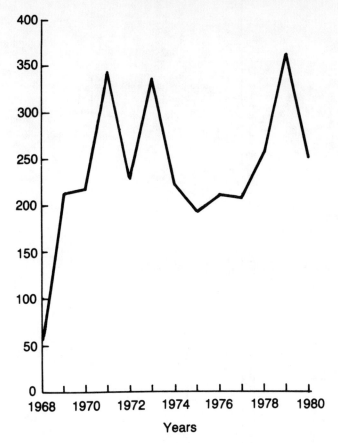

Figure 11.2 Number of houses sold in Glebe, 1968–80

mented a similar trend in house values and turnover rates (Centre for Urban Research and Action, 1977). This unprecedented surge in house values (and rents) is a major factor limiting the participation of lower-income groups in these housing markets. Fundamental to the private rehabilitation of a neighbourhood is the revalorisation of the housing stock through capital reinvestment (Table 11.3). An initial trend of large inexpensive renovations occurred in the early 1970s. By the late 1970s, the trend had shifted towards more expensive rehabilitation work, suggesting a change in the class character of the rehabilitation process in Glebe.

Unlike incumbent-upgrading, gentrification is not just a physical but also a social process. It involves the movement of upper-middle income people into neighbourhoods, usually accompanied by an

Table 11.3 Number and value ($) of alterations and additions approved to Glebe's private dwelling stock, 1968–80

	1968	1969	1970	1971	1972	1973	1974	1975	1976	1977	1978	1979	1980
$0–500	9	35	43	46	44	33	13	13	10	3	7	14	21
$501–1000	3	16	20	22	19	17	9	9	7	8	6	15	10
$1001–2000	3	8	17	13	18	17	10	5	8	8	10	20	11
$2001–3000	2	5	5	12	16	10	4	8	8	5	8	9	9
$3001–4000	—	5	1	9	2	6	6	9	4	7	7	4	5
$4001–5000	—	1	3	3	2	5	4	4	8	5	6	11	18
$5001–10000	1	5	8	3	3	2	18	11	12	11	16	27	28
$10001–15000	—	1	—	1	1	2	3	2	—	2	5	6	8
$15001–20000	—	—	2	—	—	—	—	1	—	1	2	4	9
$20001 plus	—	—	—	—	—	—	—	1	7	1	1	4	2
Total	18	76	99	109	105	92	57	63	64	51	68	114	121

Source: Building department, Leichhardt Municipal Council

upsurge in owner occupancy compared with the previous tradition of 'privately rented accommodation and limited worker-class owner-occupancy' (Hamnett and Williams, 1979:19). Between 1966 and 1981, public renting and owner occupancy in Glebe increased with a corresponding drop in private renting (Table 11.4). Far more dramatic tenure changes have taken place with boarding and lodging houses, which have been converted and sold for single residency purposes (Leichhardt Municipal Council, 1983:42). Thus the gentrification of these and other private rental housing stock has produced an increase in owner occupancy in Glebe, although a sizeable proportion of Glebe's housing stock still remains privately rented.

Table 11.4   Tenure types in Glebe, 1966-81

	Private rental		Public rental		Owner occupancy		
	Total	Percent	Total	Percent	Total	Percent	Tot. no. dwgs
1966	3375	67.8	147	2.9	1452	29.1	4974
1971	3836	61.1	186	2.9	2250	35.8	6273
1976	3480	57.5	240	3.9	2322	38.4	6042
1981	2974	57.1	163	3.1	2065	39.6	5202

Source: ABS Censuses of 1966, 1971, 1976 and 1981

Occupation change in Glebe

The preceding discussion on inner Sydney noted a change in occupational groups with a decline in the working class and an increase in professional white-collar groups (cf. Lang, 1982), and this is generally true of Glebe (Figure 11.3). Some indication of the relationship between the types of redevelopment and rehabilitation of housing and occupational changes can be obtained by examining the occupation trends in 21 census collectors districts (CDs) between 1966 and 1981 and comparing the trends in each CD with the type of residential process dominant in the area. The process of occupational change is spatially uneven. Although a clear decline in the number of blue-collar workers occurred in all CDs, a noticeable increase in white-collar workers (professionals, technical, administrative and clerical occupations) occurred in all the CDs except those located primarily in state-managed redevelopment and rehabilitated CDs (Figure 11.1). This indicates that gentrification has indeed taken place in neighbourhoods where rehabilitation of the housing stock is the predominant form of residential restructuring, but also that the same occupational changes are taking place in areas where private redevelopment is the

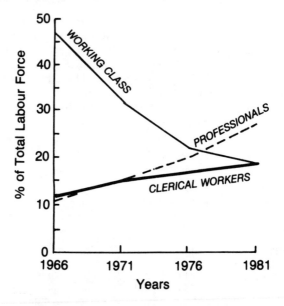

Figure 11.3   Occupational groups in Glebe, 1966–81

dominant process. <u>State-managed rehabilitation and redevelopment is not accompanied by a detectable social change</u>, whereas private rehabilitation — gentrification — and redevelopment conforms to the broader trend of inner-city social restructuring.

Conclusion

Global capitalism is in the process of rending obsolete current landuse and socio-geographic models of the inner city. Furthermore, this restructuring crisis affecting capitalism would appear to be taking place at all geographical scales — international, national, regional, and metropolitan. Thus the purpose of this essay was to determine how one inner-city area and then one inner-city suburb within that area is changing. The evidence presented supports the view that changes in inner Sydney and Glebe are both considerable and are tied to the current metamorphosis of the capitalist mode of production. The residential aspect of this change is seen in the massive investment in the residential built environment which follows decades of disinvestment. Within this process, gentrification as a socio-economic expression of the current restructuring crisis occurring within inner cities of advanced capitalist nations is but one aspect of the changes taking place.

We wish to thank Libby Freeman for her assistance in collecting some of the data used in this essay.

12 Have we been operating under the wrong paradigm? A reinterpretation of urban residential property markets

RICHARD CARDEW

The 1970s saw the flowering of a political economy (Sandercock and Berry, 1983; Kilmartin and Thornes, 1978) interpretation of the property market. This was a spectrum of perspectives ranging from strict Marxist views (Berry, 1983; Horvath and Engels, ch. 11; Kemeny, 1978) to a more generalist socio-democratic approach advocating greater government involvement to ease apparent problems of the market (Sandercock, 1975, 1983; Troy, 1978). But it was the dominant paradigm so far as popular academic interpretation was concerned and particularly that in which interventionist government policy was formulated. Ironically too, the interpretation of the property market by the development industry tended to reinforce this perspective.

The origins of this paradigm lie in the urban reformist movement of the later 1960s which achieved considerable political influence through the federal Labor Government of 1972–75. That government came to power on a platform of urban reform, reflecting public concern over soaring land prices and inadequate services to the suburban fringe. The underlying motivation was not so much a new philosophy but a concern that 'private entrepreneurs should not benefit from the process of urban growth' (Troy, 1978:6). It was a desire to capture the unearned increment in the land conversion process, to close off any opportunity for more than normal profit. The real-estate entrepreneur was seen as the bogeyman, and the structure and operations of the industry as leaving too many opportunities for abnormal profits, graft and corruption.

In viewing developers and imperfections within the industry as the problem, with the consumer apparently the loser through escalating land prices, the interpretation of the market and its problems was concentrated on the supply side. This was reinforced as Marxist ideology came to prominence, since popular Marxism does not draw a clear distinction between consumption and production, nor does it see housing as a consumption good. Marxism lacks a theory of consumer demand, though some argue a supplier-induced demand theory (Castells, 1977) and in its common form implies that those who do not own the means of production become progressively worse off (Berry, 1983). With escalating land prices in boom and then escalating interest rates in recession, it seemed their interpretation was validated. Their concern was heightened by discovery of exploitive activities involving inner-area property markets. Demand tended to be seen as a source of urban problems such as high prices, inadequate services and endless suburbia at a national level only when government economic policy induced it to fluctuate. It was rarely translated to the individual level, nor examined in the sort of detail that could reveal price increases attributable to substantial increases in real household incomes, liberalised credit facilities, and development costs that resulted in a substantially improved bundle of services.

Inevitably land and house price inflation was seen as cost push rather than demand pull. Developers reinforced this view by emphasising the increasing costs of land development in their explanations of market trends (Tyler, 1973). Costs they emphasised were those imposed by government relating to betterment levies, road standards, water and sewerage services, and lately charges for community facilities; occasionally they indicated that they were squeezed by raw (broadacre) land prices (HIA, 1971). There were very few people saying that prices were high because demand was high, that demand was high because people were affluent and had access to easy credit, or more importantly up to 1973, that speculation in subdivided lots was a major contributor to price escalation.

Failure to consider the demand side also meant that the substantial rise in mortgage interest rates accompanying the collapse of the property boom in the 1970s was seen as exacerbating the affordability problem. The notion that house and land prices might adjust to interest rates was not widely explored, and some of the research investigating the effect of interest rates on affordability focused on the affordability of mortgages rather than houses. Thus the housing crisis which began in the 1970s was seen to remain, indeed and to get worse rather than better over the next decade or so.

There were several other factors reinforcing the perspective that saw consumers as the losers and arguably led to an exaggeration of the housing crisis. Major economic and social changes occurred in the 1970s. The world economy entered a long recession with high rates of inflation, interest and unemployment. Unemployment created by recession and economic restructuring meant economic hardship for prospective and existing households with uncertainty heightening risk for lending authorities. High interest rates brought substantial increases in mortgage repayments. Rapid inflation heightened uncertainty, but also obscured the reality of changes in prices and incomes. People were not used to evaluating in constant dollar (real) terms, and responded mostly to movements in current money terms.

Socio-demographic change was a significant factor. Population growth rates slowed, casting uncertainty over economic prospects. Liberalised social attitudes towards divorce and mixed-sex households, increased support services for women with child dependants, and legislative change, all enabled a higher rate of marriage dissolution. The proportion of households headed by divorced persons doubled between 1976 and 1981, and the proportion headed by permanently separated households also increased. Birth rates and marriage rates fell. More support for young single people may have encouraged living separately from parents despite heightened unemployment. So the problems of homelessness, and of single-parent families grew substantially in the 1970s, reinforcing the perspective of a general housing crisis.

An alternative paradigm

An alternative paradigm is one that embraces neo-classical economics and fully incorporates socio-demographic considerations. Neutze (1977) has been the champion of this perspective, but it could be argued that he has not given sufficient emphasis to the demand side. Not all neo-classical economists give adequate consideration to socio-demographic factors, partly because the latter are not easily incorporated in conventional economic methods of analysis. There are difficulties in translating the monetary units of measurement in economics to the physical units of production, i.e. houses (Bowden, 1980). So the alternative paradigm is not strictly an economic one, and the incorporation of neo-classical economics need not imply a strong market-oriented perspective as the work of Apps (1980) and Priorities Review Staff (1975) demonstrate.

The strength of neo-classical economics is that it provides a set of rigorously defined concepts and techniques that allow less ambiguous interpretations of market economies than other paradigms. And of particular value is that the demand side of the equation can be assessed in as much depth as the supply side. Using this approach, the argument to be presented in the balance of this paper is that the housing crisis is not nearly as great as claimed, is more one of distribution and equity than of absolute cost. This interpretation differs only in degree from that of the political economists (Sandercock, 1983).

The neo-classical economics and socio-demographic paradigm suggest that: land price inflation is demand pull in the short run; package prices adjust to interest rates, and affordability of houses may improve in recession; long-term cost pressures are almost entirely a consequence of developer charges; developer charges have captured a large part of the unearned increment in land conversion; speculation is a much less significant feature of urban property markets than it used to be; and the real value of the land and house package may be greater than it has been at any time in the last twenty years.

Reinterpretation of residential property development

The reinterpretation starts with the lead up to the 1970s property boom which occurred in its most spectacular form in Sydney. Daly (1982) attributes much of this boom to movements of international capital associated initially with a national mineral boom. The link between mineral and property booms is well attested in history, and may well explain the Perth property boom of 1966–69. But the factors contributing to the early 1970s boom are more complex. The role of domestic capital may well have been equally important in fuelling the suburban fringe property boom. Domestic capital, much of it the savings of individuals, provided the consumer finance for land and housing. Overseas finance tended to be concentrated in the commercial sector and in broadacre land acquisition by speculators who did not intend to develop the land. It also financed some developer land purchases. Only indirectly was it channelled into end finance via finance companies.

The 1960s was a period of strong real income growth and rapidly increasing female workforce participation rates. Disposable household income rose steeply, and investment outlets for it were mainly insurance and the stock market, particularly during the mineral boom. With the collapse of the mineral boom, small investor funds were diverted to building societies and finance companies, both direct lenders to consumers for housing. Deposits in financial institutions rose strongly in this period, so major institutional lenders for housing experienced such growth in assets that they liberalised housing finance considerably. Two major forms of liberalisation were increasing loan-to-valuation ratios from 66 per cent to 85 per cent up to 95 per cent, and taking into account second incomes in calculating the size of the loan.

The former was assisted by mortgage insurance. Discrimination between new and second-hand houses was considerably relaxed, and discretionary powers of officers screening applicants were exploited in favour of maximising the amount lent. Finance for land purchase also moved from the vendor (developer) to finance companies.

Finance companies also became the preferred source of development finance for land subdivision. They became the least conservative lenders, offered higher gearing ratios (loan-to-equity ratios) than other institutions, accepted higher property valuations, were faster in approving and renegotiating loans, and allowed finance to be drawn as needed. The penalty of higher interest rates was more than offset by the higher gearing permitted (Holloway, 1972; Daly, 1982). Another source of domestic finance, never explored in any detail, is the illegal proceeds of gambling, vice and latterly drugs. McCoy (1980) records estimated annual turnover in SP (starting price) bookmaking in 1977 at $1.4 billion; narcotics were estimated at only $59 million. Real estate is one of the easiest ways to launder money, often through purchase, but also through development.

The effect of such increases in domestic savings being channelled into real estate at the consumer end is to increase demand and shorten the savings period for house and land acquisition. Also contributing to increases in demand were the entry of the post-war baby boom cohort into the household formation stage, and the increased propensity for young people to leave home and set up single-sex and mixed-sex households.

Speculation in subdivided lots

A further demand factor of considerable but largely unrecognised significance was speculation in previously subdivided and serviced lots. Speculation is mostly identified as a feature of broadacre land, where people or organisations buy property to capture for themselves a substantial windfall gain in the passage of land from rural to urban use. This sort of speculation was a feature of the property markets until the 1970s, but is now much less significant. The unearned increment appears to have been captured by developer charges. Speculation or investment in subdivided lots is an age-old phenomenon (Cannon, 1966; Fisher, 1933; Yearwood, 1970) but is now confined largely to resort land markets. It was no less common in Australia. So much land was subdivided in the Melbourne property boom of the 1880s (Cannon, 1966), for example, that surpluses were still available in 1950.

Premature subdivision was a particular concern of the planners who prepared the County of Cumberland Planning Scheme for Sydney

(Fraser 1947). They too could point to the 1880s residential sub-divisions in Sydney that had remained undeveloped, for example, the very small lots with eight-metre frontages in Fairfield and River-stone. Later, the McCarrey Committee (1968) which examined the property boom in Perth 1966–69, recognised the role of small-lot speculators in driving up land prices. According to one committee member there were so many speculators that no matter how much land was released their appetites could not be satiated (Cartwright, 1970), yet a formal measurement was not attempted.

Very few attempts have been made to measure the level of this type of investment in urban property markets. For the Wollongong urban area it was shown to fluctuate in step with the property cycle between 1956 and 1973, ranging from less than 10 per cent of transactions in the trough of the cycle to over 50 per cent of transactions in the expansionary phase (Cardew, 1977). The results were consistent with the reports of developers who indicated that up to 80 per cent of a subdivision might be sold to such persons, leaving 20 per cent to builders, both individuals and companies (McGrath, 1972). Paterson (1974) in a study of Melbourne arrived at a figure of 45 per cent for the early 1970s boom. More recently Wastell identified resale rates of 45 per cent for Adelaide (quoted in Badcock, 1984).

This sort of speculation involved a range of people, often young single people with spare funds. A common procedure in New South Wales was to buy land before title to the land was available. A 10 per cent deposit was required and the balance payable when titles were issued. The land would be resold just as title became available so that settlement on the first and second sales would occur on the same day. This avoided any payments beyond 10 per cent for the first purchaser. As the land would usually rise in price by at least 10 per cent between the first purchase resale, the profit was 100 per cent in less than a year. Clear evidence of this for subdivision in Sydney has been obtained by Taylor and McNamara (1976).

Thus the combination of small-lot speculations, rising household incomes and liberalised credit for land purchase meant that market demand was racing upwards. Clearly if supply could not keep pace with demand, price inflation was inevitable. And supply could not hope to keep pace, even with the pre-selling tactics that provided the most lucrative opportunities for speculators.

Constraints on supply of land

There were several constraints on supply. In the 1960s developer charges had been introduced to improve services in new subdivisions and cover the cost of those services. By the early 1960s in Sydney, develops were required to construct roads and install or pay for the installation of water and sewerage services including the offsite amplification of these services. Similar requirements were introduced in other States of Australia. The construction and administrative aspects of these requirements created a lead time for subdivision of twelve to eighteen months. The capital cost of development acted as a brake on the scale of development.

Further constraints were the need to link subdivision to existing infrastructure networks and residential zoning to apply to the land. There was often a mismatch between what was zoned and what could be serviced without delay. Also, the zoned residential area had steadily contracted during the 1960s, and developers' claims of inadequate land were treated frequently with an attitude that ranged from scepticism to contempt. So supply was a constraint. In Sydney, Melbourne, Adelaide and Perth between 1968 and 1973 inclusive more houses were commenced than lots created. Only in Sydney for 1972 and 1973 did land subdivision overtake house commencements, and then by a margin that was insufficient to cover the speculative/investment demand (DURD, 1974). So demand-pull price inflation resulted on a scale unprecedented in Sydney and Wollongong, and on a lesser scale in other capital cities. The difference between Sydney and other capital cities could well be related to the role of overseas finance and the emergence of Sydney as Australia's finance capital (Daly, 1982), but it could also be attributed to the tighter planning and servicing constraints in Sydney.

Price inflation of up to 25 per cent per annum took its toll on first-home buyers. Their affordability crisis peaked with the boom and actually subsided in the high-interest-rate recession which followed (Cardew, 1979; The cost of housing, 1978). During the boom small-lot investors were able to outbid first-home buyers for land, and in the building sector the demand for labour and materials had driven up building costs and blown out dwelling construction times to the point where builders were often not willing to offer fixed price contracts for houses. These contracts would include a rise and fall clause which made the final price uncertain.

The introduction of rise and fall clauses was a significant feature of the turning point in the structure of the industry. Finance institutions such as building societies would not lend on such contracts to first-home buyers stretched to their financial limit, because of a higher risk of default. So buyers turned to package deals (joint acquisition of land and house) rather than separate purchase of the land and later contract with a builder for a house. This change in practice coincided with a larger scale of spec-builder operation, companies building several hundred houses a year, and the filtering down of the project house to the bottom end of the market. The project house was introduced in the mid-1960s, and was essentially an architect-designed house for limited-scale mass production, an alternative to the double or triple fronted red-texture brick bungalow of the 1950s and 1960s. The incorporation of architect-designed houses with more efficient space utilisation meant that there was less reason to buy land and contract separately with a builder. The package deal was competitively priced and could be sold in such a way as to avoid stamp duty on the house component.

Package dealing became commonplace in urban property markets from about 1973. Instead of perhaps 10 per cent of dwellings being sold as package deals, the proportion rose to over 50 per cent and towards the 75 per cent claimed for the USA (Schmid, 1968). In Britain it is near to 100 per cent. Coincident with this trend was a fall in small-lot investment, even during a subsequent boom in 1979–81 in Sydney, again a resource development related one. Opportunities for small-lot investment were also curbed by restrictions on pre-selling of land and restrictions on resale of land. Government land agencies, including land commissions, required purchasers to build within three years and private developers were encouraged to do likewise. The property crash of 1974 brought down a number of the companies most inclined to encourage small-lot investors.

Interest rates and affordability — is there a crisis?

In 1974 interest rates rose by nearly 50 per cent, from 8 per cent on mortgages to 12 per cent. This accompanied the property collapse in Sydney and appeared to signal an era of hardship as mortgage repayment levels rose commensurately. But affordablility improved during the recession, in Sydney substantially. In that city the cost of access fell in real (constant dollar) terms 20–40 per cent between 1973/74 and 1977/78 (Cardew, 1979). And this applied to households with below average income levels and purchasing packages below median house prices. Comparable results were obtained by other investigators using average and median data only (The cost of housing, 1978; Paterson, 1981).

The reason for the improvement in affordability was a decline in land prices in money terms, hence a rapid decline in constant dollar terms, and a stabilisation of the package price in money terms for several years. The improvement was greatest in Sydney but also occurred in Melbourne and Adelaide a few years later (The cost of housing, 1978), and in Perth in 1969–71 (Worthington, 1973). In

Sydney the fall was partly a reflection of the scale of the boom; demand fell so dramatically and developers were so highly geared that they could not afford to do what they preferred in a recession — simply hold money prices constant for as long as possible. Even if money prices were held constant, they would have fallen in real terms with double digit inflation, and have led to an improvement in affordability. The pattern has been repeated in Sydney between 1981 and 1984.

Improvements in affordability during recessions are entirely consistent with the notion of demand-led price trends in the short term, for example demand-pull inflation. The fall in demand with the recession would have been a product of the loss of homesite investment demand, reduced effective housing demand because of an initial lift in the deposit gap in money terms, and uncertainty due to economic recession. Additional factors include the relative price of substitutes such as second-hand houses at the fringe and in established areas. The proportion of mortgages to second-hand houses rises appreciably in the downturn phase of the market. Other factors are a fall in the rate of population growth probably through reduced inter-urban migration, and perhaps a slackening in marriage rates.

Another implication of the demand-led thesis of short term price movement is that broadacre prices are determined by the final price of land in the form of subdivided lots. Unless there are monopolistic elements in the supply of broadacre sites, increases to land development costs including betterment levies are likely to be passed back to broadacre land holders or absorbed by the developers. Only in the long run will they be passed on and in a situation in which normal profits in development are made.

The notion that broadacre prices are determined by final lot prices is recognised by the development industry; that is the way they do their feasibility studies. They begin with gross realisation, that is, final sale prices, deduct profit and risk, selling, interest and development costs, which leaves a residual that they can afford to offer the owner of the broadacre site. If the asking price is above this then the project is not feasible and they do not proceed unless desperate for land. So to paraphrase Ricardo's dictum, the price of broadacres land is high because the price of serviced lots is high (and their price is partly a function of house prices); lot prices are not high because broadacre prices are high.

The betterment levy and developer requirements

Paradoxically, while developers are aware that broadacre land prices are a residual, they do not see that the betterment levy, and developer charges generally, either erode that residual or their profit margins. Entrepreneurs, however, are not good micro-economists. But many academics, even economists have fallen into the same error and argue that the betterment levy was passed on. Developers claimed this because the betterment levy of the early 1970s was a separately itemised component of the costs involved in acquisition of the broadacres.

It is quite easy to demonstrate in principle that the betterment levy was not passed on in the short term. Developers do all in their power to charge what the market will bear. Since the presence or absence of a betterment levy makes no difference to the quality of land as far as the end purchaser is concerned it should have no effect on what that purchaser is prepared to pay. Therefore, the price the market will bear is not affected by the betterment levy and so the cost must be absorbed or passed back. A bit of both probably occurred, in which case the price of broadacres probably rose slower than it would had a betterment levy not existed.

The same principle applies to other developer requirements but in varying degrees. Requirements that the developer contribute to the cost of offsite infrastructure works, for example, would not be known to the majority of land buyers in an urban area. So whether the developer or governments paid for them would make no difference to the price people were willing to pay for land. Road construction, water and sewerage reticulation costs and underground electricity are a different matter, but actual costs of these would invariably be underestimated by buyers, even by planners who should know and often do not. Again in principle at least a portion of these costs should be passed back or absorbed.

But what happens in the long run? Developers cannot absorb increased costs indefinitely. In the long run costs are more likely to be passed on. Marxist and classical economists at least agree that long-run costs are equal to prices. The question to ask then is whether developer charges have captured the unearned increment in land conversion. If so current land prices are largely a function of developer charges, i.e. supply costs.

The argument can only be presented in outline here. Developer charges now include installation of roads and drainage, footpaths, underground electricity and telephone lines, water and sewerage services, sign posting, open-space contributions and, in New South Wales, contribution to community facilities. The costs in a block of land developed in the outer-western Sydney suburb of Penrith, typical of most low-priced areas would amount to $15 100 including professional fees (Griffiths, 1984). With interest charges of $1500, selling costs of $1400 and a broadacre price per lot of $6000, a final sale price of $25 000 would provide a profit margin of $1000. This is hardly an attractive proposition for a twelve to eighteen month project filled with uncertainties, and suggests that broadacre prices could be nearer to $4000 per lot.

If there were virtually no developer charges, basically the situation applying in the late 1950s, the land could be sold for $10 500 per lot with the same broadacre cost of land ($6000 per lot). In constant dollar terms this is slightly higher than low-priced land in Sydney in the late 1950s ($7500 in 1984 prices) but lower than the price of equivalent land in the late 1960s ($11 500 in 1984 prices). The difference in land prices between the late 1950s and the present is mostly due to developer charges.

The late 1950s was chosen as a base year because then developer charges did not apply and the late 1950s property boom had not begun in earnest. If we take the price of land in 1972 and express it in 1984 prices, the figure is $30 500, about $5000 higher than current selling prices but not that much higher in terms of replacement cost. At least one can conclude from these figures that the real value of land at current prices has not increased substantially faster than the consumer price index in twenty years. Given the propensity for people to maximise expenditure on housing, for housing expenditure to generally rise as fast as income, and the supply constraints which exist, it is more than likely that land prices would have risen faster than the consumer price index even in the absence of developer charges.

Developer requirements were introduced progressively through the 1960s. In Sydney they were substantially increased during each of the two property booms. The impact on the development industry was felt in the recession, with widespread bankruptcy in the 1970s and a dramatic fall in lot production. In the 1980s recession, the bottom end of the land market was increasingly left to the Land Commission of New South Wales whose share of development activity and sales in lower-priced areas rose to more than 50 per cent of the market (in Adelaide the Land Commission share was greater still). Their pricing policy left no room for competition by the private sector who had to geographically separate themselves and exploit any product differentiation in order to gain a reasonable return. The problem facing Sydney is a substantial hike in infrastructure charges in the future, charges which must be passed on, or subsidised by the taxpayer in general.

Developer requirements apply in all States, and though land and housing prices are seen to be higher in Sydney than elsewhere, the picture is more complex. A study of developer requirements in thirteen local government areas (LGA) in capital cities in 1976 (The cost of housing, 1978) found a range from $4000 to $9800, and by rank order, the dearest was a Melbourne LGA, followed by a Sydney LGA, two

Melbourne LGAs, one in Sydney, one in Brisbane, one in Sydney, one in Hobart, one in Brisbane, one in Adelaide, one in Perth, one in Canberra, and one in Perth. Land prices in low-priced areas show less variation than prices in higher priced parts of each city. Part of the reason for Sydney's average housing prices being much higher than other capital cities, is the presence of more higher priced housing i.e. a wider range of house prices.

The foregoing explanation of the market would lead to expectations of a more buoyant urban fringe property market than currently exists in some cities, particularly Sydney. Demand by first-home buyers has been well below expectations of the industry and planners, despite considerable government financial assistance to home buyers. The answer may lie in higher levels of substitution of second-hand houses for new houses, since housing approvals have periodically reset record levels. But then one needs to explain why there might be a relative surplus of second-hand stock, and here an understanding of socio-demographic trends is necessary.

Conclusion

In this paper a neo-classical economic perspective has been used to challenge some of the widespread, arguably conventional wisdom about housing issues in the past two decades. Trends in the real cost of housing are shown to be a function of excess demand in the short term and increases in requirements upon developers to provide infrastructure in the long term. The consequence of this interpretation is that while housing prices may be perceived to be high, the value represented in these prices could also be at an historically high point. In other words, currently buyers may be getting more for their money than they did at most times in the last twenty years. This view of the market contrasts with that commonly derived from or implicit in the political economy perspective, a perspective which has had the greater influence in new housing policy initiatives such as Land Commissions. But a neo-classical perspective is only advocated within the context of a broader paradigm which incorporates socio-demographic trends.

13   Urban conflict patterns

JAMES FORREST

> Large cities are devices for shifting resources from poorer
> to richer while the planners look on, baffled but com-
> placent.
>
> (H Stretton, 1970 *Ideas for Australian cities*)

If conflict is to be regarded as endemic in our modernised, industrialised society (Eyles, 1974), nowhere is this more likely to be true than in
the city itself, with its diverse occupational structures, its subcultures
and ideological subgroups, and its social area segregation; in short the
proliferation of conflicting interests, economic and social. However
much planners and policy makers may seek to avoid such conflict, it is
generally regarded as a consequence of market forces, reflecting the
capitalist mode of production and its constant search for surplus value
which play a dominant role in all aspect of city form and development
(Janelle and Millward, 1976; cf. Horvath and Engels, ch. 11).

It is little more than a decade since the theme of conflict in cities became of interest to geographers (Cox and Johnston, 1982:1), although
over that period issues of locational conflict, of conflict generating
forces and the role of institutions have come very much to the fore in
geographic work. The purpose of this chapter is to review the nature of
urban conflict along with the context, scale and location of conflict
occurrences. This is approached within the context of an adaptation
and major extension of an earlier, ecological model of locational conflict
by Janelle and Millward (1976:103–106). The model is shown graphi-
cally in Figure 13.1.

Conflict generating forces

In a recent approach to a framework of ideas for understanding conflict
in the urban context, Cox and Johnston (1982:2–11) identify several

major themes of relevance to the Australian scene. These are summarised under their headings of externality effects, land-rent competition and institutional impacts.

Externality effects

These may be either positive or negative. They relate to aspects of the social and physical environment, positively, for example, in terms of proximity to one's friends or peers, or to a pleasant residential environment in which to live; negatively regarding proximity to some adverse environmental impact such as a noxious landuse or major traffic artery or problem of access to services and facilities. Though not specifically 'commodified' or priced, these effects involve important social costs (and are hence regarded by economists as 'externalities'). Conflict most commonly occurs with the threatened intrusion of a negative externality or in some cases where a promised positive externality, for example a promised open space provision in a property development proposal, fails to eventuate.

Externality effects have an important *local* expression; their impact declines with distance from the source of the problem or attribute, and has a greater initial though not long term impact on higher compared with lower socio-economic status areas (Holsman and Aleksandric, 1977). This is illustrated in the results of a mayoral election in Christchurch, New Zealand, (Taylor and Johnston, 1979:290–94) where a protest vote against the candidate of the party which supported a proposed new motorway development resulted in lost votes at booths along the proposed route, but not at booths away from the line of development (a negative externality field); and a gain in votes at booths where the candidates promised to support the erection of a major Commonwealth Games stadium in that area (a positive externality field effect). Within these externality fields, there are important pecuniary effects, the most obvious of which is on property values. Hence the intensity, in our property owning democracy, with which people react to some kinds of environmental threat. Thus the important aspect of externality effects as a positive element in conflict generation is the role it gives to collective intervention aimed at structuring externality fields to local advantage, or to ward off local disadvantage (Cox and Johnston, 1982:5).

Land-rent competition and locational conflict

Land rent, or land (property) value, is partly the result of social costs, the perceived balance between positive and negative externalities.

Hence the importance attached to 'spillover effects' seen to be associated with the proposals discussed in the preceding paragraph. These impart value to some properties (better access in the case of the motorway proposal) but subtract it from others (noise, disruption and general loss of amenity for those along the line of the motorway). But more important, land rent reflects competition to achieve at least a degree of spatial monopoly. Problems associated with this competition occur as conflicts over the location of business landuses, especially new, or new forms of shopping centres. The rent obtainable for a particular type of store or business landuse reflects the proximity of competitors. In land markets the addition of one competitor at a particular site can have a very considerable adverse effect (Poulsen, 1982). This is because of the fragmentation of the (retail) market created by the friction of distance separating consumers from an otherwise fixed source of supply (Cox and Johnston, 1982:6). Resolution of conflict over land-rent competition of course goes beyond business interests alone, and eventually leads into urban politics as a competition among spatially based groups: chambers of commerce, local retailing organisations and property developers, for example, concerned with land-rent competition and the quest for surplus value; resident associations concerned with externality effects; and local government cast into the role of arbiter or as the instrument of a market based urban economy.

Institutional effects: the role of government

Activities by institutions, in particular the activities of government, whether at the local or national level, or by government instrumentalities, become a focus of urban conflict through their ability both to modify the intensity of externality effects and to limit, or indeed enhance, scope for extraction of rents. For these reasons, particularly as they affect location decisions, business people are often as anxious to be represented on local government councils as some resident groups are to see that they are not. At the local level, zoning and development control are devices aimed both at mitigating negative externalities and controlling land-rent competition effects. The working out of contradictions between these two objectives often brings conflict between citizens, business people and (local) government. At higher levels, conflict can often occur among levels of government and government instrumentalities, as well as important social groups, notably around issues of future forms of urban growth and development. Perhaps the best example of this is Logan's (1982b) discussion of strategic planning during the 1970s and early 1980s aimed at controlling the shape of Melbourne for the remainder of the century.

An alternative view

Over the past decade or so, a different kind of perspective on urban conflict has gained ground among social geographers, a radical-Marxist view of the city as a 'growth machine' aimed at the generation of surplus value (Cox and Johnston, 1982:12–15). Institutions such as lending bodies or more importantly local and State governments are to be seen not as independent elements but as part of an underlying system of largely property based social relationships among people for whom or to whom they provide some instrumental function. These social relations are, of course, class relations. Similarly, locational conflict is no longer to be seen in terms of environmental problems but rather in terms of the nature of society, in this case class antagonisms associated with inequalities generated by capitalism and the social structuring of preferences for residential amenity (positive and negative externalities). Now, as well as confronting each other in the workplace, capital and labour also confront each other over externality effects and the social costs of land-rent competition, of investment–disinvestment decisions such as those described by Horvath and Engels (ch. 11). Thus *local effects*, instances of which are shown on the right hand side of Figure 13.1, *are but the localised realisation of much more basic conflicts within urban capitalist society*. Badcock (1984:274–88) refers to two instances of the working out of these basic conflicts.

Restrictive practices and the defence of property

> Exclusionary zoning represents the institutionalising of territorial inequity ... In the United States ... it has been refined to the point where it is utilised by local government (responding to pressures from domestic property owners) to deny access to unwanted activities or households. (Badcock, 1984:274)

In Australia the effect, though perhaps not the overt intention, is similar in its impact on the location of lower income and flat (medium density) housing in particular. Techniques of exclusion include building controls on flat development; setting minimum standards for dwelling size, boundary set backs and external walls; 'excessive' provision for car parking and open space; and the 'over-design' of street and service systems in new suburbs (Badcock, 1984:276). Nearly half of Melbourne's suburbs, for example, restrict flat construction to zoned areas, the effect being to exclude flat and town house dwellers (generally non-familism or late family cycle, post-child or widowhood groups) from about 50 per cent of eleven municipalities and more than 90 per cent of five others (Paterson, 1975:392).

CONFLICT GENERATING FORCES

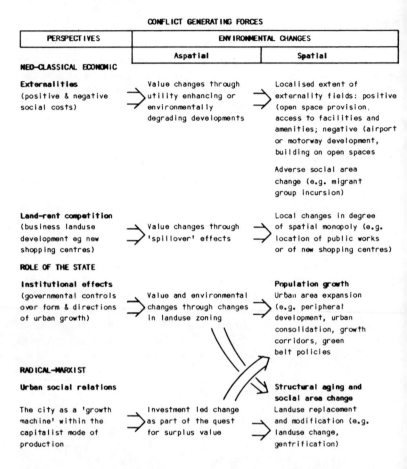

PERSPECTIVES	ENVIRONMENTAL CHANGES	
	Aspatial	Spatial

NEO-CLASSICAL ECONOMIC

Externalities
(positive & negative
social costs)

Value changes through
utility enhancing or
environmentally
degrading developments

Localised extent of
externality fields: positive
(open space provision,
access to facilities and
amenities; negative (airport
or motorway development,
building on open spaces

Adverse social area
change (e.g. migrant
group incursion)

Land-rent competition
(business landuse
development eg new
shopping centres)

Value changes through
'spillover' effects

Local changes in degree
of spatial monopoly (e.g.
location of public works
or of new shopping centres)

ROLE OF THE STATE

Institutional effects
(governmental controls
over form & directions
of urban growth)

Value and environmental
changes through changes
in landuse zoning

Population growth
Urban area expansion
(e.g. peripheral
development, urban
consolidation, growth
corridors, green
belt policies

RADICAL-MARXIST

Urban social relations

The city as a 'growth
machine' within the
capitalist mode of
production

Investment led change
as part of the quest
for surplus value

**Structural aging and
social area change**
Landuse replacement
and modification (e.g.
landuse change,
gentrification)

**Figure 13.1 Conflict generation and conflict types by major areas of
occurrence**

In Adelaide, inner city residential values have been maintained
through the practice of 'downzoning' (amending zoning regulations to
reduce the permissible intensity of development) usually in response to
collective pressure from middle class homeowners (Young, 1981) in
areas undergoing 'gentrification' (the redevelopment of formerly lower
income inner city housing areas for middle to higher income groups).
Much of this campaign was directed against medium density flat
development which was permitted under planning regulations then in
force. Such action brought reaction, from three main quarters (Bad-

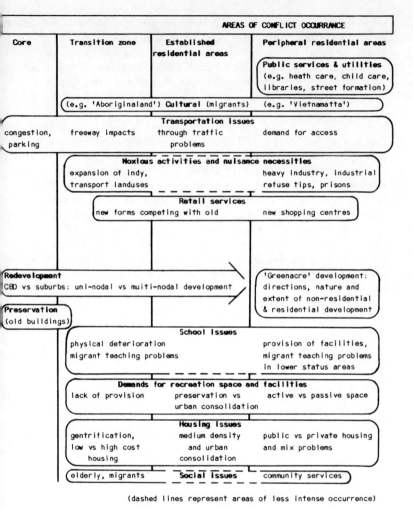

		AREAS OF CONFLICT OCCURRANCE	
Core	Transition zone	Established residential areas	Peripheral residential areas
			Public services & utilities (e.g. heath care, child care, libraries, street formation)
	(e.g. 'Aboriginaland')	**Cultural** (migrants)	(e.g. 'Vietnamatta')
		Transportation issues	
congestion, parking	freeway impacts	through traffic problems	demand for access
		Noxious activities and nuisance necessities	
	expansion of indy, transport landuses		heavy industry, industrial refuse tips, prisons
		Retail services	
	new forms competing with old		new shopping centres
Redevelopment CBD vs suburbs:	uni-nodal vs muiti-nodal development		'Greenacre' development: directions, nature and extent of non-residential & residential development
Preservation (old buildings)			
		School Issues	
	physical deterioration migrant teaching problems		provision of facilities, migrant teaching problems in lower status areas
		Demands for recreation space and facilities	
	lack of provision	preservation vs urban consolidation	active vs passive space
		Housing Issues	
	gentrification, low vs high cost housing	medium density and urban consolidation	public vs private housing and mix problems
	elderly, migrants	**Social Issues**	community services

(dashed lines represent areas of less intense occurrence)

cock, 1984:278). Property developers were concerned at the loss of investment potential in sought after areas close to the city centre. The State Planning Authority was concerned about the diseconomies of urban sprawl and aimed at medium density redevelopment of aging, inner city areas as a form of urban consolidation (cf. Stone, ch. 16). Local councils involved in pro-growth policies also supported medium density redevelopment. In some cases, however, such as Melbourne's Burwood Council, the extent of support for downzoning made it politically expedient for a majority of councillors eventually to side with their constituents against pro-growth elements on council. Successive downzoning amendments eventuated between 1973 and 1975 (Young, 1981). In other cases, however, it was not until local resident groups gained control, as of Unley Council in Adelaide for instance, that it was possible to put into effect sought after downzoning amendments.

Inner city redevelopment

Aspects of 'property-based social relations, the social base of urban politics, the distribution of power .. and the role of the state in urban change' (Badcock, 1984:281) are all to be found in the 'green bans' movement which occurred in Australian cities in the early 1970s. On the one hand, in New South Wales and Victoria were the conservative governments and their bureaucracies, seemingly committed to large scale private capital investment in property redevelopment in inner city areas. On the other hand were a variety of interest groups brought together for a variety of reasons to preserve the existing social and physical fabric. These comprised resident action groups built around nuclei of middle and working class owners and tenants concerned about displacement and adverse environmental effects, real estate agents and small scale developers who saw themselves threatened by 'big business' developers, and local councils such as Leichhardt in Sydney, Fitzroy and Collingwood in Melbourne. This second group of interests only gained real teeth, however, through the involvement of the Builders Labourers Federation (BLF) and their imposition of 'green bans'.

A green ban involved the union in withholding labour from any proposed demolition or site development considered detrimental to the environmental or historic character of an area, or thought likely adversely to affect the social cohesion of a neighbourhood. Green bans were only imposed at the request of a neighbourhood organisation and after a positive determination of a properly convened public meeting of affected residents (see Mundey, 1981). The effect of involving the union movement in environmental and planning issues in this way was of course to bring the classic confrontation between wage labour and capital firmly into urban politics (Badcock, 1984:282).

From the proclamation of the first green ban (to preserve Kellys Bush in Sydney's prestigious Hunters Hill) in 1971 to 1974, the bans stopped an estimated $4 billion in construction projects in Sydney alone (Roddewig, 1978:30). The nature of known green bans is set out in Table 13.1. There were differences between Sydney and Melbourne, however, in terms of the nature of the targets themselves (Roddewig, 1978:33). Most of the bans in Melbourne were directed against *private* developers, and tended therefore to be site specific; about half of the bans in Sydney were directed at *public* development proposals, and to

Table 13.1   Green bans in Sydney and Melbourne, 1971–75

Underlying issues	Sydney	Melbourne
Preservation of historic buildings	10	5
Inner city development and redevelopment	7	4
Retention of parkland and open space	5	9
Redevelopment incompatible with existing housing; refusal to build flats	6	4
Anti-expressway, car park development requiring housing demolitions	8	1
Inadequate compensation in compulsory purchase	3	—
No new sources or air/water pollution	—	2

Source: Carmina (1975:233) for Sydney; Roddewig (1978:33) for Melbourne

embrace whole suburbs or neighbourhoods, in The Rocks, Woolloomooloo and North Newtown in inner Sydney, for example. The
reason for this was that the Victorian Government became environmentally aware much sooner than the New South Wales Government.
Other cities also had green bans, but none on the scale of Sydney or
Melbourne: three in Adelaide, four in Perth, including one against the
demolition of old buildings in the port area of Fremantle; and one in
Hobart against the piecemeal redevelopment of old warehouses and
villas in the historic Battery Point neighbourhood (Roddewig, 1978:
34).

Action and reaction

The heyday of the green bans movement was in the early 1970s. By the
middle of the decade the movement had largely petered out. Partly this
was caused by intensification of union infighting within the BLF and
internal disagreement about environmentally oriented industrial action
as boom turned to bust (Daly, 1982). Partly too there had been a
softening of governmental attitudes on environmental matters and the
acceptance, however begrudgingly, of the concept of planning *with*
people, a concept adopted in the United States a decade previously.
Partly too there had been a radicalisation and certainly a politicisation
of the many resident action groups which were formed during this
period (Power, 1969). From the prototypal Carlton Association formed
in Melbourne in the late 1960s, resident action groups developed a
basis of expertise, resources and a sense of solidarity associated with the
formation of city-wide movements like the Coalition of Resident Action
Groups with seventeen affiliates in Sydney; the Committee for Urban

Action comprising some fourteen inner-suburban associations in Melbourne, and the Federation of Adelaide Metropolitan Residents Associations (Badcock, 1984:284).

In their encounters with corporate developers, resident groups were able to achieve their objectives only after their actions managed to enlist another level of government (mainly local government) to their cause, or to unsettle a State government politically. Otherwise the resident action movement was relatively powerless except when the BLF was persuaded to impose green bans (Badcock, 1984:285). One of the major impacts of their success in bringing about a significant pause to development through green bans and the entry of resident group activists into local government, however, was the proclamation by many municipalities of environmentally conscious planning schemes (Nittim, 1980:246). Ironically, the high standards then demanded brought about an appreciation of property values and in general a reduction in areas where the poor and their housing, governmental or private, could locate. Aspects of urban consolidation policy now being pursued by the New South Wales Government are in part a reaction against this process (ee Stone, ch. 16). Thus in their formulation of demands for local determination of local issues, resident action achieved the acceptance of general environmental and conservationist ideas as an aspect of property based social relations which gave little consideration to the likelihood that, in the context of the existing social structure, their demands could only aggravate the situation of the less advantaged in our urban society (Nittim, 1980:247). Indeed the effect of such urban action was often simply to preserve intact the quality and amenity of previously working class neighbourhoods for subsequent gentrification by upper middle class home buyers (Badcock, 1984:287; see also Johnston and Rose, 1977).

Sydney's Botany Bay port development project

An assessment of resident action in theory and practice in Sydney is provided by Nittim (1980; see also Roddewig, 1978). One example, drawing on Morone (1976) helps to give an idea of some of the problems involved in citizen reaction to a proposed major development. The decision in 1969 to develop a major deepwater port in Botany Bay arose from the view of the Maritime Services Board (1971:3) that:

> Botany Bay ... has large areas available for the construction of deep waterways and the development of large reclamation areas close to the metropolis [with] opportunities for the development of a completely modern

port and industrial complex which could be integrated with the existing facilities in the Port of Sydney.

It would also take account of the westward spread of the city resulting in the changed direction of land movement of inward and outward cargo (Butlin, 1976:6).

Though conceived in the early 1960s, it was not until 1976 that full details of the proposed port development became known. Various reports in the early 1970s touched on port side related aspects of the proposal, but there were practically no comments on the development of hinterland rail and other essential services. This was because the Maritime Services Board had no power over hinterland planning (Butlin, 1976:2). Two later reports, one on the impact of a proposed coal loader (Dames and Moore, 1974), the other on a container terminal (Maunsell and Partners, 1975) were among the first to reveal the full extent of port development, but considered environmental impacts to be minimal. The former report (1974:4) for example, estimated that environmental effects of the proposed coal loader as a port facility 'should only be minor by comparison with other schemes', but gave no details. Criticism of these reports relates to the way in which they confined their analyses to the impacts of specific aspects of port development, each of which in themselves judged to have minimal environmental effects on surrounding areas. This had the result of confounding any attempt to appreciate the overall impacts of the development (Morone, 1976:68; for a review of the policy issues involved in the Port Botany proposals, see Sanders, 1984). Not until the State government set up a general inquiry in 1976 were people able to examine the extent of the port development proposal as a whole, or attempt their own assessment of its likely impacts.

Based on submissions to the inquiry, Morone (1976:89–90) identified four main group roles involved in the Botany Bay situation:

1 *Resident action and co-ordinating groups* adopted a strong activist role voicing opinions on behalf of wide areas and large communities. Two groups figured prominently in attempts to co-ordinate the many groups opposed to port development. The Botany Bay Planning and Protection Council was formed in mid-1975, but lasted only a year. Affiliated members fluctuated considerably, but in early 1976 some ten environmental, resident action and union groups were associated with the Council's Co-ordinating and Policy Committee. During 1976, however, their co-ordinating role lapsed, to be taken up by the Botany Bay Co-ordinating and Action Committee. Like its predecessor, its objective was to liase between resident action and environmental groups, trade union and political party branches.

Neither of these two co-ordinating groups was able effectively to unite the various action groups in any longer term sense, however. Reasons for this lay partly in the different goals of each action group, but mainly in their largely unstructured nature. Most were quite small, the majority having a small membership, widely distributed. Their primary concern was with their own local areas. Among action groups with some interest in the port development, for example, neither the Hurlstone Park Progress Association nor the Towra Preservation Group appeared before the inquiry; one leader had family commitments, the other was on a trip overseas (Morone, 1976:75).

2 *Environmental groups* performed a similar function to that of academics and professionals — an advocacy role (Hartnett, 1975). Such groups are concerned with many issues throughout the State and nationally, and do not necessarily confine their interests to one specific area. Their concern with the Botany Bay project stemmed from a concern with wider national issues, especially matters of policy. Perhaps most involved was the Total Environment Centre, which played a role similar to that of the co-ordinating groups, collecting data, producing and distributing leaflets, organising and speaking at public meetings in conjunction with action groups. Among government environmental agencies, the State Pollution and Control Commission, for example, was mainly concerned about problems associated with the lack of adequate planning for the development (Morone, 1976:82).

3 *Local government authorities* have a responsibility to their ratepayers, and this was reflected in the type of submissions lodged with the inquiry (Morone, 1976:90). Those in the vicinity of the port stressed local environmental impacts, negative externalities associated with concern with traffic flows through the surrounding residential and business areas and the lack of provision for such movements, and detrimental effects on surrounding residential areas. Councils further afield, notably those in major coal producing areas, emphasised anticipated economic advantages associated with an important coal loading facility to be included in the port development.

4 For *the proponents*, the Port Botany project was originally put forward by the Maritime Services Board following a policy statement by the then Liberal (conservative) State Government (Morone, 1976:90). The Board therefore had official government sanction, in addition to complete jurisdiction over all New South Wales foreshore areas. Other proponents were transport or transport related companies interested in the economic returns of the project.

The Botany Bay case is but one example of the way in which a major government instrumentality, backed by government and in association with major private transport interests, initiated an action for development, and in turn brought forth a reaction from resident groups, environmentalists and local government authorities. By and large the reaction was unsuccessful (Sanders, 1984:145–49). So much of the port development was already in train by the time of the inquiry in 1976 as to be irreversible. There were minor victories. The Maritime Services Board agreed, for example, to major landscaping proposals around the port area. And at a later judicial inquiry into the proposed Chullora-Kyeemagh port access expressway, a decision was made against the Department of Main Roads in favour of upgrading rail facilities instead (on this issue, see Rimmer and Black, 1982:240–43). However, this ruling has not been implemented. The expressway is still a possibility.

Conclusion

The geography of conflict in cities began to become important a decade or so ago. Over that period, the emphasis has changed from relationships between patterns of conflict and urban ecological structure to a much broader concern focusing particularly on conflict generating forces. Thus a concern with areas of conflict occurrence, with local manifestations of conflict has come to be seen as the localised realisation of much more basic conflicts inherent in the nature of our economy and society. Increasing attention has also been paid to the role of the state and its instrumentalities, as arbiter or instrument, principally for their ability to modify the impact of externality effects and to control the worst aspects of land-rent competition. The general conclusion reached here would tend to see the state in an instrumentalist role as an agent of the capitalist mode of production, rather than in the alternative role as arbiter. In a property owning, private enterprise democracy, this is perhaps inevitable. Conflict arises first in defence of property, of investment, whether in terms of the social costs of externalities or land-rent realisations, and only second in terms of the improvement of social well-being in the city. Some of the consequences of this are now being worked out through opposition to aspects of current consolidation policies in New South Wales. Other consequences are being realised in that the effect of much urban action is but to preserve previously working class, inner city areas for later gentrification, for the displacement of the former, lower income residents in favour of higher income, middle class groups. Only when locational conflict patterns are placed within the broader context of generating forces reflecting conflicts and contradictions in the nature of our economy and society itself can urban conflict and its spatial manifestations be fully understood.

Part IV

Migrant Groups in the City

14 Cities of immigrants: migration, growth and heterogeneity

IAN BURNLEY

Australia has been a country of net growth through immigration throughout most of its history since 1788: during the convict era, and the goldrushes of the 1850s; during the first two decades of this century, and especially in the 1920s. The Great Depression and World War II brought a substantial halt to the immigration program. But again, following World War II, immigration became the main instrument of population building and labour-force expansion (Birrell and Birrell, 1981). The theme of this chapter is to assess the impacts of immigration on the social geography of Australian cities. To understand the nature of these impacts, we have to consider the migration processes whereby settlement took place, and also the policies of the state in fostering immigration and resettlement.

Migration types and policies

As a result of the long fertility decline to very low levels during the Depression, it became evident that the Australian labour force would shrink in absolute terms in the 1950s unless replenished by immigration. If Australia was to embark on a program of economic expansion, and also to defend herself in the event of another war, substantial immigration was required, a goal espoused by government and opposition alike.

When it became apparent that immigration from the United Kingdom and Ireland would not be enough, assisted migration agreements were concluded in turn with the Netherlands and West Germany, with Malta, Greece and Italy and, in the late 1960s, with Yugoslavia and Turkey. Meanwhile, criteria for private sponsorship were broadened with prospective migrants from Malta, Greece and Italy in the 1950s and Lebanon from the mid-1960s. Because of the great distance of Australia from traditional migrant-source nations, and the competition of other immigrant-receiving countries, an assisted migration scheme was necessary to sustain the desirable volume of migration, and to keep the more 'assimilable' immigrant intake, persons from Britain, the Netherlands and Germany, buoyant. Over 90 per cent of British and Irish settlers were officially assisted, and 65 per cent of the Dutch and Germans. While assisted immigration agreements were later signed with the Italian and Greek governments only a quarter and a third respectively of those from Greece and Italy were officially assisted. Thus those groups least able to afford the costs of migration by virtue of their socio-economic background in fact had to bear the brunt of the costs themselves (Burnley, 1974).

While officially assisted immigration is a distinct migration category, in practice, chain migration has often taken place within an assisted-migration framework. Persons in Australia have been able to nominate relatives in the home country for an assisted passage, and the Australian or home country governments have subsidised most of the passage costs for individuals and their families. The most important criterion has been relationship to the nominator who, in the case of non-British settlers has often been required to guarantee initial accommodation, and sometimes employment. Naturally, these requirements tended to reinforce chain migration and group settlement.

Refugee migration is, of course, another form of officially assisted migration, and up to 1984, over 500 000 persons had settled in Australia as refugees, most notably 170 000 refugee displaced persons from eastern Europe between 1948 and 1952, refugee waves from Hungary after the 1956 revolution, another wave from Czechoslovakia after 'The Prague Spring' was crushed in 1968, and over 80 000 from Indochina between 1975 and 1984. There was also significant refugee migration from Latin America during the 1970s, particularly from Chile after 1973. In addition, there was substantial 'quasi' refugee migration, such as the influx of almost 20 000 Lebanese after the civil war of 1975–76.

Apart from family reunion, officially assisted migration and refugee migration, persons have been able to migrate privately and individually and the term applied here to this migration is 'free migration'. It is termed 'free' because migrants are not constrained by contractual obligations to nominators, sponsors, employers or the government with regard to the costs of migration or resettlement. Such immigrants tend to be well educated, highly qualified, and/or have capital on arrival. In theory they have more choice as to region or area of residence, and more economic choices in their new country.

A special type of 'free' migration has been termed 'transilient' by Richmond (1969) and this migration type is becoming increasingly more common in more advanced economies. Transilient migration is typified by professional or managerial persons taking up contractual or medium-term appointments in their new country. Commonly, they may be much less concerned with either 'assimilating' to their new society or relating to their own ethnic community in the new land.

These socio-demographic categories of migration translate broadly into the formal migration categories used by the Department of Immigration and Ethnic Affairs (DIEA): family reunion (chain migration); refugees; and general eligibility, including persons who could make a social and economic contribution to Australia. This latter category could include assisted immigrants with required skills, independent migrants, and also 'transilient' migrants.

The migration sequence

While British migration was absolutely dominant in immigration to Australia between 1788 and 1947, more attention will be given to non-British migration because of its often distinctive contribution to the human ecology of the cities and to local community and economic structures.

Immigration 1788–1947

Irish immigration was disproportionately large during this period because of overpopulation in Ireland, and phases of repression by the British. In the years 1788 to 1820, the Australian population born in Ireland rivalled that from England. The Irish were prominent in the cities after the goldrushes as the goldfields population migrated to the metropolitan areas. While Daly (1982) was essentially correct in his assertion that the Irish, in contrast with their experience in the United States at the time, dispersed quite widely within Australian cities, there were strong neighbourhood concentrations of an intergenerational nature in Redfern, Chippendale, Surry Hills and Ashfield in Sydney, and in Fitzroy, Collingwood, Richmond and Footscray in Melbourne, all inner districts of those cities today. This Irish-Australian presence has been influential in inner-city Roman Catholic parish activities, and in local municipal and Labor Party politics.

As a result of the United State's immigration quota acts of the early 1920s, Italian migrants increasingly turned their attention to Australia (Price, 1959). Most of this pre-World War II migration went to rural areas (Cronin, 1975). In some cases, the rural migration flows shifted later to the southern cities as Galvin (1984) has noted in the case of a village chain migration from Lettopalena in the Abruzzi which first went to the canefields of north Queensland and later to Newcastle, New South Wales, as information spread about vocational opportunities in the Broken Hill Proprietary's steel works.

Migration 1947–84

There were three distinctive. features of postwar migration: first, its volume, over 3.3 million by 1984; second, the ethnic diversity of the intake; and third, the heavy bias towards urban, and particularly metropolitan settlement. Opportunities were limited in rural areas. Structural changes were affecting agriculture, resulting in fewer holdings and a diminishing farm workforce. Instead, the opportunities were in the cities, especially in the manufacturing, building and construction industries. Gaps occurred in the manual labour force because of the low fertility of the 1920s and 1930s, and because many Australian children of working-class origin did not enter their parents' occupation.

There was a major migration surge between 1948 and 1952 consisting of assisted British immigrants, almost 170 000 displaced persons and the first major intake of Italian immigrants. In Sydney, Melbourne, Adelaide and Perth, the Italian settlers found small Italian communities which had been established in the 1920s. In Sydney, some 6000 Italians, mostly men, settled temporarily in rooming and boarding houses in central Sydney, with similar trends in central Melbourne. By the early 1960s, however, these numbers had fallen considerably as men met and married Italian women in Australia, or were joined by their sponsored fiances, and moved out. Many formed residential concentrations of considerable size, such as the 5000 Italian-born in Leichhardt in Sydney in 1966, with almost as many in nearby Petersham and Five Dock, 6000 in Fitzroy in Melbourne, and 10 000 in Brunswick to the north by 1966.

The British and the displaced persons, on the other hand, tended to bypass the inner city — the British settling in a range of suburbs, according to purchasing power and their socio-economic status. However there were some concentrations of British in apartment developments or in old, formerly substantial houses which had been subdivided into flats in Randwick and North Sydney in Sydney, and in Prahran and St Kilda in Melbourne, although most British went to the suburbs, including Housing Commission estates.

The displaced persons, however, spread into low-cost housing in

intermediate and outer suburbs, and formed specific residential con-
centrations in middle to outer industrial suburbs, notably Ashfield,
Burwood, Bankstown, and Blacktown in western Sydney, and in
Sunshine and Keilor in western Melbourne. Equivalent areas were
Woodville in Northern Adelaide, and Corio in Geelong. In Sydney,
Melbourne and Adelaide, communities formed where lots could be
bought for under $320, or older detached cottages and land for about
$500. Because most were unnaturalised, they were not eligible for State
Housing Commission accommodation, a situation that has been
rectified with later waves of refugees since the late 1960s. The local
communities were strong: there were over 2200 Polish-born in Bankstown in Sydney in 1961, and as many in Sunshine in Melbourne. An
examination of the Sands Street Directories for 1961 reveals that up to
70 per cent of the names at the street block level were Slavic.

There were two basic processes responsible for the concentration of
displaced persons. Both have relevance to the more recent settlement
concentration of Indochinese refugees. The first was the location of the
major hostels for accommodating refugees and other officially assisted
immigrants. Areas with which they became familiar were those
districts near the hostels. Most found work in suburbanising factories
nearby. Their knowledge of the cities was spatially confined. Many
found opportunities for low-cost housing nearby. The second process
was what Price (1959) called 'gravitation' migration, whereby persons
gravitate together from other parts of the cities, and form communities
of compatriots speaking their native languages at the neighbourhood
level. This process also occurred with officially assisted southern
Europeans who moved away from hostels but joined established
concentrations in the inner city, by gravitation (Whitelaw and Humphreys, 1980).

By 1961, distinctive patterns of immigrant settlement had emerged
in Australian cities, as documented for Melbourne by Jones (1962)
and Stimson (1970). These were: the inner ring suburbs, comprising Melbourne, Fitzroy, Collingwood, Richmond, Prahran and
South and Port Melbourne in particular. These areas of 'high ethnicity'
comprised Italian, Greek and Maltese settlers, along with Macedo-
nians from both Greece and Yugoslavia. The second distinctive pattern
was in the western LGAs of Altona (Maltese), Sunshine and Keilor
(east European refugees). The third was in the higher income parts of
St Kilda, Caulfield and adjacent areas (Jewish settlers). To these could
be added a fourth trend, Dutch settlement in the southeastern suburbs.

In 1961–62, there was a further brief economic downturn, so
immigration was reduced. Nevertheless, strong economic recovery in
1963, and falling unemployment allowed the Australian Government to
expand the sponsorship categories to include more distant relatives,

and this was allowed with nominations under the assisted-passage schemes. Thus the Greek-born population in Australia doubled during 1961–66 to more than 150 000 to whom should be added Greeks born in Cyprus and in Egyptian cities such as Cairo and Alexandria.

These changes were in turn reflected in immigrant foci within the cities. In Melbourne, the Greek-born population grew to over 20 per cent of the total population of Richmond municipality. There were over 6000 in Prahran and as many in Northcote by 1971. The general trend was for Greeks to concentrate in Melbourne's inner eastern and southern suburbs and Italians in the inner northern suburbs in the first instance. Apart from the Northcote and Brunswick areas, population succession whereby one immigrant group succeeds another has not taken place in Australian cities. Indeed in Sydney, Matiwijiw and Rose (1979) have shown that discrete ethnic concentrations formed, and tended to survive rather than be replaced by the process of population succession.

In Sydney, Greek settlement spread from Redfern, where the first Greek community had been established prewar, into nearby Newtown, Stanmore and Dulwich Hill, and in Marrickville municipality. Indeed, Marrickville LGA supported the largest Greek-born populations, some 13 000 in 1971, in the whole of Sydney. The main thrust of Greek secondary group settlement, was south and southeast into middle-inner suburbs, whereas the main movement of the Italians was west into Ashfield, Drummoyne and Burwood where secondary and even third group settlements formed in a similar manner to those of the Greeks. This regrouping process took place as families, once in the owner-buyer market, wished to provide ample space for their children, and as wider kinship groups wished to regroup in relatively close proximity to each other. This process has been documented for the Greeks in Sydney by Sinclair (1980) and for Sydney's Maltese by Yoo (1978).

In Melbourne, this regrouping process took place in the western suburbs during the 1970s, as over 2000 Maltese moved from their core concentrations in Altona LGA, into Sunshine and Broadmeadows LGAs. Furthermore, as with the Greeks and Italians, new arrivals from overseas were now tending to bypass the old core concentrations and settle with relatives or fellow villagers in the second and third group concentrations, or with the many other compatriots who had dispersed outright.

In 1967, assisted migration agreements were signed with Yugoslavia, with two aims in mind: to reverse the marked sex imbalance in favour of males, and to provide more labour for heavy industry. The latter was a miscalculation since the manufacturing sector had already begun to contract in absolute terms, as the result of structural changes prior to the onset of recession and higher unemployment in 1973–74

(Linge, 1979). The impact of this large intake of Yugoslavs, some 70 000 in five years and many of them from Macedonia, was felt immediately in the cities. Thus the Yugoslav-born population in Footscray in Melbourne's inner west grew from 1400 in 1966 to over 5000 in 1971. In Marrickville in Sydney, numbers increased to almost this figure while in neighbouring Rockdale to the south, there was growth to over 4500 by 1976. The older, outer suburban market-garden foci, or former displaced person settlements, were also augmented by several thousand settlers, as in Fairfield west of Sydney, and in Sunshine west of Melbourne. Meanwhile in Wollongong, the Yugoslav-born became the next largest immigrant group after the British, with 8500 in 1981.

Lebanese migration to Australia also accelerated during the 1960s, the size of the Lebanese-born population increasing four-fold following the relaxation of sponsorship categories, thus allowing the rejuvenation of long-term chain migrations, and the beginning of new chain movements. Whereas almost all previous Lebanese migration to Australia had consisted of Christians, Moslem migration now began in earnest, a migration which was reinforced by the Lebanese civil war in 1975–76, and subsequent conflict. By 1984, the Lebanese-born population in Australia had grown to over 45 000 making them one of the larger immigrant populations. Three-quarters resided in metropolitan Sydney.

Lebanese settlement began first in Redfern, some two kilometres south of the central business district, in an area of terrace houses built in the 1870s. Indeed the Maronite and Melkite churches were established in Redfern well before the turn of the century. The inhabitants were virtually all first-generation persons, as the peaks and troughs of chain migration rejuvenated the neighbourhood, and as successive waves of settlers moved out to the much larger second settlements (Burnley, 1982).

Perhaps paradoxically, the Moslem migration began by Christian Lebanese businessmen sponsoring Moslems in neighbouring villages of the Bekaa valley, and Moslem residential concentrations formed in Lakemba, and Wiley Park. The influx after the civil war in Lebanon during 1975–76 doubled the size of the main Lebanese settlements in Sydney, with the number in Canterbury LGA growing to over 9000 by 1981, with substantial numbers in Marrickville, and a major second settlement in Harris Park and Granville of over 5000 first generation persons.

The last major wave of immigrants was the influx of refugees from Indochina. Between the end of 1975, when the first 'boat people' arrived, to mid-1984, over 80 000 refugees from Southeast Asia settled in Australia, the largest refugee intake after the postwar displaced persons program. Almost all eventually settled in the large metropolitan cities, particularly Sydney, Melbourne and Adelaide. In Sydney, three hostels located in the western LGAs of Liverpool and Fairfield were used to accommodate the refugees, the major reception centre being the Cabramatta hostel in Fairfield. In 1981, approximately 30 per cent of the Indochinese settlers in metropolitan Sydney were resident in Fairfield, with appreciable numbers in Liverpool and Bankstown. Despite growing concern about the extent of residential concentration in western Sydney, the proportion of new arrivals leaving the hostels intending to settle in Fairfield LGA, had fallen to 21 per cent in 1982–83.

In common with previous migrant streams, the Indochinese concentrated in the lower rental outer suburbs principally because of their proximity to the major migrant hostels. Perceptions of housing opportunities were spatially constrained to adjacent areas they saw on their journey to work or to local services and social institutions, especially as the refugees did not have private transport. Cheap rental accommodation comprising flats recently built near railway stations was becoming available, and in older suburban neighbourhoods where deceased persons' homes were also becoming available, or homes vacated by retirees moving to alternative accommodation elsewhere. Further, the main residential receiving areas for lower-income immigrants were no longer in the inner city, but in Sydney's case were now in the southwestern and central western suburbs. The inner-suburban housing market had changed from a predominantly rental one to an owner-occupier one, and with changing residential preferences on the part of some 'middle-class' groups, the cost of housing was now greater in many inner-city districts than in the outer western areas.

Another reason was the establishment of government and private agencies to help the refugees adjust. A wide range of community assistance organisations, State, federal, municipal and charities, were established in the southwestern region of Sydney. Assistance, with language instruction, translation, finding employment, arrangements for relatives to migrate, channelled through these agencies was a natural incentive for concentration. Finally, Indochinese communal organisations were established locally.

The regional impact of immigration

In the 1947–71 period, Melbourne was the main immigration magnet, largely because of the relatively greater thrust towards industrialisation in the postwar period, compared with Sydney. Indeed mainly because of immigration, and natural increase accruing to migrant families,

Melbourne's population growth between 1947 and 1972 was greater than that of Sydney. But between 1971 and 1981, the immigration flow to Sydney was relatively and absolutely greater than that to Melbourne. This was partly due to the greater migration from Asia to Sydney, and the more substantial settlement there of Middle Eastern and New Zealand-born immigrants. Partly it reflected some of the economic changes documented by Daly (1982), with Sydney becoming the new financial centre of Australia and with expansion of employment in the information processing and communication industries. A high proportion of the highly skilled, educated and professional persons from Asia entered these new growth sectors.

By 1981, the foreign-born comprised 28 per cent of the population of metropolitan Melbourne and 27 per cent of that in Sydney and Perth, compared to 22 per cent of the national population. (For an urban area comparison for Australia as a whole see Forrest, 1984b.) While immigration accounted for 43 per cent of national population growth (excluding births in Australia to immigrants) during 1947–71, it contributed over 52 per cent of Sydney's growth and 56 per cent of Melbourne's growth. Because of the age selectivity of the immigration flow, the impact on the growth of Melbourne's labour force was over 70 per cent up to 1971, and over 60 per cent in Sydney. Almost half the population of metropolitan Sydney, and over half the population of metropolitan Melbourne were first or second generation immigrants in 1981.

The secondary industrial cities which expanded rapidly postwar attracted many immigrants, notably the larger cities of Wollongong in New South Wales and Geelong in Victoria, and as Zubrzycki (1964) noted in a detailed study, the Latrobe Valley resource-based urbanising area in eastern Victoria; the industrial and shipbuilding second city of South Australia, Whyalla; and the petro-chemical town of Kwinana in Western Australia near Perth. In Wollongong-Shellharbour, immigrants and their Australian-born children constituted almost 52 per cent of the more than 220 000 people there in 1981. In Whyalla, immigrants and their Australian-born children constituted over 60 per cent.

These regional impacts were associated with sectoral concentrations of specific parts of the labour force: in Melbourne in 1981, first-generation immigrants constituted 46 per cent of the male workforce in tradesmen, production process workers and labouring occupations; in Sydney, 40 per cent; in Wollongong, 54 per cent; and almost 59 per cent in Whyalla. It was the northwestern Europeans and British that tended to be well represented in the professions, managerial and clerical occupations, while the immigrant groups from the Mediterranean countries and from east Europe were mainly in the craftsman, factory worker and labouring occupations.

Nevertheless, these observations do not suggest a class structure layered on ethnic lines; there is limited structural pluralism of the type noted by Gordon (1964) in American cities where class and ethnic segregation are strongly interrelated. However there have been strong concentrations of some immigrant groups, particularly their female members in specific occupations in the food, clothing and textile industries. This relates to the lesser education and formal skills of southern European and Levantine women and associated problems in the use of English. These trends also reflect gender inequalities in Australian society as a whole. The tendency towards the residential concentration of many of those from southern Europe, the Middle East and some eastern European countries meant that significant proportions of school enrolments in specific areas of the major cities, and in suburbs of Wollongong and Whyalla were of non-Australian parentage. The impact on school enrolments was often much greater than census figures would suggest. There are several reasons for this.

Most migration streams to Australia have been heavily age selective, this being reinforced by official immigration policy. Most immigrants from southern Europe were under age 35 on arrival, and indeed many were in their twenties. It was normal for family formation to occur in Australia and thus birth rates were raised in areas of residential concentration, especially in the inner city, although immigrant fertility patterns conformed with those prevalent in Australia. In the inner city, the host-society population during the 1950s and the early 1960s tended to be an aging one. Relatively few young Australian couples chose to raise their families in the inner city. The markedly different ages, then, of the immigrant and Australian-born in inner city localities inevitably meant that children of immigrant parents formed proportions of the primary school enrolments frequently in excess of 75 per cent.

More teachers had to be allocated to inner-city schools in both the public and Catholic school systems where hitherto they had experienced declining enrolments. Gradually there were improvements in pupil-teacher ratios, the appointment of teachers' aides, bilingual teachers, and the establishment of remedial English classes. Not all problems were solved; there were strikes over staffing in individual schools, as in Arncliffe in Sydney's southern inner suburbs in 1974, while in 1984, with the impact of Indochinese settlers being felt in Liverpool in Sydney's southwestern suburbs, teachers were threatening a State-wide strike over class sizes and the inadequate provision of special language teachers. Similar conditions now prevailed in older outer suburbs such as Liverpool and Fairfield, as had occurred almost a generation earlier in the inner city, for the Australian and older immigrant populations who settled there post-war were now aging and were contributing relatively few children to the schools relative to the newer immigrants. Meanwhile, school enrolments were falling precipitously in the inner suburbs as earlier southern European immigrants began to move out, or as their children moved out of the schools into adulthood, and as the process of 'gentrification' took place where middle-class couples with fewer children moved into older, inner-city housing which was being revitalised.

Finally, mention can be made of the impact of immigrant populations on the business structure of old 'string street' shopping districts. It was in the areas of strong Greek, Italian and Yugoslav concentration, through which these arteries ran, that enterprising families established small businesses. Later, comparison goods stores and professional services were established so that in the main residential communities, all the supportive needs of settlers could be met. In Leichhardt as late as 1976 there were 175 Italian shops and services around and near the Parramatta Road and Norton Street intersection, with an additional 60 in Great North Road in adjacent Five Dock. In Newtown-Stanmore, there were as many Greek businesses, with another 40 in Dulwich Hill. In Melbourne there were 100 Italian businesses and institutions in Lygon and Drummond Streets in Carlton, and over 300 along sections of Sydney Road in Brunswick and Coburg. The shops did far more than retail goods: they often provided a 'gatekeeper' advisory role.

Conclusion

Immigration has profoundly altered urban social environments in Australia, especially since World War II. The impact on the large cities was greater, partly because of the relatively greater concentration of immigrants and their children there. Otherwise, the 1981 population of metropolitan Sydney would have been little more than 1.6 million of today's 3.3 million and Melbourne would have had less than 1.3 million compared with the actual 2.72 million.

It was immigrants from southern Europe and the Levant that began the residential revitalisation process in the inner city. Buying old, formerly rented dwellings, they removed the subdividing partitions and renovated the dwellings, often painting the terraces white, pink or blue. Many of the building applications for additions approved by inner-city municipal councils were to southern European applicants.

Emphasis has been given to residential concentrations of immigrants from culturally dissimilar backgrounds and the migration processes which resulted in the formation of these concentrations, but as early as the 1961 census, all but the Maltese had less than half their populations resident in definable ethnic concentrations. The residential concentrations, although large in the case of the Greeks, Italians, Maltese, Yugoslavs and Lebanese, were not monolithic ethnic quarters or zones of minimum choice. Nevertheless the Survey of Living Conditions in Melbourne conducted in 1966 (Harcourt, Harper, and Henderson, 1970) found that many recently arrived Greeks and Italians were below the poverty line. Burnley and Walker (1982) in a more recent survey found significantly higher unemployment among Greeks, Yugoslavs and Lebanese in their inner-city concentrations in Sydney while Young and Petty (1980) found high youth unemployment with Lebanese in Sydney and also considerable evidence of overt discrimination against them in the Sydney labour market. The ethnic concentrations of southern Europeans became much smaller during the 1970s: there was significant return migration to southern and central Italy as noted by Thompson (1982) and to Greece as documented by Bottomley (1980). More, however, moved out to second settlements or to suburbia in general.

Despite the concentrations in lower-income districts, and in less skilled manual jobs on the part of the first-generation southern Europeans, unpublished 1981 census information indicates that the second generation have been occupationally mobile, more so the men; the second generation Greek, Australian and Yugoslav children had proportions of their workforces in professional and managerial occupations equal to those of the Australian-born of Australian-born parents. Among those of European origins at least, there is little evidence of labour market segmentation or structural pluralism on an intergenerational basis. However, less is known about the fortunes of less able second generation persons from culturally or 'racially' dissimilar backgrounds. Despite the controversy over Indochinese and other Asian immigration which erupted in the first half of 1984, there is every reason to assume that a modest intake of refugees can be sustained. Much depends on the level of unemployment in Australia.

15   Aboriginal migration to inner Sydney

IAN BURNLEY AND NIGEL ROUTH

Gale (1972:1) has observed that the urban Aboriginal is a new element in the population in the Australian city. The task of this chapter is to explore this observation and to compare the adjustment of Aboriginal migrants to inner Sydney with Gale's earlier, but wider, study of Aborigines in Adelaide. We examine the extent to which there are common processes at work in the two cities which condition or constrain settlement, opportunities and adjustment of Aboriginal newcomers to the city. We ascertain the causes of cityward migration of Aborigines, and the extent to which this means a fundamental change in the settlement and social circumstances of Aborigines in New South Wales.

The impact of western man on the Aboriginal people has been one of almost unrelieved tragedy: a massive increase in mortality caused by the accidental introduction of European diseases, against which Aborigines had little resistance. Violence and genocide also played their part and, in the sum, the collective impact of disease and oppression may have decimated the Aboriginal population to a greater extent than hitherto supposed (Butlin, 1983). And while the Aboriginal presence in metropolitan Australia may be a comparatively recent phenomenon, it must be remembered that there was a substantial Aboriginal population settled around the bays and estuaries of Sydney and other metropolitan areas before European colonisation began.

The decline in the Aboriginal population reached a nadir in 1921, then recovered to 'moderate growth' overall (Jones, 1970). In New South Wales, the great majority of Aborigines are of mixed ancestry but this has not lessened their subordinate status. A high proportion of those in country districts have experienced high unemployment, have been displaced from ancestral lands to a far greater extent than in the Northern Territory or in Western Australia, and have been relegated to a marginal existence. Their population has grown considerably faster than the total population. In a 1965 survey of part-Aborigines in rural and non-metropolitan urban areas, Rowley (1972) found that 56 per cent were children under fifteen years of age and 51 per cent were under 30. This implies that the part-Aboriginal population will increase rapidly in the near future as the mothers of the second generation have already been born. This suggests a potential impetus for outmigration from country districts to find better opportunities in the cities.

There is evidence, however, that overall Aboriginal fertility has been falling and this has certainly taken place in the country districts (Gray, 1984). But it should be remembered that Aboriginal birth statistics for New South Wales are inadequate. Gray estimates that between 1971 and 1981, the Aboriginal fertility rate fell by 46 per cent from 5.9 to about 3.3 while the overall Australian rate fell by 31 per cent to 2. It is against these demographic indicators, plus continued high adult mortality, with life expectancies for men still under 60 years (Smith, 1979), that the discussion of factors with potential to precipitate outmigration from country districts is set.

Factors predisposing Aborigines to migrate to the cities or not

While Aboriginal fertility has been falling, the rates of natural increase and the number of young people entering the labour market have been substantially above those of the total Australian population. Given levels of unemployment, especially for persons with limited occupational skills, higher in the country than in the metropolis, there would be strong push factors propelling Aborigines to migrate from such conditions. The question here then is, why has the outmigration of Aborigines from country districts not been greater? Reasons for this apparent inertia may be local ties to family or kindred group in the country to whom persons turn for support in times of need; housing costs in the city; discrimination in the housing and employment markets, and in places of social interaction, such as hotel bars and sports clubs in the city.

On the other hand, Aboriginal unemployment has traditionally been high in country districts, partly due to lack of skill, and partly to a reluctance of graziers and farmers to hire Aboriginal workers. Accepting that inertia existed because of communal ties and uncertain opportunities in the European world of the cities, powerful forces were propelling the Aboriginal migration to Sydney. Indeed Rowley (1982) found that in 1980, 53 per cent of the males in his longitudinal survey were unemployed compared with 21 per cent in his 1965 survey.

The Sydney sample survey: sample characteristics

During the second half of 1982, a questionnaire survey was conducted in Sydney of 150 people, only 21 of whom had been born in Sydney. Two approaches were adopted in carrying out the interviews. Approximately 60 per cent of the interviews were conducted by the authors, either working through several of the major Aboriginal organisations in the inner city, or conducted with their knowledge and approval. The other 40 per cent were obtained by an Aboriginal interviewer who was employed on the project amongst Aborigines living in the city area.

The majority of those interviewed lived in South Sydney, or in the suburbs of Chippendale, Newtown, Redfern and Leichhardt. Table 15.1 shows the age structure of the sample and the 1981 census population of Aborigines in these localities. With the exception of hostel interviewees, most of whom were young, and who thus introduced some bias in the age distribution, the sample resembled the census population.

Table 15.1   Age and sex distribution of adults in the census and sample Aboriginal populations %

	Age group			Sex	
	15–24	25–34	34+	Male	Female
Sample survey	47	31	21	53	47
Census	39	26	35	54	46

Source: Sample survey, 1982 and unpublished 1981 census tabulations, microfiche

Stated reasons for leaving the country

Whereas employment problems were the most frequent category of reasons for leaving the country, family reasons were the most frequently cited for migrating to Sydney, followed in order of importance by job opportunities (Table 15.2). Negative factors — unemployment, poor health facilities, poor housing, discrimination, bad memories and poor health — in sum accounted for 51 per cent of the reasons for leaving the country. Positive factors — more job opportunities, family ties, education, urban opportunities (including better welfare help), better health and housing facilities — accounted for 89 per cent of the reasons for moving to Sydney. However, unemployment levels for the sample in Sydney, over 40 per cent, were almost as high as those in the country.

There are some parallels between the reasons for migration to Sydney and those found by Gale (1974) in her earlier study of movement to Adelaide, which found that kinship was the major cause of Aboriginal migration to Adelaide. Gale also found that the nature of

Table 15.2 Main reasons of Aborigines for leaving the countryside and for migrating to Sydney

Leaving country:	Number	Percentage	Migrating to Sydney:	Number	Percentage
No jobs, few opportunities, unemployed	98	41.2	More job opportunities	67	30.5
Family reasons	48	20.2		69	31.4
Education (for self or children)	25	10.5	Opportunities (more welfare help, assistance)	24	10.9
Opportunities (elsewhere, or to see the city)	16	6.7		20	9.1
Welfare/law (trouble with police, to be near relative in trouble)	14	5.9	Welfare/law (transfer by authorities)	8	3.6
Involuntary reasons (moved with parents when young)	13	5.5		8	3.6
Poor facilities in country (medical, housing)	10	4.2	Better facilities in city, housing	16	7.3
Negative reasons (discrimination, bad memories, disliked the place)	8	3.4			
Personal problems (poor health, family split, ran away)	6	2.5	Personal reasons (choice, came to visit and stayed)	8	3.6
Reasons total	238	100.		220	100.0

Source: Sample survey 1982–83

kinship, and the extent of its power, as a force attracting Aboriginal migrants to the city, varied considerably from one regional group to another. This had been the result of Aborigines having been placed on reserves, particularly those in the southern part of South Australia where the characteristic form of their Aboriginal community became that of an interrelated cluster of families in close mutual contact, but isolated from other Aboriginal groups. In Sydney, such divisions were less in the inner city; there was no modern reserve system in rural New South Wales.

Another resemblance to the Adelaide situation was involuntary migration on the part of a minority of movers: movement with parents when young; the forced movement of children from families which had been labelled as indigent by the State authorities (before World War II); trouble with police; or movement to Sydney to be near a relative in trouble. However, the relative frequency of such responses was less than that found in the Adelaide study.

The migration process and immediate adjustment in Sydney

A total of 30 people (23 per cent of migrants) had lived in Sydney previously for a period of over six months. They had then left to live elsewhere, including return to the country town they came from, and then moved back to Sydney to live. Eight people had done this four or more times. However the majority, 74 per cent, had not lived in Sydney previously. A high proportion, 40 of those interviewed, had lived in Sydney for two years or less.

The regional origins of Aboriginal migrants to Sydney conformed to the geographical distribution of Aborigines in New South Wales. Of the sample which included those born in Sydney, 24 per cent were born in the Mid-North Coast Statistical Division, 21 per cent in the North Western Division, 1 or 2 per cent in the Northern Division, and 9 per cent in the Murray and Murrumbidgee regions. The remainder were evenly distributed by origin, though with relatively few from the Illawarra, in contrast to the known migrational linkage between the long-established La Perouse Aboriginal settlement and the Illawarra and South Coast regions. For most, there were no intervening options between remote source regions and Sydney: differences among local Aboriginal communities in the country and the risk of discrimination, particularly in local employment and housing, precluded stepwise migration, i.e. movement to larger towns before movement to Sydney.

Of those from the north coast, half (16) were from the town of Kempsey where there is a sizeable Aboriginal population. A fifth of those from the North-Western Division were from Brewarrina, but over half the total sampled were born in a range of small towns rather than major country urban concentrations or fringe settlements. Few were from rural areas.

Duration of residence in Sydney of the migratory part of the sample (Table 15.3) shows that while almost half had been resident under five years, 27 per cent had lived in Sydney for over ten years. A minority had visited Sydney as migrants four or more times (eight people), and 30 had lived in Sydney 'permanently' (for six months or longer) more than once. The 'permanent residents' were understated because 26 persons had not been resident six months on their present visit.

Table 15.3 Aboriginal internal migrants: duration of residence in Sydney

	Time in Sydney					
	< 6 mths	7 – 12 mths	1 – 2 yrs	3 – 5 yrs	5 – 10 yrs	> 10 yrs
Number	26	9	16	25	18	35
Percentage	20.2	7.0	12.4	19.4	13.9	27.1

Source: Sample survey

Persons were asked whether their current dwelling was their first address in Sydney. Over 67 per cent (87) of the 129 internal migrants to Sydney had resided elsewhere in Sydney (Table 15.4). There was considerable movement within the inner city, especially in South Sydney (containing part of Redfern, Surry Hills, and Chippendale). The mobility within defined areas of concentration resembles that found among the early stages in Greek settlement in Cringila, Wollongong by Robinson and Kambesis (1977). The major difference between the Aboriginal experience and that of the Greeks in Wollongong and in the inner city of Sydney, however, has been that home ownership has not been the normal outcome for the Aborigines.

It is difficult to compare Aboriginal home ownership as found in the Sydney inner-city study with that in Adelaide as reported in Gale's (1974:124–7) wider survey. Gale found that the larger proportion of Aboriginal households in Adelaide had limited housing choices. Less than 7 per cent were owners or owner buyers in Adelaide. Because the South Australian Housing Trust had a much greater stake in the metropolitan housing market in Adelaide (one third of all homes built since World War II) it was to be expected that a large proportion of Aborigines would be so accommodated. The renting and boarding proportions in the inner districts of both cities, even at different points in time appear to have been very similar.

Of the people who had moved to Sydney and had lived in more than one place, half had been boarding with friends or relatives immediately prior to their present residence. As well as the importance of kin ties in migration, and in initial residence, this also indicates the necessity of

Table 15.4 Local government area and suburb of residence in Sydney prior to current residence

LGA of previous residence[a]	Number	Percentage	Suburb of previous residence[b]	Number	Percentage
Blacktown	3	3.4	Alexandria	4	5.5
Leichhardt	3	3.4	Chippendale	3	4.1
Marrickville	11	12.6	Newtown	4	5.5
Randwick	3	3.4	Redfern	30	41.1
South Sydney	55	63.2	Surry Hills	3	4.1
Sydney	5	5.7	Mt Druitt	3	4.1
Other Sydney LGAs	7	8.1	Other Sydney areas	26	35.6
Total	87	99.	Total	73	100.0

Source: Sample Survey
Notes: [a] Not applicable, i.e. born in Sydney, and/or still living at first address = 2; not stated = 1
 [b] Not applicable here and not stated = 77, including those born in Sydney, and/or still living at first address, and some of the hostel residents

boarding to ease the financial burden of seeking rental accommodation on an individual basis. Boarding contributed to an overall larger household size than that found by Rowley (1981) in his recent wider Sydney study of Aborigines, and was reinforced by some discrimination by real-estate agents and small investor home/absentee landlords. Some 41 per cent had been renting from private sources, but only a few from the Aboriginal Housing Company (formerly Co-Operative) Ltd, and the Housing Commission. Both the proportion of people boarding, and renting privately, were higher than the boarding and renting proportions of the total survey population at the time of interviewing, for a far higher proportion (28 per cent) were now renting from the Aboriginal Housing Company Ltd.

The necessity to rent from private landlords, with the resulting insecurity of dwelling tenure generated much of the intra-urban mobility of Aborigines in the inner city. Discrimination was also a factor in this mobility: persons were asked whether they had experienced serious problems when they first arrived in Sydney. Forty-eight persons, or 38 per cent of in-migrants stated that they had experienced serious problems. Of these, 14 per cent were directly associated with racial discrimination or associated tensions with police.

Major problems, in order of importance, were adjusting to city life and finding their way around the city (29 per cent); finding employment and associated problems of making ends meet while the search for employment continued (22 per cent); the search for accommodation (in which discrimination was implicit in the standard of housing offered and in the rent to be charged); and making friends (10 per cent). Indeed, over 20 per cent of the problems had to do with social isolation, despite the importance of kinship ties in the migration process. Nevertheless, over 60 per cent stated they did not have serious problems when they first arrived in Sydney.

Table 15.5   Reasons for residential location in particular areas of Sydney

	Number of Reasons	Percent
Family and friends there	80	47.1
Like the area, Aboriginal organisations nearby	29	17.1
Accommodation: hostel, cheap area, Aboriginal Housing Company or Commission home	26	15.3
Only place available	19	11.2
Close to work, school, hospital	12	7.1
Away from other Aboriginals	4	2.3
Total reasons	170	100.0

Source: Sample survey

Persons were asked why they 'chose' their part of Sydney to live in (Table 15.5). The main category of reasons was associated with kin and friends (47 per cent). This was a much higher proportion than that found with other Australians in parts of Redfern, Newtown and Marrickville (Burnley, 1985), and resembled that observed with Lebanese, Greeks, Italians and Yugoslavs in those same areas. While employment was the most important reason for moving from the country to Sydney, kinship and friendship was the most important reason for specific destinations in Sydney. Here there was a certain parallel in the informal social organisational structure of Aboriginal and southern European settlement in particular areas, although formal immigration requirements distinguished southern European settlers. Ties with the area was the second most important reason, (17 per cent) with the cheap accommodation third (15 per cent). However, when specific housing (hostel, Aboriginal Housing Company and Housing Commission accommodation) and only place available are seen together, 26 per cent of the reasons were 'minimum choice' or institutional.

Ongoing adjustment to Sydney: survival and institutions

Persons were asked whether they had experienced problems in Sydney and if so, what these were. Seventy persons (47 per cent) had experienced problems. Over 35 per cent of these were inability to meet commitments (e.g. paying food, clothing and electricity bills), paying rents (21 per cent), general financial problems (16 per cent) and the cost of essential services, e.g. travelling costs (17 per cent) with an additional 12 per cent specifically associated with unemployment. These figures illustrate the difficulties involved for people trying to cope financially when the cost of living was so expensive, relative to their incomes.

The high level of unemployment, 40 per cent, amongst those in the labour force, contributed to these financial problems, to the pattern of boarding with relatives and the larger household size discussed earlier. Boarding mitigated some of the difficulties when the dole could be obtained by other than husband or spouse in the same household. However, there was no diminution of high unemployment with longer residence in Sydney and their relative poverty precluded many households from having a car. This in turn forced an element of residential segregation, especially continuing dependence on Aboriginal organisations by a significant minority of interviewees. When people were asked which agencies they would go to if they needed assistance of any kind, 38 per cent would turn to Aboriginal-controlled and staffed organisations.

The two main agencies, however, from which people had received assistance were the Department of Social Security (31 per cent of interviewees) and the Commonwealth Employment Service (29 per cent). This total of 60 per cent seeking assistance from federal government bodies was five times higher than the proportion indicated in response to the question on where people would go if they were in need of assistance. This is mainly because all of those visiting the CES and most of those going to the Department of Social Security did so because they were unemployed at some stage. Over 80 per cent of the total sample had received aid from a federal, State or Aboriginal organisation.

The main Aboriginal-managed organisations of a supportive nature in the inner city in 1984 were the Aboriginal Children's Service, the Aboriginal Housing Company Ltd, the Aboriginal Medical Service, the Aboriginal Legal Service, and Tranby Co-operative College. The branches of government departments which focused on Aboriginal needs, and which were staffed by Aborigines at the 90 per cent level in their agencies in Redfern and adjacent areas, were Aboriginal Hostels Ltd, and the Gullema Aboriginal Contact Centre, a branch of the Youth and Community Services Department of the State government.

There was substantial growth in the number of Aboriginal-staffed and oriented organisations from the early 1970s. These serve a crucial role in the Aboriginal community, performing welfare-oriented functions: legal aid, medical and dental services, crisis and relief services. They reflect relative deprivation of inner-city Aborigines, and the specific needs of different life-cycle groups, such as children of kindergarten and adolescent ages. The Aboriginal Legal Service is staffed by Aboriginal lawyers and law students: this profession is one being entered by Aborigines in urban Australia, with support in Sydney being given by the progressive faculty of law at the University of New South Wales. In 1984, there were still no Aboriginal doctors in the services, but there were nurses, and teachers in the Aboriginal Children's Service, Tranby Co-operative College, and Murawina Ltd, a kindergarten service. The Aboriginal Housing Company was established as a co-operative in the Whitlam years. A large block of old terraces was bought with aid from the Commonwealth government and restored. The value of the properties increased considerably and they provided accommodation for needy families.

Many of the survey respondents stated that the Aboriginal organisations were more able to meet the myriad needs of the inner-city population than the governmental organisations. By 1984, virtually all the essential services to the Aboriginal community, except for employment and related payments were provided by Aborigines and a significant proportion of Aborigines were specifically choosing to patronise these services. This was because they felt that the institutions were more 'in tune' with Aborigines' needs, and were more empathic with their lifestyle and problems. The fact that Aborigines were running these organisations means that Aborigines were beginning to control their own lives and it was also a valuable contribution towards improving their living conditions in the competitive urban environment.

Aborigines have continued to encounter entrenched prejudice in inner Sydney, and especially in the Eveleigh Street district of Redfern. A white medical practitioner was forced to set up night-surgery hours for Aboriginal patients because whites were not prepared to sit in the same waiting room with Aborigines. He faced the loss of custom. Another example was when Murawina, the Aboriginal kindergarten, was seeking Council approval to establish new premises in Eveleigh Street. A public meeting was called at which there was opposition to the proposal from residents, who in the mid-1970s were still mainly non-Aboriginal. A European migrant in Eveleigh Street spoke up at the meeting, objecting to the idea and concluding by asking Aborigines present, 'Why don't you all go back where you came from?' This anecdote illustrates the problems and prejudices Aborigines have confronted in their daily existence in the city, and it helps to explain why there is a strong concentration of Aboriginal organisations providing advice, assistance and support in the inner city.

The survey found that there was a pressing need for Aboriginal organisations which catered for social and recreational needs, especially among adolescents. The absence of such organisations highlights the point that the lifestyle of most Aborigines in the inner city does not allow them to engage in prolonged leisure pursuits. The Aboriginal Housing Company had been instrumental in opening the 'Black Market' in Redfern, a supermarket run by Aborigines. A section of the Company's offices was converted into a gymnasium in mid-1984.

Conclusion

Aboriginal migration to Sydney has resulted from rural deprivation and unemployment, the hope for better things in the city, and the bonds of kinship and friendship with people already in the city. Deprivation also occurs in the city, with inner-city unemployment at 40 per cent, a conservative estimate. There are few chances of entering the owner-buyer market, and boarding with relatives has been a major component of initial adjustment, accounting in part for a larger average household size than that found by Rowley (1984) in his wider household survey.

Residential concentration approaching segregation occurs at the street-block level in parts of Redfern and Chippendale. This results from three interrelated influences: ethnic identity and associated 'externalisation' of the Aborigines by non-Aborigines; social class and associated residential stratification/segregation relationships; and institutional factors. Ethnic or religious differences and social class factors reinforce the tendency towards segregation (Boal, 1969; 1975).

The social class factor constrains the Aborigines to low-rent districts which are found within specific pockets of the inner city. This is the spatial aspect of the residential concentration process. An aspatial aspect is discrimination within the housing market against Aborigines, which has a spatial manifestation in increased concentration. Social pressures of a more general kind operated against them and a response to this was pressures within the group to find self respect and identity, especially as reinforced by the Aboriginal-run and managed organisations and support services. Associated with this has been a strong group identity, one which transcends tribal associations among the various Aboriginal peoples of New South Wales. This represents a contrast with the situation observed by Gale in Adelaide a decade or more earlier. Not only were there distinctly separate communal-kinship groups in Adelaide with settlement and organisation being somewhat segmented, but there was movement from the Northern Territory, since at that time federal Aboriginal welfare and service organisations for the Northern Territory Aborigines were concentrated in Adelaide. While the inner-Sydney Aboriginal population was more homogeneous, some tensions were observed among subgroups in the allocation of management and fiscal resources.

The implications of this Sydney study, and that of Gale (1974) among 'urban Aborigines' in Adelaide, is that the 'culture of poverty' explanation of Aboriginal settlement and adjustment in the inner city is inappropriate (Langton, 1981:19). Nevertheless, Gale found that there might be sound economic reasons to explain why Aborigines maintained kinship ties in Adelaide and other urban areas : 'the extended family is an economic necessity for many' (Gale, 1977:331). She suggests that it is not legitimate to attribute the persistence of extended kin ties in Adelaide to 'traditional or social values'. There is a contradiction in that while poverty may contribute to maintaining their larger households, in the situation of boarding with relatives or friends as was found both in the Adelaide and Sydney studies, the adjustments to city life reflect 'Aboriginality' and cultural tradition (Langton, 1981:17).

The institutional completeness being established in inner Sydney with the Aboriginal voluntary organisations and services, a 'black' supermarket, and the housing company, augurs well for the eventual improvement of living conditions. Indeed, almost two-thirds of those persons interviewed in the sample survey felt they were 'better off' in the city than the country. This was despite the poverty and unemployment experienced by most on a transitory basis, and a substantial minority on a long-term basis. Support by the Aboriginal institutions may be a transition necessity as social adjustment to the wider urban society proceeds. It may also be required until Australian society accepts Aborigines on an equal footing.

Part V

Our Future Urban Condition

16 Urban consolidation: problems and prospects

CAROLYN STONE

In Australian cities since the war, population growth and the 'cult of the quarter-acre block' have meant a very rapid rate of urban expansion, of 'urban sprawl' as it is often called. Probably no concept in urban thinking has attracted more unanimous condemnation than that of sprawl, the idea that urban expansion is unplanned, inefficient and wasteful. Yet rarely have efforts to contain urban sprawl been successful and where they have, as described in Hall et al. (1973), the resultant benefits and costs have usually been regressive.

Attempts to deal with urban sprawl have either been in terms of increasing densities within existing urban areas or directing metropolitan population growth to smaller centres. In Australia both measures have been tried, but for the most part the cities have continued to spread and have lost population from their older, inner-city areas from a combination of gentrification, the aging of the population and declining household size. Sydney's inner-area population has been shrinking since the war, despite a brief period of stabilisation from 1966 to 1971 when the rate of flat construction was at its highest. Between 1971 and 1981 the loss of population from the Central Sydney Subdivision (Leichhardt, Marrickville, Randwick, Sydney, Waverley, Woollahra) was in the order of 70 000 people (NSW Department of Environment and Planning, 1984). Parallel trends occurred in inner Melbourne.

As Paterson (1980:106) points out, metropolitan planning in Australian cities has always facilitated low-density suburban development, but 'goes through occasional paroxysms of guilt and, appalled by what it has done, repents and is for a time born again, getting very committed to "densification".' Densification or urban consolidation was a concern in the 1948 County of Cumberland Scheme and although it did not feature in the 1968 Sydney Region Outline Plan it was, during the 1960s, part of the justification for inner-city housing renewal and high-rise public housing developments. It re-emerged in full force in the late 1970s, primarily in response to the crisis in urban public finance and the anticipated inability of the state to make ends meet in the provision of new urban services and facilities (Sandercock, 1983). In the debate that ensued the justification for urban consolidation was broadened to suggest that it would promote a greater variety of housing and thereby extend housing choice; it would reduce the rate of house-price inflation; it would ensure the more efficient use of existing urban infrastructure; it would reduce public sector costs, primarily by reducing the need for expansion at the fringe; and it would promote metropolitan accessibility and cause an associated reduction in energy consumed for travel.

Housing variety

Proponents of consolidation argue that housing renewal — infill, redevelopment, conversion, rehabilitation and recycling (Archer, 1980) — will increase the variety of housing available. This is considered especially significant in the demographic context of an aging population, reduced household size and increasing variation in household structure. One of the assumptions is that older people will vacate large dwellings to occupy smaller ones in the vicinity, a more 'efficient' use of existing housing stock. Through conversion better use could also be made of warehouses, factories and offices that have become obsolete for their initial purposes (Roseth, 1980).

Housing renewal, however, is inhibited by the regulation of residential development. Zoning, minimum lot sizes, minimum flat sizes, height and setback provisions, and parking, landscaping and other requirements combine to discourage the development of medium-density dwellings (Reid, 1980). Costs are inflated by residential development standards. The subsequent adherence to minimum standards produces uniformity and a further lack of variety in residential provision (de Monchaux, 1980). Any attack on the lack of variety in housing is therefore bound up with adjustments to the regulation of residential development.

A number of moves have already been made in this direction. The State of New South Wales' dual occupancy policy, for example, 'allows the addition of an attached self-contained dwelling to an existing house or the conversion of an existing house into two dwellings' (NSW Department of Environment and Planning, 1983). Potentially, this promotes the more efficient use of housing stock. However, the rating system, the taxation system and eligibility for pensioner benefits promote the retention of larger dwellings by people who may not 'need' the space (Roseth, 1980; Troy, 1982).

Planning policies on housing for the aged and disabled and group homes provide for further potential variety in the housing stock. New South Wales State Environmental Planning Policies (SEPPs) 5 and 9 allow the development of aged and disabled persons housing and 'group homes' in all zones which permit residential development. However, they are generally dependent on other conditions being met and are therefore not likely to increase housing choice to any great extent. For example, under an amendment to the original SEPP 5 designed to prevent development in isolated locations, adequate support services for aged and disabled persons need to be provided 'at reasonable cost' to the residents, and the land on which development takes place needs to adjoin land already zoned for urban uses and 'have reasonable access to community facilities and shops'.

The State's SEPP on the strata subdivision of buildings used for residential purposes helps to retain the variety in housing stock that still exists where boarding houses and flats have not been converted to strata title units. The SEPP requires that councils consent to any subdivision under the Strata Titles Act and in doing so 'assess the impact of any . . . subdivision on the supply of, and demand for, rental accommodation in the council's area'. The aim is 'to facilitate the conservation of rental accommodation provided in buildings used for residential purposes for people on low to moderate incomes'.

SEPP 2, which allows for reduced minimum standards for residential flat development in certain inner areas, and SEPP 8, which allows 'surplus public land' to be used 'to promote the social and economic welfare of the community' should also increase the variety of housing available in established urban areas. SEPP 8 specifically recognises 'that particular types of development, including development for . . . housing, may be . . . carried out as [a] matter . . . of priority'.

There are thus a number of existing policies which, collectively, may increase housing variety and housing choice in established urban areas. Those who support consolidation on the basis that it provides for wider consumer choice in housing envisage easier access to housing for marginal groups as a result. In their view, apart from providing strata and torrens title accommodation for single and smaller households, consolidation will provide more opportunities for rental accommodation in relatively convenient locations. Opponents of consolidation, on the other hand, have argued that encouraging the development of multi-unit dwellings in established areas will promote gentrification and through the supply of such housing even lead to a reduction of average household size.

The debate in this respect seems to hinge largely on the location of consolidation. Private consolidation in inner and 'middle-ring' suburbs — whether it be by infill, redevelopment, conversion, rehabilitation or recycling — will be largely out of the financial reach of lower-income rental-housing groups. The impact on the housing market as a whole may be to release some rental accommodation vacated by occupants of new or renewed accommodation but this may be counterbalanced by the continuing conversion of rental accommodation to owner occupation. Consolidation in less desirable areas may increase the supply of rental accommodation and genuinely provide for greater variety and housing choice for lower-income groups. To suggest though that consolidation will lead to greater housing choice in all areas for all groups is not to recognise the cost of that development in the more convenient locations. Without substantial involvement by the public housing sector, consolidation will mostly provide greater choice of housing type, not of location for those groups whose access to housing is currently most difficult.

Housing cost

Consolidation is intended to reduce house-price inflation by increasing the supply of housing overall and by lowering costs as a result of adjustments to the standards demanded for multi-unit housing. A positive side effect of both reduced standards and an increase in supply would be the dismantling of segregative local government practices, designed in the name of environmental standards but with the social effect of excluding certain housing groups by restricting the types and sizes of dwellings allowed.

If consolidation were to increase the overall supply of housing, there would be grounds for arguing that it would lead to a reduction in house-price inflation. However, although the housing market is not monolithic, an increase in the supply of dwellings in established areas may have the effect of reducing the construction of new housing on the fringe. If this occurred, house prices in these locations could become inflated. An increased supply of dwellings in established areas may have an effect on prices, in particular submarkets, but for these effects to be translated into reduced house-price inflation in general, supply across all submarkets would need to be maintained. To assist in this, consolidation would need to pay relatively more attention to public housing and dual occupancy (especially in middle and outer areas) and relatively less attention to private development (especially in inner areas).

Another plank in the consolidation argument regarding costs is that if construction costs per multi-unit dwellings were lower, house prices would decline, even with a constant overall supply. This position argues for a reduction in building standards since the cost of multi-unit housing is seen to be inflated unnecessarily by excessive environmental planning requirements. It is argued that sound environmental standards could be maintained and costs simultaneously reduced if standards were carefully and selectively adjusted. This perspective is particularly important for established but not inner areas since the land cost component of the dwelling unit has been highly significant in the latter. This would account, to some extent, for the simultaneous increases in the supply and cost of inner urban multi-unit dwellings in recent years.

Some critics of consolidation see a reduction in standards leading to wholesale environmental degradation and a reduction in surrounding property values. According to this view, consolidation might serve to break down exclusionary zoning but it will 'downgrade' local areas, environmentally and otherwise. In view of likely land prices in (previously) exclusionary zones and continuing environmental controls, this scenario seems less likely than the one where additional housing has a gentrifying effect on local neighbourhoods. In either case, however, those most in need of private rental housing would not be the primary beneficiaries.

Use of existing urban infrastructure

One of the central arguments in favour of consolidation concerns the more efficient use of existing urban infrastructure. Although consolidation is not aimed at inner areas exclusively, the debate in this respect has focused on inner areas where, it is claimed, population decline has resulted in excess service provision and the wasteful use of urban resources. The counter view (for example, Troy, 1982; Bechervaise, 1982; Orchard, 1982; Sandercock, 1983) is that declining inner-area populations have not necessarily resulted in spare capacity in urban services; the level of provision of many services in areas which have lost population is still below the metropolitan average, or below the 'recommended' standard; there is little evidence of spare capacity in the physical infrastructure of established areas; many of the 'pipes and drains' type of services are in poor repair and would require substantial amplification were they required to support a higher population; with most social and community facilities there is little spare capacity in inner areas and, in any case, the trend is towards relocating such facilities as hospital beds to the periphery; and many service and secondary jobs are decentralising to outer locations so urban consolidation in inner areas may result in longer average journeys to work.

This assessment of limited capacity in urban infrastructure in inner areas may be correct, but capacity for urban consolidation may well be greater in the middle and particularly the outer areas. However, even if significant capacity exists in middle and outer areas, the cumulative impact of consolidation in any one locality still needs to be anticipated. Monitoring systems should be established to keep track of the local effects of increased dwelling unit or population densities.

The local impacts of consolidation are likely to be quite complicated. There may be a declining public-school population, for example, and a simultaneous increase in motor vehicles. Or public-transport patronage could increase to such an extent that extra services are required, adding to rather than preventing further expense. Notions as to how consolidation might result in a more efficient use of urban infrastructure need to take issues such as this into account. Consolidation plans for particular areas need to be specific to those areas; in some areas consolidation may be the least desirable social result.

As far as the more efficient use of social and community infrastructure is concerned, more consideration may need to be given to alternative uses for those facilities, to meet existing community need. School and hospital facilities, for example, could be used for a much wider range of purposes than those which have been contemplated so far.

Public sector costs

At the very heart of the argument for consolidation is the notion that it will reduce the requirement for expansion at the fringe, thereby reducing public sector costs. Recent research has indicated that the cost of new medium-density residential development in selected middle-ring areas is indeed much less for the public sector than new development on the fringe. On the basis of a case study analysis, average expenditure for servicing per lot in release areas was put at $14 000 compared with $4000 in selected 'middle-ring' areas (NSW Department of Environment and Planning, 1984). Although the cost of servicing additional lots in other 'middle-ring' areas could be higher, so too could the costs of servicing new areas — in a separate analysis the costs of providing a limited number of services for lots on the periphery was estimated to be in the order of $13 500 per lot for the State government and $5000 per lot for local government (Wilmoth, 1982). Substantial per lot savings at the fringe could therefore be achieved through consolidation.

Consolidation in established urban areas may not, however, have sufficient impact on the requirement for new urban land at the fringe to bring about substantial public sector savings. In the Wollongong region it has been estimated that consolidation would reduce the demand for new urban land by less than 10 per cent (Cardew and Pratt, 1984). A similar situation in the Sydney region would mean that it may not ultimately be worthwhile, on the basis of savings in public sector costs alone, to pursue consolidation.

Energy and accessibility

A further argument for consolidation is that it could promote metropolitan accessibility, conserving energy and providing for greater equity in the urban structure. Declining inner-area populations and the decentralisation of industrial and office activity have meant a mode shift to private transport for the journey to work and decreased accessibility to employment for those without access to private transport. The containment of population and the concentration of jobs in metropolitan or suburban centres would provide for shorter journeys to work by public transport, conserving energy and promoting more equal accessibility to jobs, services and facilities in the region.

For the long-term future of the city, energy conservation remains an essential consideration. Evidence on the relationship between energy use and urban form remains uncertain, depending on a range of variables whose future is equally unclear. Thus, it is not known what effect consolidation would have on the travel patterns of 'consolidated' households. Proximity to job opportunities might add to rather than decrease the use of private transport for the journey to work. Shorter travel times for work trips might increase the amount of travel undertaken for other purposes, leading to greater total energy consumed for transport.

The optimistic view of the relation between consolidation and energy sees significant possibilities for the increased use of public transport for the journey to work in particular. This, of course, would depend on jobs being located in central places accessible by public transport. Greater use of public transport may, however, result in increased peak deficits (Morison, 1980), thereby eroding benefits derived from urban consolidation. Moreover, it is estimated that if other travel behaviour were to remain the same, a diversion of 200 000 people from outer to middle-ring areas in the Sydney Region would save only 1 per cent of all energy used for transport (McNeill, 1980).

This is not to say that urban consolidation should not be pursued on energy grounds. As Morison (1980) has pointed out, the best response to urban development in energy terms is likely to involve both expansion at the fringe and consolidation. The precise location of consolidation in relation to existing or potential public transport facilities and employment is an important question too. The private promotion of consolidation in the most accessible areas, however, will largely exclude lower-income households. Those most in need of improved accessibility by public transport may therefore be the last to benefit and the higher private vehicle usage among higher-income groups may work against consolidation's energy objectives.

Conclusion

This chapter has outlined the arguments at the basis of the consolidation policy in an effort to show that they are more complicated and possibly less convincing than they may first appear. Consolidation may not improve housing opportunities for those most in need of housing. It will not necessarily reduce house-price inflation and may further segregate housing submarkets through gentrification. Whether consolidation can make housing more accessible to lower-income groups will depend largely on the extent of public sector involvement and a shift in focus from the inner to the outer areas. But even in the outer areas the capacity for consolidation may be insufficient to bring about significant public-sector costs savings on the fringe. In specific cases consolidation might lead to the more efficient use of existing infrastructure but this would need to be closely assessed and monitored for particular proposals. The relationship between urban consolidation and energy conservation is also not axiomatic. Consolidation plans for particular areas should therefore be carefully made and closely watched. They should be well integrated with concerns about lower-income housing stock and with policies and practices in this regard. Substantial public sector involvement would be a prerequisite if the costs of consolidation were not to outweigh its possible advantages.

17   Planning the future of Sydney

CAROLYN STONE

The plan that has guided Sydney's growth in the last fifteen years has come to the end of its useful life. Produced in 1968, the Sydney Region Outline Plan (SROP) identified land for urban development until the year 2000. Most of this land has already been developed or 'released' for development, despite a much lower rate of population·growth than anticipated. The future of the Sydney region is thus once again under consideration. In the interim, however, economic crisis and demographic decline has shifted the physical planning emphasis to an economic policy orientation with a much shorter time perspective. Metropolitan planning, with its traditional focus on future land uses, has fallen into disfavour (Self, 1980). The 'future', meanwhile, has largely become the intellectual and professional preserve of 'futurologists'. Their work, while relating to the city (Gappert and Knight, 1982), has had little impact on planning.

An equally important reason for the decline of metropolitan planning has been its failure to produce its own image of the future. Apart from the rosy economic prospects that have invariably been implied by metropolitan planning, plans for large urban regions have generally envisaged an orderly distribution of the future regional population (whose size, it was thought, could be fairly accurately anticipated) and a more even spread of jobs, services and facilities. Metropolitan planning in Sydney and elsewhere has largely been unable to achieve this. Yet the traditional issues remain important. How big is the city's population likely to be? Where will the future population be accommodated? Where should jobs and other activities be located so that the region operates more efficiently or equitably?

The crucial issue now for metropolitan planning is whether it can deal with its usual concerns in such a way that it does not create an ideal-type notion of the future. Can metropolitan planning provide a better basis for decision-making in the longer term? This chapter suggests that it can, but the form metropolitan planning takes and the

223

functions it fulfils need to be different from the past. Three issues which have always been central to metropolitan planning in Sydney are examined to illustrate this proposition: (a) future population size; (b) future regional population distribution; and (c) the future location of jobs in the region. These are considered in terms of the way in which they have been treated in the past, the problems that have arisen and possible directions for the future. The underlying view is that despite its current unpopularity, metropolitan planning still has an important role to play in providing a forum in which various objectives and values can be pitted and measured against one another and where a holistic perspective can be taken on the development of the urban region. Implicit in this perspective is a view of the state which emphasises the *contradictory* nature of the state's activities (McDougall, 1982). The state functions by means of planning to facilitate the accumulation of capital (Castells, 1977, 1978; Lojkine, 1976) but it also can and does promote and protect the interests of non-dominant groups in the society. Metropolitan planning provides one of the arenas in which various social classes and class 'fractions' pursue their respective interests in the pattern of urban growth and development.

Population size and metropolitan planning

The likely future size of the region's population was a major concern of both SROP and the 1948 County of Cumberland Scheme (CCS). CCS estimated that Sydney's population in 1980 would be 2.3 million. The 1981 population was in fact 3.25 million, CCS dramatically underestimated postwar immigration and fertility rates. This led to irresistible pressure for conversion of the green belt, a central feature of the scheme, to provide for urban land. The Melbourne and Metropolitan Board of Works' equivalent projection for Melbourne contained a similar error and much of Melbourne's rural and green belt land was also rezoned for residential development.

SROP's projections were equally inaccurate but in the opposite direction. Like the 1971 population estimates for the Melbourne region, it seriously overestimated the rate of future population growth, not anticipating the decline in economic growth, the associated decrease in immigration and the fall in fertility rates that characterised the 1970s. SROP expected a year 2000 population of 5 million for the Sydney region (5.5 million actually, but 500 000 people were to be 'steered' to growth centres in other parts of the State). This may well prove to be an overestimate of 20 per cent.

Because SROP anticipated such an increase in population, it

identified huge areas of non-urban land on Sydney's fringe for urban development. The apparent availability of such large tracts of land implicitly condoned the urban development patterns which are proving problematic in the planning of the Sydney region today. The loss of population from older urban areas, the low-density spread of development in new suburbs and the nondevelopment of large amounts of suitably zoned and serviced urban land may not have been as severe had SROP not provided for massive expansion in anticipation of rapid population growth.

The demographic problem in metropolitan planning is not simply how better to 'predict' the future but rather, how to take account of a range of possible demographic outcomes and plan in such a way that none of the possible outcomes cannot be accommodated. Wilmoth (1983:5) suggests a novel approach to circumvent the problem — that of promoting a *size*-related rather than a *time*-related growth path. '. . . Critical events such as the release of major new sectors for urban development or the development of new town centres are to be tied to numerical population and household thresholds. These critical dates may be advanced or brought back according to yearly monitoring . . .'. This is a workable approach for some problems, mostly in the shorter term, but in the longer term, as Self (1984:1) has pointed out, it is 'not altogether convincing, because employment patterns and preferred life styles are changing all the time'. In other words, it makes an important difference in planning whether a forecast population level is reached in a given year or rather later since in the interim there would be substantial social and economic changes which should affect the planning adopted at the start. The timing of investment programs also requires a demographic focus.

Two major population projections to 2001 have been prepared for the Sydney region in recent years. That by the NSW Department of Environment and Planning (1983; 1984), based on their official projections for the State (NSW Population Projections Group, 1982), adopted the same fertility and mortality assumptions. Fertility was assumed to continue declining, stabilising after 1986 at slightly different levels for the low, medium and high projections. The mortality rate for the low projection was assumed to remain as it was between 1977 and 1979 and to be slightly lower than the 1977–79 rate for the medium and high projections. Net migration to Sydney was estimated from recent trends and the 1981 census: overseas migration estimates of 40 000, 70 000 and 100 000 annually; and an annual loss from New South Wales of 10 000, 5000 and 5000 for the low, medium and high levels respectively. This gave a projection for the Sydney region of between 3.53 million and 4.24 million. In the second recent projection for Sydney, Burnley (1983) arrived at very similar conclusions, though

Table 17.1   Low, medium and high population projections for the Sydney region, 1981–2001

Source	Year	Low	Projection level Medium	High
Department of	1981	3 253 250[a]	3 253 250	3 253 250
Environment	1986	3 351 000	3 438 000	3 446 000
and Planning	1991	3 439 000	3 653 000	3 715 000
	1996	3 497 000	3 857 000	3 973 000
	2001	3 534 000	4 059 000	4 235 000
Burnley	1981	3 273 500	3 273 500	3 273 500
	1986	3 361 600	3 456 700	3 491 700
	1991	3 431 800	3 635 500	3 725 400
	2001	3 529 300	3 971 900	4 170 800

Sources: NSW Department of Environment and Planning (1984) Burnley; (1983)
Note: [a] The 1981 population used by the Department of Environment and Planning (1984) was 'an unpublished estimate of the census estimate of the census count adjusted for underenumeration, supplied by the Australian Bureau of Statistics'

with some differences at the medium level (Table 17.1).

There are two important questions that arise from the time frame and construction of these projections. The first is that metropolitan planning often requires a perspective beyond that which can be provided by demographic projection. For example, given the 'lead times' involved in urban development (the time required to plan new urban development and provide the necessary services), and the fact that new urban lots are not completely taken up as they become available, land that may only be required for a population level to be reached in 2001 needs already to have been identified (Figure 17.1). The major metropolitan planning task is therefore to look beyond the end of the century. The second question is whether the size and composition of a regional population can and should be influenced by metropolitan planning and, if so, how. This involves the distinction that is made in the literature between projections and forecasts and between normative forecasts and contingency forecasts. Isserman's (1984:208–15) definitions in this regard are helpful:

Projections are conditional ... statements about the future. They are calculations of the numerical consequences ... of the underlying assumptions ... The projection is merely a hypothetical, technical exercise and not a prediction of what will occur in the future.

A *forecast*, on the other hand, *is* such a prediction. It is a statement of the *most likely* future. Unlike the analyst who prepares projections, one who forecasts accepts the responsibility for evaluating alternative 'ifs' and identifying those that are most likely to be true.

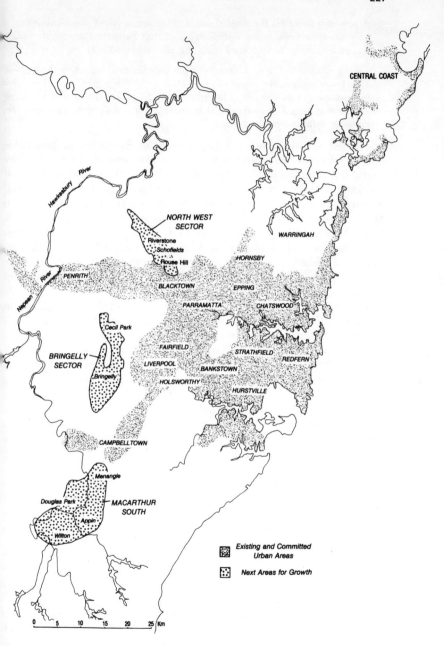

Figure 17.1   Designated future growth areas in the Sydney region

A *normative forecast* is the desired future. It is not an elitist pronouncement, a utopian statement, or an unrealistic goal, but rather an attainable future whose definition has evolved from the planning process.

Contingency forecasts are statements of possible futures, including the highest and lowest plausible population levels ... If the range of contingency forecasts suggests too much uncertainty exists about the future, planning action may be taken to reduce that uncertainty or to prevent undesirable, possible futures from occurring.

Neither Burnley's nor the Department of Environment and Planning's estimates are projections in the narrow sense of the word. They would fall somewhere along Isserman's (1984:210) 'projection/forecast continuum' since some assessment of likely possible futures is implicit in their methodology. However, for the purposes of metropolitan planning more attention needs to be given to forecasts and specifically to 'normative contingency forecasts, each portraying the desired, attainable future under certain conditions' (Isserman, 1984:215). The demographic future needs to be seen not as an exogenous factor but one that is integrally bound up with social and economic events and subject to influence by planning action.

In the Sydney region the ability of planners to influence population growth and change is closely related to immigration. The history of recent immigration has seen one third of all immigrants to Australia locating in Sydney (Australian Council on Population and Ethnic Affairs, 1982). The estimate is that for every six or seven migrants to Australia, one additional dwelling is required in Sydney (Neilson Associates, 1982). Yet, while also the most volatile, immigration is a variable over which metropolitan planning and State policy makers have had little influence. Immigration policy has traditionally been highly centralised in Canberra, in formal consultation with the States but with little apparent regard for the impact of immigration on Sydney or Melbourne in particular.

In the immediate future, therefore, the ability of planners and/or the State to influence population levels in the Sydney region is limited. This may be all the more reason why the difficult and unpopular task of promoting State-wide decentralisation of population, particularly to coastal zones and in conjunction with regional economic development, should be pursued. Whatever the case, possible economic and social futures for the Sydney region need to be related to possible demographic futures and vice versa. For example, there may be little point in pursuing a high technology economic future if the population structure works against the development of such an economy. Similarly, if the forecast rates of unemployment in the Sydney region and/or the rest of the State are high, this may well affect the nature and rate of internal migration and, therefore, Sydney's future size.

Population distribution and metropolitan planning

In a plan that was typical of its time, CCS provided Sydney with a green belt to contain its population within prescribed limits and consign the overflow to 'satellite' towns and villages. There was to be an increase in densities within the city limits where the 'principles of district planning' were to apply, providing for:

> urban communities or groups of communities, largely self-sufficient in shopping, entertainment, education, culture and amenities, with local industrial areas and representing population groups which can function efficiently as independent units but with the special advantages derived from proximity to the central zone. (Cumberland County Council, 1948:65).

The SROP, on the other hand, did not pay much attention to existing urban areas. By the time it was produced, the green belt had largely disappeared and in the climate of economic growth and prosperity that prevailed, the expansion of the city seemed inevitable. SROP failed, however, to anticipate the substantial loss of population from established areas that ensued, underestimating the rate at which households would form and overestimating residential densities. The land SROP allocated for a population of 5 million in the year 2000 is therefore already largely occupied by a population of 3.5 million.

The problems and prospects associated with the consolidation of these areas to accommodate a higher population have already been described (ch. 16). What is significant for metropolitan planning is that even with the most ambitious targets for consolidation being reached, additional urban land will still be required in the near future. Areas for growth in the 'medium term' have been identified (Figure 17.1), but questions remain concerning the rate and sequence in which this land should be developed and the social, environmental and other impacts of such development.

Options for development in the Sydney region in the medium and longer term are affected by a range of physical constraints. There are purely natural features such as steepness of land or liability to flood which put a brake on development. But these constraints are not absolute. At a price they can be overcome. Restrictions are clearer when natural difficulties overlap with other constraints such as water catchments, parks, other recreation areas, coastal protection zones and areas of significant scenic beauty or cultural/historical significance. Further limitations are provided by land set aside for other specific purposes such as that used by the army (e.g. around Holsworthy) and areas that have been identified as suitable for the land-based treatment of effluent water (Anderson, 1982). Also included are sites that may be required for a second Sydney airport. However, the future use of some of these areas is subject to change: gravel extraction areas in western Sydney, for example, may become part of the ambitious Penrith Lakes Scheme, a scheme to provide for substantial water-based recreation in western Sydney; agricultural land may be urbanised; the Holsworthy military area is clearly regarded as essential for army purposes now but in thirty years time army requirements may well be different; of the sites set aside for a second Sydney airport only one will eventually be used for this purpose.

An equally changeable situation applies to the development of the Central Coast and Warringah. The capacity of the Central Coast for urban development, put at 500 000 in SROP and reduced to 400 000 in the subsequent NSW Planning and Environment Commission (1975) Gosford-Wyong Structure Plan may be much further reduced by the unavailability of land subject to mine-related subsidence. In addition, the limited capacity of rail links with the Central Coast have tended to encourage a conservative approach to urban land development there. Similarly, with Warringah, the view since SROP, reinforced by the findings of the Warringah Transport Corridor Inquiry (Kirby, 1983), has been that development should be restricted due to the limited capacity of transport infrastructure connecting the Warringah peninsula with the rest of Sydney and the relative costs of servicing urban development itself.

Air pollution effects in particular of further development in western Sydney may, however, give greater weight to the development of the Newcastle-Sydney-Wollongong conurbation, along the coastal zones. SROP, which recognised the linkages between the three metropolitan areas, went mainly in the opposite direction with its development of western Sydney but future metropolitan planning may reduce this trend, on the basis of better road and rail connections between Newcastle and Sydney and Sydney and Wollongong and an increasingly integrated job market between Sydney and Wollongong. In any case, residential location decisions may automatically reinforce this option, despite the regionalised nature of housing demand and, therefore, population growth (Burnley, 1983). The limitations of planning, including metropolitan planning, need to be recognised (Masser, 1980; Wissink, 1980).

The general point is that the pattern of constraints and opportunities for urban development in the Sydney region is not static. Consequently, although lead times for development require decisions about land to be taken many years in advance, metropolitan planning should not be geared towards the production of an isolated plan. It should facilitate continual assessment of the events, trends and patterns that bear on future decision-making, providing the basis for public debate and political action.

Table 17.2 Objectives for metropolitan planning as expressed by the County of Cumberland Scheme (1948), the Sydney Region Outline Plan (1968) and the Review of the Sydney Region Outline Plan (1980)

County of Cumberland Scheme	Sydney Region Outline Plan	Sydney Region Outline Plan Review
To plan the County as a region — and one which (since it embraces the State capital and Australia's largest city and port, together with a natural background of farms and forest, towns and villages) is greatly affected by any government policies influencing State or National development.	The development of Sydney should be integrated with that of the State as a whole.	The development of Sydney should be interrelated with that of the State as a whole.
	Sydney should remain Australia's greatest city, commercial centre and port.	Maintain Sydney's role as a major international commercial centre and port.
	Sydney-Newcastle-Wollongong should be regarded as a closely related urban complex.	The economic linkages between the three cities should be fostered to maximise the efficiency of operations of the larger urban complex.
As a matter of national concern, to protect and enhance the beauty and natural resources of the County.		Manage, conserve and enhance the natural environment. Manage and enhance the built environment. Identify and conserve the heritage of the Region. Identify, conserve and manage the natural resources of the Region. Seek to have a regional resource strategy formulated.

Table 17.2 (Cont'd)

Within the scope of town and country planning to provide the people of the County with the best conditions of living, working and recreation, all properly located to ensure the utmost convenience.	This objective is retained but revised to express more clearly its purpose: Develop a balance between homes and jobs, community facilities and services.
	A wider and more balanced distribution of commercial activity should be established so that over-concentration of employment in the metropolitan centre can be avoided.
To provide for the efficient functioning of industry and commerce within the County.	Ample, well located industrial land should be available.	Opportunities for future employment growth will influence the selection of areas for residential growth and will be co-ordinated with the provision of suitable industrial land.
	A much greater level of investment in communications and public utilities is needed, coupled with the best use of existing facilities.	Make the best use of existing facilities including public transport systems and orderly and economic extension of public utility services.
To provide for the developments resulting from changes in the County's population and functions and for the redevelopment necessary for the elimination of existing or potentially unsatisfactory conditions.	Flexibility is necessary.	While the intention of this objective remains valid it is now seen as an administrative principle on which future land releases will be based. It has been deleted as an objective.
	Long term growth must be allowed for.	
To provide a framework for local and detailed planning.		
To produce a plan acceptable to an enlightened public and to the authorities responsible for facilitating the County's development.		Using an inter-corporate approach, develop a closer relationship between the community, planning and implementation.
	High quality in urban design and landscape should be established.	These concerns are met by other detailed objectives.

Comprehensive replanning of the metropolitan city centre is needed.	Difficult compromises between conservation values, civil designs and adaptation of the urban fabric in the face of changing social and economic requirements substantially increase the complexity of planning in this field. Planning provisions will facilitate suitable market initiatives in development.
The future transport system should provide optimum accessibility to and from major travel generators ...[a]	Continue a co-operative mode of transport planning and seek to ensure that new residential areas are serviced at an acceptable level.
Land use planning and transport planning should be integrated to aim jointly at minimising private costs of traffic congestion ... and facilitating the efficient movement of goods.[a]	The planning principle adopted in 1968 is re-endorsed.
	Influence urban land prices to achieve reasonable housing costs, especially for low income households. Influence also the availability of sites for medium-density housing so as to provide a real choice for all income groups.
	Manage urban growth and change to obtain the most effective use of existing resources.

Source: Cumberland County Council 1948:12

Source: State Planning Authority 1968:11–13, 44

Source: NSW Planning and Environment Commission 1980:6–9

Note: [a] In SROP these were considered as transport planning objectives rather than as general objectives of the Plan.

To do this metropolitan planning needs to be clear about its own objectives. The objectives of CCS, SROP and the 1980 Review of SROP, (Table 17.2), show considerable continuity. The location of the region in a wider context and the promotion of accessibility within the region have been enduring concerns. Environmental issues, raised in CCS but lost in SROP, are resurrected in SROP Review. Similarly, the role of the 'community' in metropolitan planning, referred to in the SROP Review objectives, was a concern in CCS. Economic development is an issue throughout but the perspective shifts somewhat from efficiency to employment issues. Recent conditions of economic crisis are also reflected in SROP Review's concern with low-income housing and urban finance.

Future planning for the Sydney region is likely to reinforce the objectives supported by SROP Review, but problems will arise if the objectives are shown in practice to be mutually incompatible. For example, some aspects of economic development may be incompatible with optimum environmental management; the mode of provision of low-income housing may be inconsistent with efforts to promote accessibility to employment. Contradictions such as these are inevitable since the pursuit of a range of objectives will always require that precedence is given to some objectives over others. The task for metropolitan planning is to clearly identify which patterns of development relate to which objectives. As Boyce et al. argue (1970:101):

> Alternative plans should be used to explore and learn about the effects and implications of a wide range of diverse assumptions about objectives, attitudes, possible policies and programs ...

The relative costs and benefits of alternative courses of action, including the social and environmental costs, need to be thoroughly evaluated.

Job location and metropolitan planning

The location of jobs was a central issue in both CCS and SROP. Like the equivalent schemes for Melbourne, these plans were concerned to see a more even distribution of employment to shorten the average journey to work, to provide more equal access to services and facilities associated with employment locations and to reduce congestion and development pressures at the core. CCS proposed a hierarchy of centres ranging from neighbourhood centres to the county centre or the city itself. The middle ground was to be held by twenty district centres, mostly located along suburban railway lines and including such centres as Chatswood, Bankstown and Hurstville. Industrial decentralisation was encouraged by restricting the availability of industrial land in inner areas and making it available further from the core. SROP sought 'to encourage the development of a limited number of large new commercial centres offering substantial employment opportunities, more particularly office employment' (State Planning Authority, 1967:22). There was less emphasis on industrial decentralisation but industrial areas were proposed for new growth areas and better access to manufacturing jobs was seen as a byproduct of the locational requirements of industry itself (State Planning Authority, 1968:29).

Since the late 1960s in particular, manufacturing has shifted west from the inner areas in response to the availability of land and buildings more suited to its technical requirements and in response to a changing market as the population has expanded (Cardew and Rich, 1982). The growth of trucking for freight transport and containerisation have promoted this dispersal (Rimmer and Black, 1982). Warehouse jobs have also left the inner city for sites more appropriate for new goods-handling techniques. Retailing, as always, followed the population, often in the form of large, integrated shopping centres rather than as additions to existing centres. Office jobs also dispersed from the central area, the proportion in the central area falling from 58 per cent in 1961 to 41 per cent in 1976 (Alexander, 1982). Trends similar to these are also evident in the Melbourne region (Newton and Johnston, 1981).

Despite the dispersal of economic activities in the Sydney region, the distribution of jobs and related services and facilities remains highly skewed (Table 17.3) (see also Black, 1977 and Maher et al. 1981 for Melbourne). The pattern of accessibility by public transport, for example, (column 1) is clearly radial, with none of the local government areas north of Willoughby, west of Concord or south of Kogarah having access to more than 10 per cent of the region's jobs within 40 minutes by public transport (Figure 17.2).

Average accessibility to employment opportunities, weighted according to the proportion of households with no car (column 3), is highest around Ashfield rather than the city centre because of higher accessibility by car in the inner west and higher levels of car ownership (column 5). Average travel time to work by car and by public transport (columns 6 and 7) reflects the relative availability of different types of jobs in various parts of the Sydney region and the socio-economic and occupational characteristics of residents. Actual travel times are a general indication of local availability of jobs. Thus from Blacktown, Campbelltown and Gosford, average travel time is 60, 62 and 73 minutes respectively while from Leichhardt, North Sydney and Woollahra travel times are 32, 29 and 32 minutes respectively.

Table 17.3 Relative accessibility to employment in the Sydney region, 1981

Local Government Area	1 Proportion of jobs within 40 minutes by public transport	2 Proportion of jobs within 40 minutes by private transport	3 Average of (1) and (2) weighted by proportion of households with no car	4 Proportion of households with no car	5 Car ownership per household	6 Average travel time* to work by car	7 Average travel time* to work by public transport
Ashfield	20.4	85.6	65.5	30.7	0.93	17.8	37.0
Auburn	9.8	39.9	32.2	25.5	1.04	20.6	42.0
Bankstown	5.7	38.8	33.7	15.3	1.35	24.2	49.0
Baulkham Hills	7.1	15.7	15.4	3.7	1.82	34.8	64.0
Blacktown	3.1	12.1	10.9	13.3	1.33	36.0	60.0
Blue Mts	4.5	5.9	5.7	15.4	1.26	35.6	63.0
Botany	15.5	71.3	56.6	26.3	1.00	10.9	37.0
Burwood	16.8	84.6	65.5	28.2	1.03	18.0	39.0
Camden	8.3	4.0	4.3	5.9	1.66	29.5	53.0
Campbelltown	3.4	3.9	3.8	11.6	1.31	37.2	62.0
Canterbury	10.5	69.9	55.5	24.2	1.06	20.3	44.0
Concord	15.2	77.4	64.6	20.5	1.19	18.9	40.0
Drummoyne	19.1	84.9	71.9	19.7	1.17	18.7	39.0
Fairfield	3.1	25.2	21.5	16.7	1.26	28.7	55.0
Gosford	4.4	4.7	4.7	16.7	1.22	39.3	73.0
Hawkesbury	4.4	4.7	4.7	8.3	1.56	39.3	72.0
Holroyd	4.9	27.3	24.0	14.6	1.33	25.8	52.0
Hornsby	2.8	18.7	16.9	11.6	1.51	34.9	63.0
Hunters Hill	9.4	70.6	59.8	17.6	1.36	23.3	44.0

Hurstville	9.2	46.1	40.0	16.4	1.31	25.0	41.0
Kogarah	10.1	56.6	49.0	16.3	1.32	23.0	44.0
Ku-ring-gai	4.2	34.2	31.8	7.8	1.66	29.2	51.0
Lane Cove	8.9	68.9	58.0	18.2	1.23	18.5	43.0
Leichhardt	28.4	82.0	62.9	35.7	0.88	14.1	32.0
Liverpool	3.3	16.3	14.3	15.5	1.35	30.5	57.0
Manly	3.3	36.1	27.2	27.0	1.07	21.4	56.0
Marrickville	35.1	81.7	64.3	37.3	0.80	13.4	32.0
Mosman	2.0	54.5	41.8	24.2	1.12	21.7	56.0
North Sydney	30.1	66.5	55.4	30.4	0.94	16.2	29.0
Parramatta	7.7	30.8	26.3	19.3	1.26	23.8	47.0
Penrith	4.5	5.9	5.8	10.3	1.38	35.6	63.0
Randwick	18.4	67.0	53.4	28.0	1.01	12.1	37.0
Rockdale	16.5	67.9	56.8	21.5	1.12	20.2	43.0
Ryde	4.8	47.7	41.0	15.6	1.31	22.9	50.0
South Sydney	39.7	78.1	58.8	50.3	0.64	8.9	24.0
Strathfield	15.6	70.8	58.9	21.6	1.22	19.2	41.0
Sutherland	3.0	13.8	12.7	9.8	1.55	33.0	58.0
Sydney	40.1	78.4	55.7	59.2	0.51	8.4	19.0
Warringah	7.0	17.8	16.5	11.7	1.47	27.5	65.0
Waverley	20.1	65.1	49.7	34.2	0.88	14.8	38.0
Willoughby	11.6	62.9	52.9	19.4	1.24	18.8	41.0
Wollondilly	3.4	3.9	3.9	7.6	1.61	37.2	62.0
Woollahra	24.7	68.6	56.4	27.9	1.07	12.6	32.0
Wyong	4.4	4.7	4.7	15.3	1.24	39.3	73.0

Source: State Transport Study Group (1981 Sydney Travel Survey)

* minutes

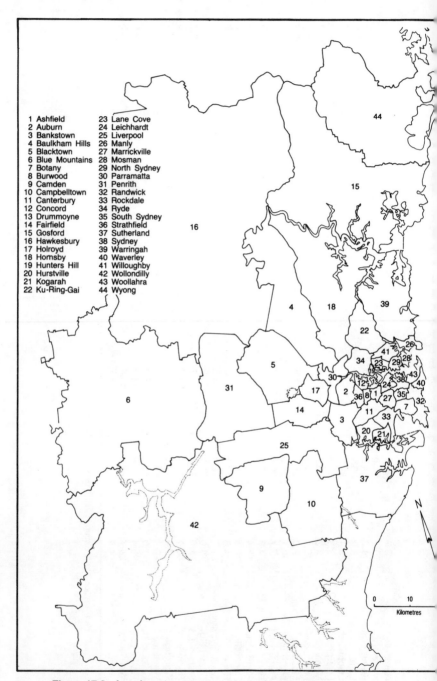

Figure 17.2   Local government areas in the Sydney region

Despite the decentralisation of jobs that has occurred since the 1950s therefore, relative accessibility to employment opportunities in the region (and to related services and facilities) remains an unresolved metropolitan planning issue. This is especially so, because to the extent that jobs have been decentralised, it has not been primarily to suburban centres accessible by public transport. As a result those without access to private transport have not had the full benefit of decentralisation. In addition, there has been an increase in cross-commuting and a decline in the overall use of public transport (Alexander, 1982; Greene, 1980). The result of job dispersal in short has been neither equitable nor energy efficient.

If better accessibility to employment opportunities remains an objective in metropolitan planning, the location of a large number of jobs in a small number of commercial centres might be an appropriate strategy (Alexander, 1982). Both SROP and CCS sought this type of urban structure but neither specified the measures necessary to promote concentrated decentralised growth. While there has been public action in the way of road building, for example, to promote the development of centres such as Parramatta, there has been no co-ordinated public commitment to achieving growth in certain strategic locations. More importantly, there has been no integration of metropolitan planning propositions with the budgeting and infrastructure financing procedures. Melbourne's failure to develop its 'district centres' has been due to the same reasons.

To some extent, the pattern of job dispersal that has developed so far can be seen to have its own inevitable logic. The 'wired city' means that there will be 'reduced travel needs, as provided by the transfer home of certain types of computer-based work, certain types of purchasing options, and certain forms of mass media ...' (Shostak, 1982:77). On the other hand, with Gottmann's (1983) 'transactional city' where technological change and specialisation have led to greater inter-dependency, interaction and exchange of information, the tendency is towards centralisation. While the two tendencies are not necessarily incompatible, Gottman's scenario has distinct implications for the CBD since more information equipment per worker means more space per worker. There can be an expansion of the CBD and a simultaneous decline in the number of workers, a pattern that is already evident in Sydney (Alexander, 1982). The continuation of this trend may not be incompatible with the high technology/high finance future envisaged by some for Sydney.

The NSW Department of Environment and Planning, in association with the State Transport Study Group, has already embarked on a modelling exercise to determine the accessibility implications of various levels of employment not only in the CBD but in all major suburban centres in the region (Searle, 1984). Initial results were confusing as there did not appear to be a difference in levels of accessibility between the scenario which spread jobs throughout the region and the scenario which concentrated jobs in centres. This 'result' might have been anticipated on the basis of a review of 'metropolitan plan making' undertaken in the USA at the end of the 1960s, a decade which saw metropolitan planning almost exclusively in terms of land use and transportation planning (Boyce et al. 1970). One of their conclusions (Boyce et al. 1970:84–86) was that:

> in those programs in which land use patterns exhibiting significant differences were used as the basis for testing a single transportation system . . ., no large difference in network performance and costs was demonstrated for the land use alternatives [because] . . . the size of districts used for forecasting development and travel demand was probably too large to detect the assumed land use and transportation interaction; the expected differences in spatial arrangements of activities and environmental quality may not exist at this aggregate district scale.

Alternative patterns of employment distribution for the Sydney region may thus yet prove to be significant.

Summary and conclusions: the form and functions of metropolitan planning

This chapter has argued that metropolitan planning in Sydney has put forward an idealised view of the structure and functioning of the urban region. Despite experience to the contrary it has persisted with the belief that the size of a regional population in the long term could be 'predicted'. It has been equally firm (often with questionable results) about the land which should be used for urban development in the long term, focusing on the development of a metropolitan plan rather than on a method of dealing with metropolitan planning problems. Similarly, with the distribution of jobs and other activities in the region, it has concentrated on the 'end state' without paying attention to the means of getting there. As Stretton (1975:243) points out, metropolitan planning for Sydney has had 'civilised purposes' and the best of intentions to promote a better, more efficient and more equitable urban structure. It has always, however, remained aloof from politics in the sense that it has not seen its *raison d'être* as integration with the process of government. The production of metropolitan plans has constituted metropolitan planning, with insufficient articulation between the plan and the decision-making process for either of Sydney's plans to have achieved any of their loftier ideals.

Metropolitan planning of this type needs to be superseded by metropolitan planning viewed as a process of bringing together for debate and discussion alternative views on the actions that affect the urban future. Metropolitan planning should provide for the monitoring of trends and events and the assessment of impacts at the metropolitan scale. It should be a means of highlighting differences in objectives and therefore values that infuse alternative perspectives and the means whereby a set of values in planning is justified and promoted. The conflicts inherent in the planning in the Sydney region at the present time would seem to make such an approach not only helpful but essential if the full implications of proceeding in any one direction are to be appreciated.

18 Conclusion: issues for the future

IAN BURNLEY AND JAMES FORREST

In this concluding chapter, we permit ourselves some crystal-ball gazing about the future of metropolitan, and indeed, urban Australia. Following the theme of the book, this involves consideration of past and present trends as they may affect the future. Manning Clark in the concluding paragraph of the fifth volume of his *A History of Australia* states that 'Men make their own history more wisely when they know what that history has been about'. The same applies to our understanding of contemporary social processes in the cities, and planning for their futures. The emphasis will be on growth as it may relate to, and reflect urbanism and social change in Australia. The city, and the national social system may almost be synonymous. Indeed the question must be asked: are metropolitan or urban social processes and social problems specifically urban? Is there an 'inner city' or an 'outer suburban' problem, or are both general society problems?

The following demographic and lifestyle trends, already underway, are considered likely to operate in Australia at least until the turn of the century:

1 The continuation of low fertility resulting in numbers of children per family of two or fewer.
2 Despite the trend towards small families and household sizes, the processes of suburbanisation are likely to continue. The ethos of the family on its own block of land has not changed greatly as indicated in the ABS Housing Survey of 1981;
3 The continuance of gentrification in the inner city, a trend which may accelerate if there is a renewed energy crisis;
4 The continuance of a multi-racial immigrant intake, but at lower levels of net migration than during the long postwar economic boom. The anti-Asian sentiments aroused in some quarters during 1984 may eventually result in the re-establishment of an assisted passage scheme which would result in an increased British intake.

5 The progressive movement to a post-industrial society (Bell, 1973) and even to a 'post-service' economy (Jones, 1982). There is uncertainty whether the new technological revolution will generate more jobs than it is displacing, but the evidence so far is that it will not. Manufacturing employment will continue to contract, and local pockets of very high unemployment may occur in the cities: in certain working-class districts in the inner city, and in the case of Sydney and Melbourne, in some outer suburban public housing estates. The contraction of manufacturing may result in a diminution in the size of the working class, while automation may displace many middle-class clerical workers. Associated technological changes in the electronic communications area may also reduce the number of management personnel. All this has implications for the income and class structure of suburbs.

6 While high levels of home ownership are likely to be maintained, there may be problems if long-term unemployment ensues, when households experiencing chronic unemployment may become of necessity, renters.

It could be argued that the main social divisions in Australian polity will be (a) the employed who are outright home owners; (b) the employed who are owner-buyers; (c) the marginally unemployed who are owner-buyers or outright owners, sometimes through inheritance; (d) the marginally unemployed who are renters; and (e) the chronically unemployed who are renters. This typology may be further refined to include persons living in cohesive families and who are employed and unemployed; and those who are living alone, are single or divorced and who are employed or unemployed. And again, renting could be divided between those who are leaseholders and thus have some security of tenure, renters of flats or houses, and renters of flatettes and rooms or inmates of rooming houses. The latter dwelling stock has been eroded continuously. As the various housing markets are spatially concentrated or dispersed, more-advantaged and less-advantaged persons come to have different social geographies within the cities. Further, as local housing submarkets change in structure, particularly in the availability of private rental housing, socio-demographic changes of considerable importance will occur.

The issue of social heterogeneity in neighbourhoods, discussed in this book, may polarise into a greater degree of segregation. Most obvious are the location of receiving areas for low income immigrants; the location of 'skid rows' or areas where the homeless or near homeless reside; the location of new elite areas, the decline of some older prestigious districts, and the intensification of other high income districts.

Demographic and lifestyle change, suburbanisation and consolidation

Growth of Australia's metropolitan cities to 2001 is likely to be slower than during the long economic boom from 1948–50 to 1973–74. During that era, the annual compound rates of growth of Sydney and Melbourne exceeded 2.2 and 2.5 per cent per annum. In fact Melbourne, although the second city of Australia, increased its volume of population more than Sydney during 1947–71, mainly because of stronger immigration to that city. After 1971, more immigrants went to Sydney than to Melbourne. However, Sydney's internal migration loss increased, through migration to coastal areas of New South Wales's and larger regional cities within the State, as well as to Queensland and Western Australia.

Recent internal migration surveys by the Australian Bureau of Statistics indicate that the movement to Queensland has slowed although that to coastal New South Wales continues unabated. The internal migration loss checks Sydney's growth somewhat. In addition, lower fertility and lesser *rates* of international migration than in the 1950s and 1960s boom periods will result in Sydney and Melbourne's growth rates ranging between 1.2 and 1.4 per cent annum and populations of between 4 and 4.3 million in the case of Sydney, and between 3.4 and 3.7 million in the case of Melbourne by 2001. These populations are significantly less than the five million in each metropolis confidently forecast in the 'heady' days of the late 1960s, but they are significantly *more* than those estimated in the conservative years of the 1970s. This means that in Sydney's case in particular, there will be pressures on available land, due to slowdowns in the subdivision and rezoning of rural to urban land consequent to the more modest projections becoming available. Even natural growth in the southern region (statistical subdivision) of Sydney, without migration, will not be able to be accommodated. This will almost certainly mean a redirection of population to the Western and South Western Statistical Subdivisions (Burnley, 1983).

There are implications here for urban consolidation strategies. This does not refute the assertions of Carolyn Stone as to the advisability, cheapness or otherwise of servicing, of urban consolidation in inner districts and middle-ring suburbs already established. Rather, it points to consolidation strategies in newly developing areas. Such developments are already underway in Housing Commission subdivisions in the Campbelltown region southwest of Sydney, and near Penrith. However unless the design, layout and servicing is handled in an enlightened manner, there is a risk, given typical Australian preferences for detached, suburban houses with land, that residential and social stratification might occur between the 'consolidation' developments and others. In this instance, the result could be the reverse of what Stone forecast in the inner city: the consolidated areas might become *low* income ones.

Demographic characteristics and associated life-style factors have been changing, notably the decline in the first-marriage rates and the rise in the median age at marriage during the 1970s with a moderate decline thereafter. These processes, along with general aging of the population resulted in falls in the average household size — in Sydney, from 3.2 at the beginning of the decade to 2.8 in 1981 with further declines thereafter. There was an associated evolution of housing submarkets, some of which had a distinct spatial bias: retirement housing (villa units, town houses, home units) of an informal organisation structure; and retirement village complexes of a formal organisational type. The latter occurred without full investigation of whether retirement villages rather than neighbourhood support systems are the most enlightened way of maintaining the urban condition of the elderly.

With persons electing to remain single, or becoming divorced or separated, housing submarkets developed for those with some savings and disposable incomes; these were owner-occupier home units, town houses or villa units. Many of these were in the inner city but often were in beachfront areas, such as in Bondi, Coogee and Manly in Sydney, and on a lesser scale in St Kilda and Elwood in Melbourne.

For less affluent persons, however, breakdown in marriage and sale of the family home could mean at least one of the partners having to rent in the private sector. Furthermore, there has been an increasing number of sole-parent families, and those with very limited means have become eligible for Housing Commission accommodation on a priority basis, so that in some estates, up to half the households comprise solo-parent families. It is not expected that there will be an alarming increase in such needy families in the future, partly because remarriage often occurs, and partly because conservative social values may be re-established. Nevertheless, many neighbourhoods, particularly in the inner-city area will be further differentiated into various types of households. Forrest's chapters indicate that the outcomes of these processes are visible at the neighbourhood level.

The trend towards smaller households, in conjunction with aging and increased longevity (Rowland, 1980; Howe, 1980), may mean that a large proportion of the existing dwelling stock may become tied up by these households, thus generating a further demand for new housing on the urban periphery.

Inequalities in the cities

The studies reported in this volume suggest that social inequalities in the cities are not being ameliorated, as evident by the observation of social indicators of various kinds. Relative variations in mortality have increased between areas of Sydney and Melbourne during the 1970s. Relative variations in unemployment have increased between areas in Sydney, Melbourne and Adelaide over time. There may be relationships between the 'breeder' and 'drift' hypotheses which can explain part of the spatial variability in mortality as discussed in Burnley and Batiyel's chapter, and the 'trapped' hypothesis discussed by Vipond with reference to local pockets of high unemployment, and suggested by Vinson and Homel's (1976) earlier work. Ultimate explanations may have to do with economic and societal change, rather than spatial explanations, but the spatial incidence suggests that local planning intervention in the community health, recreational and community planning area may help.

The incidence of plague mortality was seen to be associated with social class and crowded housing conditions, while place of employment was seen as the main source of contagion. While the analysis of heart-disease mortality by area and the problems of 'ecological correlation' and inference make conclusions tentative, it does appear that social class and living conditions, through self neglect or occupational stress may generate populations more at risk who tend to inhabit some areas more than others. Poverty, as with the plague outbreak, may not be the main factor, but poverty can be associated with crowding. Crowding in the workplace and at home influenced the diffusion of plague in Sydney, and crowding at school, and the distribution of septic tanks affected the ecology and distribution of infectious hepatitis in Sydney and Wollongong, as earlier work by Brownlea (1967) has shown. In other work, Burnley (1980a:255–294; 1980b) indicates that 'social isolation' variables statistically 'explained' much of the spatial variation in premature heart disease and cancer mortality in Sydney, Melbourne and Adelaide. Socio-economic status was also important. It seems that social isolation (living alone with detachment from communal life) can occur in areas of relative crowding — single-person households occupying only a room in medium to high-density older housing. Vinson and Homel's (1976) monograph indicates areas of overall disadvantage in Sydney by use of sensitive social indicators and there are linkages between the findings of this work and those of this volume and the cited studies.

The questions now to be asked are: (a) what are the structural factors sustaining such inequality? (b) will the location of 'at risk' groups within the cities change, and if so, will they be more or less spatially concentrated? (c) will greater or less segregation of 'at risk' groups make support for them, and the amelioration of their difficulties more or less easy to achieve? and (d) how will the future form and morphology of the cities affect access, both spatial and aspatial, of individuals and groups to the services that society offers for the amelioration of problems? (See the companion volume, *Why cities change*, Cardew et al. 1982, for amplification of these issues.)

Discussion of amelioration by public agencies suggests the 'social democratic' model of society wherein the state intervenes to regulate and modify the excesses generated through social class inequalities arising from the mode of production. Structural and Marxist models, however, suggest that the activities of the state and its administrative elite act to reinforce inequalities (cf. Troy, 1981).

A final issue will be that of mobility of people and access to work, services and leisure as the energy crisis, presently in abeyance for political reasons because of recession, returns with greater impetus. The future form of our cities, linear, multi-nuclear or mono-nuclear, has still to be fully canvassed, a consideration which relates back to the other planning options reviewed in chapters 16 and 17. An associated issue will be that of making subregions of the metropolitan areas as self-sufficient as possible: in employment opportunities, retail facilities, service provision and amenities.

References

Agnew J A and Duncan J S (1981) 'The transfer of ideas into Anglo-American human geography' *Progress in Human Geography*, 5, pp. 42–57

Aitken D (1972) *The Country Party in New South Wales: a study of organisation and survival*, Australian National University Press, Canberra

AIUS (1973) *Urban development in Melbourne*, Australian Institute of Urban Studies, Canberra

Alexander I (1979) *Office location and public policy*, Longman, New York

Alexander I (1982) 'Office suburbanisation: a new era?', in Cardew R V eds *Why cities change: urban development and economic change in Sydney*, Allen and Unwin, Sydney, pp. 55–76

Anderson D (1982) *Report of the task force on the use of reclaimed water*, New South Wales Government, Sydney

Anderson, J, Duncan S and Hudson R (1983) *Redundant spaces in cities and regions*, Academic Press, London

Aplin G S (1982) 'Models of urban change: Sydney 1820–1870', *Australian Geographical Studies*, 20, pp. 144–57

Apps P (1980) 'Housing policy and housing theory', *Housing economics*, Australian Government Publishing Service, Canberra

Archer R W (1980) 'Planning for housing renewal and urban consolidation', in Archer R W ed. *Planning for urban consolidation*, Planning Research Centre, University of Sydney, Sydney, pp. 7–18

Armstrong W G (1903) *Annual report of the medical officer of health for the year 1902*, Government Printer, Sydney

Ashburton-Thompson J (1903) *Report of the Board of Health on a second outbreak of plague at Sydney, 1902*, Legislative Assembly of New South Wales, Government Printer, Sydney

Austin A G ed. (1965) *The Webbs' Australian diary 1898*, Sir Isaac Pitman and Sons, Melbourne

Australian Council on Population and Ethnic Affairs (1982) *Population report #6: recent trends in immigration*, Canberra

Australian Dictionary of Biography, 1851–1891

Badcock B (1984) *Unfairly structured cities*, Blackwell, London

Bate W (1962) *A history of Brighton*, Melbourne University Press, Melbourne

Batiyel M (1983) Unemployment and ill health in metropolitan Sydney, unpublished BA Honours thesis, University of New South Wales

Bechervaise H (1982) 'Theory and practice: the local view', in Sandercock L ed. *Urban consolidation: the equity issue*, Centre for Environmental and Urban Studies, Macquarie University, Sydney, pp. 35–50

Beed C, Singell L and Wyatt R (1983) 'The dynamics of intra-city unemployment patterns', *Australian Bulletin of Labour*, 10, pp. 36–46

Bell D (1973) *The Coming of post-industrial society*, Basic Books, New York

Bell R (1983) Emergence of global banking: a macro economic geography, unpublished BA Honours thesis, Department of Geography, University of Sydney

Berry M (1983) 'Posing the housing question in Australia: elements of a theoretical framework for a Marxist analysis of housing', in Sandercock L and Berry M eds, *Urban political economy, the Australian case*, Allen and Unwin, Sydney, pp. 91–115

Berthoud R (1976) 'Where are London's poor?', *Greater London Intelligence Quarterly*, 36, pp. 5–12

Birrell R and Birrell T (1981) *Population and Australian society*, Longman Cheshire, Melbourne

Black J (1977) *Public inconvenience*, Urban Research Unit, Australian National University, Canberra

Boal F W (1969) 'Territoriality on the Shankill-Falls divide, Belfast', *Irish Geography*, 6, pp. 30–50

Boal F W (1972) 'The urban residential subcommunity: a conflict interpretation', *Area*, 4, pp. 164–8

Boal F W (1975) 'Social space in the Belfast urban area', in Peach C ed. *Urban social segregation*, Longman, London, pp. 245–65

Bolton C (1981) *Spoils and the spoilers: Australians make their environment 1788–1980*, Allen and Unwin, Sydney

Borrie W D (1954) *Italians and Germans in Australia*, Cheshire, Melbourne

Bottomley G (1980) *After the Odyssey*, University of Queensland Press, St Lucia

Bottomley G and de Lepervanche M (1984) eds *Ethnicity, class and gender in Australia*, Allen and Unwin, Sydney

Bowden R (1980) 'Equilibrium and disequilibrium in models of the housing market: a survey', *Housing Economics*, Australian Government Publishing Service, Canberra

Boyce D E, Day N D and McDonald C (1970) *Metropolitan plan making: an analysis of experience with the preparation and evaluation of alternative land use and transportation plans*, Regional Science Research Institute, Philadelphia

Boyd R (1978) *Australia's home: why Australians built the way they did*, Penguin, Melbourne

Brewer G (1984) *The experience of unemployment in three Victorian regions*, SWRC Reports and Proceedings, 48

Bromilow F J (1977) *What is an affordable house?*, mimeo, Division of Building Research, CSIRO, Melbourne

Bronfenbrenner U (1979) *The ecology of human development*, Harvard University Press, Cambridge, Mass.

Brownlea A A (1967) 'An urban ecology of infectious disease: City of greater Wollongong', *Australian Geographer*, 10, pp. 169–187

Bullock A (1977) 'Liberation', in Bullock A and Stallybrass O eds *The Fontana dictionary of modern thought*, Fontana Books, London, p. 348

Burke T ed. (1978) *Housing problems and housing policy*, Centre for Urban Studies, Swinburne College of Technology

Burnley I H (1974) 'The social ecology of immigrant settlement in Australian cities', in Burnley I H ed. *Urbanization in Australia, the post war experience*, Cambridge University Press, Cambridge, pp. 99–118

Burnley I H (1976) *The social environment: a population and social geography of Australia*, McGraw-Hill, Sydney

Burnley I H (1977) 'Mortality variations in an Australian city: the case of Sydney', in McGlashan N D ed. *Studies in Australian Mortality*, University of Tasmania, Hobart, 29–61

Burnley I H (1978) 'The social ecology of suicide in metropolitan Sydney', *Australian Journal of Social Issues*, 13, pp. 91–103

Burnley I H (1980a) *The Australian urban system*, Longman Cheshire, Melbourne

Burnley I H (1980b) 'The social ecology of premature mortality in three Australian cities', *Australian Journal of Social Issues*, 15, pp. 306–20

Burnley I H (1982) 'Lebanese migration and settlement in Sydney, 1970–1978', *International Migration Review*, 16, 102–32

Burnley I H (1983) 'Forecasting metropolitan and urban subregional population changes and their resource use implications: methodology and example — Sydney, Australia', *Applied Geography*, 3, pp. 277–301

Burnley I H (1985) 'Immigrant adjustment in ethnic neighbourhoods', in Burnley I H, Encel S and McCall G eds *Immigration and Ethnicity in the 1980s*, Longman Cheshire, Melbourne (in press)

Burnley I H and Routh N L (1984) *Aboriginal migration to Sydney*, interim report, School of Geography, University of New South Wales

Burnley I H and Walker S R (1982) 'Unemployment in metropolitan Sydney: spatial, social and temporal dimensions', in Cardew R V, eds *Why cities change*, Allen and Unwin, Sydney, pp. 181–204

Butlin N G (1964) *Investment in Australian economic development 1861–1900*, Cambridge University Press, Cambridge

Butlin N G (1976) *The impact of Port Botany*, Australian National University Press, Canberra

Butlin N G (1983) *Our original aggression*, Allen and Unwin, Sydney

Cain R (1975) Transportation planning and conflict in Sydney: a case study of inner-city expressways in Glebe, unpublished BA Honours thesis, School of Geography, University of New South Wales

Campbell J F (1936) 'Liberty plains of the first free settlers, 1793', *Royal Australian Historical Society*, 22, pp. 317–29

Campbell M (1981) *Capitalism and power in the UK*, Croom Helm, London

Cannadine D (1977) 'Victorian Cities: how different', *Social History*, 2, pp. 457–82

Cannadine D (1982) 'Residential differentiation in 19th century towns: from shapes on the ground to shapes in society', in Johnson J H and Pooley C G eds *The structure of nineteenth century cities*, Croom Helm London, pp. 235–52

Cannon M (1966) *The land boomers*, Melbourne University Press, Melbourne

Cardew R V (1977) 'House lot speculation is consumer led', *Royal Australian Planning Institute Journal*, 15, pp. 83–5

Cardew R V (1979) *The real cost of housing*, Australian Institute of Urban Studies, Canberra

Cardew R V (1980) 'The Future of flats and home units in Sydney', in R Archer ed. *Planning for urban consolidation*, Planning Research Centre, University of Sydney, pp. 76–85

Cardew R and Pratt I (1984) *Urban consolidation in the Illawarra*, Department of Environment and Planning, Sydney

Cardew R V, Langdale J V and Rich D C (1982) *Why cities change: urban development and economic change in Sydney*, Allen and Unwin, Sydney

Carmina M (1975) 'Public participation — an Australian dimension', *The Planner*, 61, pp. 232–34

Carter H (1978) 'Towns and urban systems 1730–1900', in Dodgshon R A and Butlin R A eds *An historical geography of England and Wales*, Academic Press, London, pp. 367–400

Cartwright D (1970) 'The price of land in Western Australia', in *The availability and cost of land conference proceedings*, Planning Research Centre, University of Sydney

Cass B and Garde P (1984) 'Unemployment in the western region of Sydney: job seeking in a local labour market', in Hooke R ed. *54th ANZAAS Congress: SWRC Papers*, SWRC Reports and Proceedings 47, June, pp. 3–56

Castells M (1977) *The urban question: a marxist approach*, Edward Arnold, London

Castells M (1978) *City, class and power*, MacMillan, London

Centre for Urban Research and Action (1977) *The displaced: a study of housing conflict in Melbourne's inner city*, Melbourne

City of Sydney (1978) *Central business district study*, 1, Pot Still Press, Sydney

Clay P (1979) *Neighbourhood Renewal: Middle class resettlement and incumbent upgrading in American neighbourhoods*, Lexington Books, New York

Cohen R (1981) 'The new international division of labor, multinational corporations and urban hierarchy', in Dear M and Scott A eds, *Urbanization and urban planning in a capitalist society*, Methuen Press, New York, pp. 287–318

Committee of Inquiry (1978) *The cost of housing*, 1, Australian Government Publishing Service, Canberra

Connell R W and Irving T H (1980) *Class structure in Australian history: documents, narrative and argument*, Longman Cheshire, Melbourne

Cormick P H (1938) *Premature subdivision and its consequences*, Institute of Public Administration, Columbia University, New York

Cox K R and Johnston R J eds (1982) *Conflict, politics and the urban scene*, Longman, London

Cronin C (1975) *The sting of change: the Sicilian family in Sicily and Australia*, University of Chicago Press, Chicago

Crough G, Wheelwright T and Wilshire T (1980) *Australia and world capitalism*, Penguin Books, Melbourne

Crough G and Wheelwright T (1982) *Australia: a client state*, Penguin Books, Australia

Cumberland County Council (1948) *The planning scheme for the County of Cumberland*, Sydney

Cumpston J H L and McCallum F M (1926) *The history of plague in Australia 1900–1925*, Government Printer, Melbourne

Cunningham J (1984) 'Egotism in prestige ratings of Sydney suburbs: where I live is better than you think it is', *Australian Journal of Psychology*, 36, 429–38

Curson P H (1985) *Times of crisis: epidemic disease in Sydney 1788–1900*, Sydney University Press, Sydney (in press)

Daly M T (1982) *Sydney boom, Sydney bust*, Allen and Unwin, Sydney

Daly M T (1984) 'The revolution in international capital movements: urban growth and Australian cities', *Environment and Planning, A*, 16, pp. 1003–1020

Dames and Moore Pty Ltd (1974) *Environmental impact investigation*, report on proposed coal loading facility, Port of Botany Bay, New South Wales, for the New South Wales Colliery Proprietors Association, Sydney

Dasvarma G L (1977) 'Causes of death among males of various occupations', in McGlashan N D ed. *Studies in Australian mortality*, University of Tasmania, Hobart, pp. 63–74

Davey C, Emery J S and Milne A K (1980) *People, places and patterns: communities, a geographical study*, Rigby Education, Sydney

Davies W K D (1984) *Factorial ecology*, Gower, Aldershot

Davis J R and Spearritt P (1974) *Sydney at the census: a social atlas*, Urban Research Unit, Australian National University, Canberra

Davison G (1979) *The rise and fall of marvellous Melbourne*, Melbourne University Press, Melbourne

de Monchaux J (1980) 'Urban consolidation and residential development standards', in Archer R W ed. *Planning for urban consolidation*, Planning Research Centre, University of Sydney, Sydney, pp. 47–64

Dennis R (1982) 'Stability and change in urban communities: a geographical perspective', in Johnson J H and Pooley C G eds *The structure of 19th century cities*, Croom Helm, London, pp. 38–52

Dennis R and Clout H (1980) *A social geography of England and Wales*, Pergamon, Oxford

[DURD] Department of Urban and Regional Development (1974) *Urban land prices 1968–1974*, Australian Government Publishing Service, Canberra

Dobson A J, Gibberd R L, Wheeler D J and Leeder S R (1981) 'Age-specific trends from ischaemic heart disease in Australia and cerebrovascular disease mortality in Australia', *American Journal of Epidemiology*, 3, pp. 404–12

Dow G M (1965) *Samuel Terry: the Botany Bay Rothschild*, Sydney University Press, Sydney

Dunlop E W (1974) *Harvest of the years: the story of Burwood 1794–1974*, Municipality of Burwood, Sydney

Durkheim E (1924) *Suicide*, New York

Echo 'The suburbs of Sydney', 4 September, 18 September and 25 September 1890

Edwards N (1978) 'The genesis of the Sydney Central Business District 1788–1856', in Kelly M ed. *Nineteenth century Sydney*, Sydney University Press, Sydney, pp. 37–53

Eggleston F W (1932) *State socialism in Victoria*, P S King and Son, London

Evans A (1980) 'An economist's perspective', in Evans A and Eversley D eds

The inner city, Heinemann, London, pp. 84–97

Evans A W (1984) 'Inside out down under? Outer city unemployment in Australia', *Urban Policy and Research*, 2, pp. 27–32

Evans A and Russell L (1980) 'A portrait of the London labour market', in Evans A and Eversley D eds *The Inner City*, Heinemann, London, pp. 72–83

Eyles J (1974) 'Social theory and social geography', *Progress in Human Geography*, 6, pp. 27–88

Eyles J (1978) 'Social geography and the study of the capitalist city', *Tijdschrift voor Economische en Sociale Geografie*, 69, pp. 296–305

Faulkner W and Nelson R (1983) *Unemployment and transport availability in metropolitan Melbourne*, Bureau of Transport Economics, Occasional Paper 53, Australian Government Publishing Service, Canberra

Feldheim J (1914) *The expansion of Sydney; a pictorial contrast 1840–1914*, Sydney

Firey W I (1947) *Land use in central Boston*, Harvard University Press, Cambridge, Mass.

Fisher E M (1933) 'Speculation in suburban lands', *American Economic Review*, 23, pp. 152–61

Forrest J (1968) 'An approach to the analysis of sub-areas in Timaru', *New Zealand Geographer*, 24, 195–201

Forrest J (1970) 'Land elevation, dwelling age and residential stratification in a New Zealand town', *New Zealand Geographer*, 26, pp. 195–202

Forrest J (1973) 'Residential patterns in smaller towns', in Johnston R J ed. *Urbanisation in New Zealand*, Reed Education, Wellington, pp. 228–34

Forrest J (1977) 'The urban people', in *Readers digest atlas of Australia*, Readers Digest Services Pty Ltd, Sydney, pp. 188–205

Forrest J (1980) 'Homogeneity and heterogeneity: on the residential segregation of occupation groups within urban sub-areas', in Irwin P (compiler) *Papers of the Newcastle (16th) Conference, Institute of Australian Geographers*, Department of Geography, University of Newcastle, pp. 133–40

Forrest J (1982) *Community profiles: a social atlas of Warringah Shire at the 1976 census*, Warringah Shire Council, Sydney

Forrest J (1984a) *Population profiles: the Municipality of Willoughby at the 1981 census, and comparisons with results of the 1976 and 1971 censuses*, Willoughby Municipal Council, Sydney

Forrest J (1984b) 'Urban migrant population', in Rose A J ed. *The Macquarie illustrated world atlas*, Macquarie Library, Sydney, pp. 128–9

Forrest J and Herborn P (1981) *Atlas of social environment: Sutherland Shire at the 1976 census*, Sutherland Shire Council, Sydney

Forrest J and Johnston R J (1981) 'On the characterisation of residential areas according to age structure', *Urban Geography*, 2, pp. 31–40

Forster C (1983) 'Spatial organisation and local unemployment rates in metropolitan Adelaide: significant issue or spatial fetish?', *Australian Geographical Studies*, 21, pp. 33–48

Fox L (1981) *Multinationals take over Australia*, Alternative Publishing Cooperative, Sydney

Fraser R D L (1947) 'Premature urban development by land subdivision — a country planning problem', *The Shire and Municipal Record*, July 28, pp.

203-11

Freemans Journal 'Opening of Santa Sabina', 24 April 1894

Freestone R (1982) 'The garden city idea in Australia', *Australian Geographical Studies*, 20, pp. 24-48

Friedmann J and Wolff G (1982) 'World city formation: an agenda for research and action', *International Journal of Urban and Regional Research*, 6, pp. 309-44

Gale F (1974) *Urban aborigines*, Australian National University Press, Canberra

Gale F (1977) 'Aboriginal values in relation to poverty in Adelaide', in Berndt R M ed. *Aborigines and change: Australia in the '70s*, Australian Institute of Aboriginal Studies, Canberra, pp. 8-9

Galvin J (1984) The Lettopalena Italian community in Newcastle, unpublished PhD thesis in Geography, University of Newcastle, New South Wales

Gappert G and Knight R V eds (1982) 'Cities in the 21st century', *Urban Affairs Annual Review*, 23, Sage Publications, Beverly Hills

Gecas V (1979) 'The influence of social class on socialisation', in Burr W, Hill R, Nye F and Reiss I eds, *Contemporary theories about the family*, 1, Free Press, New York, pp. 365-404

Gibberd R W (1982) *Changing mortality from ischaemic heart disease in Australia*, paper presented to the Australian Population Association Conference, Canberra

Gibson J and Johansen A (1979) *The quick and the dead, a biomedical atlas of Sydney*, A H and A W Reed, Sydney

Gibson V (1975) A humanist geography of people and their place: Glebe, Sydney, unpublished BA Honours thesis in Geography, University of Sydney

 Gibson V and Horvath R (1983a) 'Global capital and the restructuring crisis in Australian manufacturing', *Economic Geography*, 59, pp. 178-94

Gibson V and Horvath R (1983b) 'Aspects of a theory of transition within the capitalist mode of production', *Environment and Planning D*, 1, pp. 121-38

Glynn S (1970) *Urbanisation in Australian history 1788-1900*, Nelson, Melbourne

Gordon D (1978) 'Capitalist development and the history of American cities', in Tabb W and Sawers L eds *Marxism and the metropolis: new perspectives in urban political economy*, Oxford University Press, New York, pp. 25-63

Gordon M (1964) *Race and assimilation in American life*, Oxford University Press, New York

Gottmann J (1983) *The coming of the transactional city*, University of Maryland, Maryland

Gray (1984) *Aboriginal fertility*, mimeo, Australian Bureau of Statistics, Canberra

Greene D L (1980) 'Recent trends in urban spatial structure', *Growth and Change*, 11, pp. 29-40

Griffiths B E (1984) 'Subdivision development costs', *The Valuer*, 28, pp. 205-10

Gvelke L (1982) *Historical understanding in geography*, Cambridge University Press, Cambridge

Hall P, Thomas R, Gracey H and Drewett R (1973) *The containment of urban England*, Allen and Unwin, London

Hamnett C and Williams P (1979) *Gentrification in London: an empirical and theoretical analysis of social change*, Research Memorandum 71, Centre for Regional, Urban and Local Government Studies, University of Birmingham

Harcourt A, Harper P and Henderson R (1970) *People in poverty*, Cheshire, Melbourne

Harrison B (1972) *Education, training and the urban ghetto*, Johns Hopkins University Press, Baltimore

Hartnett B (1975) 'Advocacy planning and bureaucratic guerrillas', *Royal Australian Planning Institute Journal*, April, pp. 46–9

Harvey D (1973) *Social justice and the city*, Arnold, London

Harvey D (1978) 'The urban process under capitalism: a framework for analysis', *International Journal of Urban and Regional Research*, 2, pp. 101–32

Harvey D (1982) *The limits of capital*, Blackwell, Oxford

Head B (1984) 'Recent theories of the state', *Politics*, 19, pp. 36–45

Herbert D (1972) *Urban geography: a social perspective*, David and Charles, Newton Abbott

Herbert D T and Johnston R J eds (1976) *Social areas in cities: spatial perspectives on problems and policies*, Wiley, London

Hetzel B S (1981) 'Dietary differences and disease', *Medical Journal of Australia*, 1, pp. 113–15

Heyde Family Papers (nd) Mitchell Library, Sydney

HIA (1971) *A study of land costs in Australia*, Housing Industry Association, Melbourne

Hinchcliffe T F M (1981) 'Highbury New Park: a 19th century middle class suburb', *London Journal*, 11, pp. 29–44

Holloway A E (1972) 'Short-term finance for land development, bridging finance and end finance in housing and flat development from a developer's viewpoint', *Finance for Investment in Urban Development*, Urban Research Unit, Australian National University, Canberra

Holsman A J and Aleksandric V (1977) 'Aircraft noise and the residential land market in Sydney', *Australian Geographer*, 13, pp. 401–7

Holterman S (1975) *Census indicators of urban deprivation*, Department of the Environment, London

Homel R and Burns A (1983a) Conditions of life and child adjustment, paper presented to the Australian Family Research Conference, Canberra, November

Homel R and Burns A (1983b) Children's experience of the environment, unpublished ms., School of Behavioural Sciences, Macquarie University

Horton F and Reynolds D (1969) 'An investigation of individual action spaces: a progress report', *Proceedings, Association of American Geographers*, 1, pp. 70–75

Horvath R and Tait D (1984) *Sydney: a social atlas*, Division of National Mapping, Canberra

Howard E (1902) *Garden cities of to-morrow*, Faber and Faber, 1965 Edition, London, pp. 16

Howard E (1911) 'Town planning *ab initio*', *Transactions of the Town Planning Conference*, October, 1910, Royal Institute of British Architects

Howe A (1980) *Towards an aging Australia*, University of Queensland Press, St Lucia, Brisbane

Huber R (1974) *From pasta to pavlova*, University of Queensland Press, St Lucia, Brisbane

Hymer S (1975) 'The multinational corporations and the law of uneven development', in Radice H ed. *International firms and modern imperialism*, Penguin Books, Harmondsworth, pp. 37–62

Inskip G C (1901) 'The federal city: a few suggestions', *Congress on the Federal Capital*, 44

Isserman A M (1984) 'Projection, forecast and plan. On the future of population forecasting', *American Planning Association Journal*, pp. 208–221

Jackson P and Smith S J (1984) *Exploring social geography*, Allen and Unwin, London

Jacobs J (1961) *The death and life of great American cities*, Random House, New York

Janelle D G and Millward H A (1976) 'Locational conflict patterns and urban ecological structure', *Tijdschrift voor Economische en Sociale Geografie*, 67, pp 102–13

Jeans D N (1965) 'Town planning in New South Wales 1829–1842', *Australian Planning Institute Journal*, 3, pp. 191–6

Jevons W S (1858) 'Remarks upon the social map of Sydney', unpublished ms., Mitchell Library, Sydney

John Paterson Urban Systems (1974) *Melbourne metropolitan residential land study*, Urban Development Institute of Australia, Victorian Division, Melbourne

Johnson L (1983) 'Bracketing lifeworlds: Husserlian phenomenology as geographic method', *Australian Geographical Studies*, 21, pp. 102–8

Johnston J (1975) 'Participation in local government : Leichhardt 1971–1974', in Lucy R ed. *The pieces of politics*, 2nd edition, Macmillan Press, Melbourne, pp. 230–57

Johnston M and Rose A J (1977) 'Attitudes towards an inner-city environment', *Australian Geographer*, 13, pp. 394–400

Johnston R J (1966) 'The location of high status residential areas', *Geografiska Annaler*, 48B, pp. 23–35

Johnston R J (1971) *Urban residential patterns*, Bell, London

Johnston R J (1973a) 'Social area change in Melbourne 1961–66: A sample exploration', *Australian Geographical Studies*, 11, pp. 79–98

Johnston R J (1973b) 'Neighbourhood patterns within urban areas', in Johnston R J ed. *Urbanisation in New Zealand*, Reed Education, Wellington, pp. 204–27

Johnston R J (1974) 'Geography and the social sciences', *Geographical Education*, 2, pp. 159–68

Johnston R J (1979a) *Geography and geographers: Anglo-American human geography since 1945*, Arnold, London

Johnston R J (1979b) 'On the characterisation of urban social areas', *Tijdschrift voor Economische en Sociale Geografie*, 70, pp. 232–8

Johnston R J (1982) *Geography and the state: an essay on political geography*, 1st edition, Macmillan, London

Johnston R J (1983) *Geography and Geographers: Anglo-American human geography since 1945*, 2nd edition, Arnold, London

Johnston R J and Semple R K (1983) *Classification using information statistics*, Catmog 37, Geo Books, Norwich

Jones B (1982) *Sleeper awake: technology and the future of work*, Penguin, Melbourne

Jones E and Stilwell F (1983) 'When is an urban problem not an urban problems?', in Williams P ed. *Social Process and the City*, Urban Studies Year Book, 1, Allen and Unwin, Sydney, pp. 10–31

Jones F L (1962) The Italian population of Carlton, unpublished PhD thesis in Demography, Australian National University

Jones F L (1969) *Dimensions of urban social structure*, Australian National University Press, Canberra

Jones F L (1970) *The Aboriginal population of Australia*, Australian National University Press, Canberra

Jones K and Kirby A (1982) 'Provision and well-being: an agenda for public resources research', *Environment and Planning A*, 14, pp. 297–310

Jones R (1962) 'Segregation in urban residential districts: examples and research problems', *Proceedings IGU symposium in urban geography Lund 1960, Lund studies in geography B*, 24, pp. 433–47

Kain J F (1968) 'Housing segregation, negro employment and metropolitan decentralisation', *Quarterly Journal of Economics*, 82, pp. 175–97

Keenan D R (1979) *Tramways of Sydney*, Transit Press, Sydney

Keig G (1984) *An atlas of mortality for South Australia 1969–1978*, Division of Water and Land Resources, CSIRO, Canberra

Kelly M (1978a) *Paddock full of houses: Paddington 1840–1890*, Doak Press, Sydney

Kelly M (1978b) 'Picturesque and pestilential: the Sydney slum observed, 1860–1900', in Kelly M ed. *Nineteenth-century Sydney: essays in urban history*, Sydney University Press, Sydney, pp. 66–80

Kelly M (1978c) 'Eight acres: estate subdivision and the building process, Paddington, 1875–1890', in McCarty J W and Schedvine C B eds *Australian Capital Cities*, Sydney University Press, Sydney, pp. 48–61

Kemeny J (1977) 'A political sociology of home ownership in Australia', *Australian and New Zealand Journal of Sociology*, 13, pp. 47–52

Kemeny J (1978) 'Home ownership and finance capital', *Journal of Australian Political Economy*, 3, pp. 89–97

Kemeny J (1980) 'Home ownership and privatization' *International Journal of Urban and Regional Research*, 4, pp. 372–88

Kemeny J (1981) *The myth of home ownership*, Routledge and Kegan Paul, London

Kendig H (1979) *New life for old suburbs*, Allen and Unwin, Sydney

Kilmartin L and Thornes D C (1978) *Cities unlimited*, Allen and Unwin, Sydney

King P E (1979) 'Problems of spatial analysis in geographical epidemiology', *Social Science and Medicine*, 130, pp. 249–52

Kirby A (1982) *The politics of location: an introduction*, Methuen, London

Kirby D S (1983) *Warringah transport corridor inquiry report*, Sydney

Knibbs G H (1961) 'The theory of city design', *Journal and Proceedings of the Royal*

Society of New South Wales, 35, pp. 62–112

Lambert J, Paris C and Blackaby B (1978) *Housing policy and the state*, Macmillan, London

Lang M (1982) *Gentrification amid urban decline*, Ballinger Publishing Co., Cambridge, Mass.

Langton M (1981) 'Urbanizing aborigines: the social scientists' great deception', *Social Alternatives*, 2, pp. 16–22

Larcombe F A (1978) *The advancement of local government in New South Wales: 1906 to the present*, Sydney University Press, Sydney

Larcombe F A (1979) *Change and challenge, a history of the Municipality of Canterbury NSW*, Canterbury Municipal Council, Sydney

Lash T and Sigal H (1976) *State of the child: New York*, Foundation for Child Development, New York

Lawson R (1973) *Brisbane in the 1890s: a study of an Australian urban society*, United Queensland Press, Brisbane

Lawton R and Pooley C G (1976) *The social geography of Merseyside in the nineteenth century*, Social Science Research Council, London

Leichhardt Municipal Council (1983) *Low income housing evaluation study*, draft proposal

Linge G J R (1979) 'Australian manufacturing in recession: A review of the spatial implications', *Environment and Planning, A*, 11, pp. 1405–1430

Linge G and McKay J eds (1981) *Structural change in Australia: some spatial and organisation responses*, publication HG/15, Department of Human Geography, Australian National University Press, Canberra

Little A and Mabey C (1972) 'An index for the description of educational priority areas', in Shonfield A and Shaw S eds *Social indicators and social policy*, Heinemann, London

Logan M I, Maher C A, McKay J and Humphreys J S (1975) *Urban and regional Australia: an analysis and policy issues*, Sorrett, Melbourne

Logan M, Whitelaw J and McKay J (1981) *Urbanization: the Australian experience*, Shillington House, Melbourne

Logan W S (1982a) 'Gentrification in inner Melbourne: problems of analysis', *Australian Geographical Studies*, 20, pp. 65–95

Logan W S (1982b) 'The future shape of Melbourne', in Cox K R and Johnston R J eds *Conflict, politics and the urban scene*, Longman, London Oxford, pp. 146–69

Luffman C B (1901) 'The agricultural, horticultural and sylvan features of a federal capital', *Congress on the Federal Capital*, Melbourne

Lyman S M and Scott M B (1967) 'Territoriality: a neglected sociological dimension', *Social Forces*, 15, pp. 236–49

McCandless B and Evans E (1973) *Children and youth: psychosocial development*, Dryden Press. Hillsdale

McCarrey L E [Chairman] (1968) *Land taxation and land prices in Western Australia*, report of the committee appointed by the premier, Perth

McCarty J W and Schedvin C B (1978) *Australian capital cities*, Sydney University Press, Sydney

McCoy A W (1980) *Drug traffic*, Harper and Row, Sydney

McDonnell G (1982) *Western Sydney and regional diversification: decentralisation and autonomy*, Planning Research Centre, University of Sydney, Occasional Paper 10

McDougall G (1982) 'Theory and practice: a critique of the political economy approach to planning', in Healey P, McDougall G and Thomas M J eds *Planning theory: prospects for the 1980s*, Pergamon, Oxford, pp. 258–71

McGrath (1972) A statement in the *Second seminar on the price of land*, Australian Institute of Urban Studies, Canberra

McNeill A (1980) 'Transport users and energy implications', in Archer R W ed. *Planning for urban consolidation*, Planning Research Centre, University of Sydney, Sydney, pp. 28–36

Maher C (1982) *Australian cities in transition*, Shillington House, Melbourne

Maher C, O'Connor K and Logan M (1981) 'Employment opportunities', in Troy P N ed. *Equity in the city*, Allen and Unwin, Sydney, pp. 123–44

Manning I (1976) 'The geographic distribution of poverty in Australia, *Australian Geographical Studies*, 14, pp. 133–47

Maritime Services Board (1971) *Birth of a port: Botany Bay development stage I*, Sydney

Marjoribanks K (1979) *Ethnic families and children's achievements*, Allen and Unwin, Sydney

Masser I (1980) 'The limits to planning', *Town Planning Review*, 51, pp. 39–49

Matiwijiw P and Rose A J (1979) 'Caravans or Caravanseri? the establishment of immigrant ethnic groups in urban areas', paper presented to Manchester meeting, Institute of British Geographers

Maunsell and Partners Pty Ltd (1975) *Environmental impact statement*, report on the proposed Botany Bay container terminal for the Australian National Line, Sydney

Mayer H (1954) 'Some conceptions of the Australian party system 1910–1950', *Historical Studies*, 7, pp. 254–60

Mayne A J C (1981) 'Commuter travel and class mobility in Sydney, 1850–88', *Australian Economic History Review*, 21, pp. 53–65

Miller R and Siry J (1980) 'The emerging suburb: West Philadelphia 1850–1880', *Pennsylvania History*, 46, pp. 99–146

Moore W E (1963) *Social change*, Prentice-Hall, Englewood Cliffs

Morison I (1980) 'Urban consolidation and energy use', in Archer R W ed. *Planning for urban consolidation*, Planning Research Centre, University of Sydney, Sydney, pp. 19–27

Morone C R (1976) Botany Bay port development: an analysis of reaction to a proposed major development, unpublished BA Honours thesis, School of Earth Sciences, Macquarie University

Morris J (1981) 'Urban public transport', in Troy P N ed. *Equity in the city*, Allen and Unwin, Sydney, pp. 21–49

Morrison W J (1888) *Aldine centennial history of New South Wales*, 2

Moses L and Williamson H F (1964) 'The location of economic activity in cities', *The American Economic Review*, 57, pp. 211–222

Mumford L (1961) *The city in history: its origins, its transformations and its prospects*, Penguin, Harmondsworth, pp. 480–86

Mundey J (1981) *Green bans and beyond*, Angus and Robertson, Sydney

Myers G C and Manton K G (1977) 'The structure of urban mortality, a methodological study of Hanover, Germany, part II', *International Journal of Epidemiology*, 6, pp. 213–23

National Population Inquiry (1975) *Australia's population and the future*, Australian Government Publishing Service, Canberra

Neilson Associates (1982) Immigration and housing demand in New South Wales and Sydney, study prepared for the Australian Population and Immigration Research Program, unpublished paper

Nelson H (1980) 'The politics of decontrol in New South Wales', in Albon R ed. *Rent control: costs and consequences*, Centre for Independent Studies, Sydney, pp. 83–102

Neutze G M (1977) *Urban development in Australia*, Allen and Unwin, Sydney

New South Wales Department of Environment and Planning (1983) *Dual occupancy: how it works*, Sydney

New South Wales Department of Environment and Planning (1983) *Sydney region population estimates for local government areas 1981–2001*, Sydney

New South Wales Department of Environment and Planning (1984) Urban consolidation policy: a position paper, unpublished paper

New South Wales Department of Environment and Planning (1984) *Planning issues in the Sydney region: population*, Sydney

New South Wales Department of Health (1984) *Trends in mortality New South Wales 1975–1977 to 1980–1982*, States Health Publication 105, pp. 84–106

New South Wales Electoral Office (1894) *Electoral Rolls*, Canterbury Electorate

New South Wales Electoral Office (1899) *1899–1900 New South Wales Electoral Rolls*

New South Wales Planning and Environment Commission (1975) *Gosford–Wyong structure plan*, Sydney

New South Wales Planning and Environment Commission (1980) *Review of the Sydney region outline plan*, Sydney

New South Wales Population Projections Group (1982) *Interim population projections for New South Wales 1981–2001*, from a report prepared by the New South Wales Department of Environment and Planning

New South Wales Statistician's Office (1903–4) *Census of New South Wales, 1901*, Government Printery, Sydney

Newton P W and Johnston R J (1976) 'Residential area characteristics and residential area homogeneity: further thoughts on extensions to the factorial ecology method', *Environment and Planning A*, 8, pp. 543–52

Newton P W and Johnston R J (1981) 'Melbourne', in Pacione M ed. *Urban problems and planning in the developed world*, Croom Helm, London, pp. 71–119

Nittim Z (1980) 'The coalition of resident action groups', in Roe J ed. *Twentieth century Sydney: studies in urban and social history*, Hale and Iremonger, Sydney, pp. 231–47

Onokerhoraye A G (1977) 'The spatial pattern of residential districts in Benin, Nigeria', *Urban Studies*, 14, pp. 291–302

Openshaw S and Taylor P J (1981) 'The modifiable areal unit problem', in Wrigley N and Bennett R J *Quantitative geography: a British view*, Routledge and Kegan Paul, pp. 60–69

Orchard L (1982) 'Has the homework been done?', in Sandercock L ed. *Urban consolidation: the equity issue*, Centre for Environmental and Urban Studies, Macquarie University, Sydney, pp. 51–63

Pahl R E (1968) 'The rural-urban continuum' in Pahl R E ed. *Readings in urban sociology*, Pergamon Press, Oxford, pp. 263–305

Pahl R E (1970) *Whose city? And further essays on urban society*, Longman, London

Pahl R E (1973) *Patterns of urban life*, Longman, London

Painter R (1980) *Glebe project*, Department of Housing and Construction, Australian Government Publishing Service, Canberra

Park R E (1926) 'The urban community as a spatial pattern and a moral order', reprinted in Peach C ed. 1975 *Urban social segregation*, Longman, London, pp. 21–31

Parkin A (1982) *Governing in cities: the Australian experience in perspective*, Macmillan, Melbourne

Parkin F (1979) *Marxism and class theory: a bourgeois critique*, Tavistock, London

Paterson J (1974) *Melbourne metropolitan residential land study*, report for the Urban Development Institute of Australia (Victoria), John Paterson Urban Systems, Melbourne

Paterson J (1975) 'Social and economic implications of housing and planning standards', in *Priorities review staff report*, office of the prime minister, Canberra, pp. 373–434

Paterson J (1980) 'Urban consolidation: lovelier the second time round?', in Archer R W ed. *Planning for urban consolidation*, Planning Research Centre, University of Sydney, Sydney, pp. 106–12

Paterson J (1981) 'Major planning issues' in *Proceedings Sixth Conference*, Local Government Planners Association of New South Wales, Sydney, pp. 41–9

Peach C (1975) 'The spatial analysis of ethnicity and class', in Peach C ed. *Urban social segregation*, Longman, London, pp. 1–17

Peach C (1981) 'Conflicting interpretations of segregation', in Jackson P and Smith S J eds *Social interaction and ethnic segregation*, Academic Press, London, pp. 19–33

Plague Register (1902) *Register of cases of bubonic plague 1900–1908*, Archives Office of New South Wales, Sydney

Plowden Report (1967) *Children and their primary schools*, report to the Central Advisory Board for Education, HMSO, London

Poland J and Barnes R (1979) 'Plague', in Stoenner H, Kaplan W and Torten M, *CRC Handbook series in zoonoses*, A(1), CRC Press, Florida

Pooley C G (1982) 'Choice and constraint in the nineteenth-century city: a basis for residential differentiation', in Johnson J H and Pooley C G eds *The structure of nineteenth century cities*, Croom Helm, London, pp. 199–233

Poulsen M P (1982) 'Retail development: competition versus governmental control', in Cardew R V eds *Why cities change*, Allen and Unwin, Sydney, pp. 165–80

Poulsen M and Spearritt P (1981) *Sydeny: a social and political atlas*, Allen and Unwin, Sydney

Poverty Report (1975) *Poverty in Australia*, first main report of the Commission of Inquiry into Poverty, 1–2, Australian Government Publishing Service, Canberra

Powell J M (1978) *Mirrors of the new world: images and image makers in the settlement process*, Australian National University Press, Canberra

Power J M (1969) 'The new politics of the old suburbs', *Quadrant*, 13, pp. 60–65

Price C A (1959) 'Immigration and group settlement', in Borrie W D ed. *The cultural integration of immigrants*, UNESCO, Paris, 259–73

Priorities Review Staff (1975) *Report on housing*, Australian Government Publishing Service, Canberra

Reid H (1980) 'Local government regulation of housing development' in Archer R W ed. *Planning for urban consolidation*, Planning Research Centre, University of Sydney, Sydney, pp. 37–46

Richardson and Wrench Contract Books, (1867–1890), 10–40 (Old Firm), 1–2 (New Firm), Mitchell Library, Sydney

Richmond A H (1969) 'The sociology of immigration in industrial and post-industrial society', in Jackson J A ed. *Migration*, Cambridge University Press, Cambridge, pp. 238–81

Rimmer P J and Black J A (1982) 'Land use transport changes and global restructuring in Sydney since the 1970s: the container issue', in Cardew R V et al. eds *Why cities change*, Allen and Unwin, Sydney, pp. 223–46

Roberts A M (1970) The development of the suburb of Annandale, 1876–1899: from 'model farm' to 'model suburb', unpublished BA Honours thesis in History, University of Sydney

Roberts A M (1978) City improvement in Sydney: public policy 1880–1900, unpublished PhD thesis, University of Sydney

Robinson R and Kambesis A (1977) 'Ethnic residence: aspects of spatial adjustment and residential choice of Greeks in urban Illawarra', in Robinson R ed. *Urban Illawarra*, Sorrett, Melbourne, pp. 267–82

 Roddewig R J (1978) *Green bans: the birth of Australian environmental politics*, Hale and Iremonger, Sydney

Roseth J (1980) 'Urban consolidation possibilities in Sydney', in Archer R W ed. *Planning for urban consolidation*, Planning Research Centre, University of Sydney, Sydney, pp. 1–6

 Ross R and Trachte K (1983) 'Global cities and global classes: the peripheralisation of labor in New York city', *Review*, 6, pp. 393–431

Rowland D T (1977) 'Theories of urbanization in Australia', *Geographical Reivew*, 67, pp. 161–76

Rowland D T (1979) *Internal migration in Australia*, Census monograph 1, Australian Government Publishing Service, Canberra

Rowland D T (1980) 'Sixty-five not out: towards a demography of aging in Australia', Australian Institute of Public Affairs, Sydney

Rowley C (1972) *Outcasts in white Australia*, Penguin Books, Melbourne

Rowley C (1981) 'Rural aboriginal households in New South Wales', mimeo, Australian National University

Rowley C (1982) *Equality by instalments: the aboriginal householder in rural New South Wales 1965 and 1980*, Australian Institute of Aboriginal Studies, Canberra

Rowley C (1984) *Aboriginal households survey, Sydney, 1984*, Australian Institute of Aboriginal Studies, Canberra

Runciman W G (1967) 'The three dimensions of social inequality', in Betaille

A ed. *Social inequality*, Penguin Books, Harmondsworth, pp. 45–63

Russell R (1885) in Evidence, *Royal commission on land titles and surveys*, Victoria Parliamentary Papers, 2, p. 49

Sandercock L (1983) 'Urban development on the cheap', *Plan, Journal of the Local Government Planners' Association of NSW*, 2, pp. 14–17

Sandercock L and Berry M eds (1983) *Urban political economy: the Australian case*, Allen and Unwin, Sydney

Sanders W (1984) 'Sectoral politics and urban development: the case of Port Botany', in Williams P ed. *Conflict and development*, Urban Studies Yearbook, 2, Allen and Unwin, Sydney, 135–53

Saunders P (1980) *Urban politics*, Penguin, Harmondsworth

Saunders P (1981) *Social theory and the urban question*, Hutchinson, London

Schmid A A (1968) *Converting land from rural to urban uses*, Johns Hopkins Press, Baltimore

Searle G (1971) *The rush to be rich: a history of the colony of Victoria, 1883–1889*, Melbourne University Press, Melbourne

Searle G (1984) Geographies of employment in Sydney in the year 2015, paper presented to Section 21 (Geographical Sciences), 1984 ANZAAS Congress, Canberra

Self P (1980) 'Whatever happened to regional planning?', *Town and Country Planning*, July/August, p. 209

Self P (1984) Report on the development of a metropolitan strategy for the Sydney region, unpublished report to the New South Wales Department of Environment and Planning

Semple R K and Scorrar D A (1975) 'Canadian international trade', *Canadian Geographer*, 19, pp. 135–48

Semple R K, Youngman C E and Zeller R E (1972) *Economic regionalisation and information theory: an Ohio example*, discussion paper 28, Department of Geography, Ohio State University, Columbus

Shostak A (1982) 'Seven scenarios of urban change', in Gappert G and Knight R V eds *Cities in the 21st century*, Urban Affairs Annual Reviews, 23, Sage Publications, Beverly Hills, pp. 69–93

Sinclair D A (1980) 'The resettlement of Greek immigrants in Sydney', in Burnley I H, Pryor R J and Rowland D T eds *Mobility and community change in Australia*, University of Queensland Press, St Lucia, pp. 142–150

Sjoberg G (1960) *The pre-industrial city: past and present*, The Free Press, New York

Smith D M (1977) *Human geography: a welfare approach*, Arnold, London

Smith L (1978) *The aboriginal population*, Australian National University Press, Canberra

Smith M P (1980) *The city and social theory*, Blackwell, Oxford

Smith N (1979) 'Toward a theory of gentrification: a back to the city movement by capital not people', *Journal of the American Planning Association*, 45, pp. 538–68

Smith N (1982) 'Gentrification and uneven development', *Economic Geography*, 58, pp. 139–55

Smith N (1983) Gentrification, frontier and the restructuring of urban space, unpublished paper

Soja E (1980) 'The socio-spatial dialectic', *Annals of the Association of American Geographers*, 70, pp. 207–25

Soja E, Morales R and Wolff G (1983) 'Urban restructuring: an analysis of social and spatial change in Los Angeles', *Economic Geography*, 59, 195–230

Solling M (1972) Glebe 1790–1891: A Study of patterns and processes of growth, unpublished MA Honours thesis, Department of Geography, University of Sydney

Springett J (1982) 'Land owners and urban development: the Ramsden Estate and 19th century Huddersfield', *Journal of Historical Geography*, 8, pp. 129–44

Stannage C T (1979) *The people of Perth: a social history of Western Australia's capital city*, Perth City Council, Perth

Stapleton C M (1980) 'Reformulation of the family life-cycle concept: implications for residential mobility', *Environment and Planning A*, 12, pp. 1103–18

State Planning Authority (1967) *Growth and change, prelude to a plan*, Sydney

State Planning Authority (1968) *Sydney region outline plan 1970–2000 AD: a strategy for development*, Sydney

Statistician's report on the eleventh census of New South Wales, Sydney, 1893

Stevenson T L (1979) 'Light and living conditions: mortality in nineteenth century Adelaide', *Proceedings of Tenth New Zealand Geography Conference and Forty Ninth ANZAAS Congress, Geographical Sciences*, 10

Stillwell F J and Hardwick J M (1973) 'Social inequality in Australian cities', *The Australian Quarterly*, 45, pp. 18–36

Stilwell F (1979a) 'The current economic depression and its impact on Australian cities', *Australian Quarterly*, 51, pp. 5–16

Stilwell F (1979b) 'An urban crisis', *Current Affairs Bulletin*, 56, pp. 22–31

Stilwell F (1980) *Economic crisis, cities and regions: an analysis of current urban and regional problems in Australia*, Pergamon, Sydney

Stimson R J (1970) 'European immigration settlement patterns in metropolitan Melbourne, 1947–1961', *Tijdschrift voor Economische en Sociale Geografie*, 61, 114–26

Stimson R J (1982) *The Australian city: a welfare geography*, Longman Cheshire, Melbourne

Stokes C J (1962) 'A social theory of slums', *Land Economics*, 38, 187–98

Stretton H (1970) *Ideas for Australian cities*, Georgian Press, Melbourne

Stretton H (1976) *Capitalism, socialism and the environment*, Cambridge University Press, Cambridge

Sunday Telegraph 'Strathfield: oasis in the heartland of Sydney's west', 22 August 1982

Sweetser F L (1983) *Urban residential areas in Australia*, Australian National University Press, Canberra

Sydney Morning Herald 'In Strathfield buyers tend to knock 'em down, build anew', 17 August 1983

Szelenyi I (1977) Class and beyond: further dilemmas for the new urban sociology, unpublished paper, Flinders University, Adelaide

Szelenyi I (1981) 'The relative autonomy of the state mode of production', in Dear M and Scott A J eds *Urbanization and urban planning in capitalist society*,

Methuen, London

Taylor A and McNamara A (1976) Case studies of the conversion of rural land to urban residential uses, unpublished report, Diploma in Urban Studies, Macquarie University

Taylor G A (1914) *Town planning for Australia*, Building Limited, Sydney

Taylor P J and Johnston R J (1979) *Geography of elections*, Penguin, Harmondsworth

The Cost of Housing (1978) *Report of the committee of inquiry into housing costs*, 1, Australian Government Publishing Service, Canberra

Thompson L (1982) *Australia through Italian eyes*, Oxford University Press, Melbourne

Timms D W G (1969) 'The dissimilarity between overseas-born and Australian-born in Queensland', *Sociology and Social Research*, 53, pp. 363–74

Timms D W G (1971) *The urban mosiac: towards a theory of residential segregation*, Cambridge University Press, Cambridge

Troy P N (1978) *A fair price*, Hale and Iremonger, Sydney

Troy P N ed. (1981) *Equity in the city*, Allen and Unwin, Sydney

Troy P N (1982) 'Urban consolidation: the equity issue', in Sandercock L ed. *Urban consolidation: the equity issue*, Centre for Environmental and Urban Studies, Macquarie University, Sydney, pp. 7–16

Tyler A S (1973) *Report on the price of land*, Institute of Real Estate Development, Sydney

Urry J (1981) 'Localities, regions and social class', *International Journal of Urban and Regional Research*, 5, pp. 455–74

Vance, J E (1964) *Geography and urban evolution in the San Francisco Bay area*, Institute of Environment Studies, University of California, Berkeley

Vance J E (1971) 'Land assignment in the precapitalist, capitalist and post-capitalist city', *Economic Geography*, 47, pp. 101–20

Vinson T and Homel R (1976) *Indicators of community wellbeing*, Australian Government Publishing Service, Canberra

Vipond J (1980a) 'The impact of higher unemployment in areas within Sydney', *Journal of Industrial Relations*, September, pp. 326–41

Vipond J (1980b) 'Intra-urban unemployment differentials in Sydney, 1971', *Urban Studies*, 17, pp. 131–8

Vipond J (1981) 'Changes in unemployment differentials in Sydney, 1947–76', *Australian Geographical Studies*, pp. 67–77

Vipond J (1982) *The suburban unemployed*, Centre for Applied Economic Research paper 16, University of New South Wales

Vipond J (1984) 'The intra-urban unemployment gradient: the influence of location on unemployment', *Urban Studies*, 21, pp. 377–388

Walker R (1978) 'The transformation of urban structure in the nineteenth century and the beginnings of suburbanization', in Cox K ed. *Urbanization and conflict in market societies*, Methuen Press, London, 165–212

Walker R (1982) 'A theory of suburbanization: capitalism and the construction of urban space in the United States', in Dear M and Scott A eds *Urbanization and urban planning in capitalist society*, Methuen Press, London, 383–430

Ward D (1968) 'The emergence of central immigration ghettoes in American cities: 1840–1920', *Annals, Association of American Geographers*, 58, pp. 343–59

Ward D (1975) 'Victorian cities: how modern', *Journal of Historical Geography*, 1, pp. 135–51

Ward D (1980) 'Environs and neighbours in the two nations: residential differentiation in mid-19th century Leeds', *Journal of Historical Geography*, 6, pp. 133–62

Ward R N (1969) 'The copper town', *Architecture in Australia*, 53, pp. 668–71

Waugh and Cox (1858) *Directory of Sydney and suburbs, 1855*, Sydney

Weber A F (1963) *The growth of cities in the nineteenth century: A study in statistics*, Cornell University Press, Ithaca

Whitelaw J S and Humphreys J S (1980) 'Migrant response to an unfamiliar residential environment', in Burnley I H, Pryor R J and Rowland D T eds *Mobility and community change in Australia*, University of Queensland Press, St Lucia, Brisbane, pp. 151–69

Whitlam Report (1984) *Report of the committee established by the Premier of New South Wales to report on the steps necessary to establish offshore banking activity in Australia with particular reference to Sydney*, Government Printer, Sydney

Wilmoth D (1982) 'Urban consolidation policy and social equity' in Sandercock L ed. *Urban consolidation: the equity issue*, Centre for Environmental and Urban Studies, Macquarie University

Wilmoth D (1983) Population issues and metropolitan planning in Sydney, paper presented at a seminar on Australian Population Issues, Department of Demography, Research School of Social Sciences, Australian National University Canberra

Wirth L (1938) 'Urbanism as a way of life', *American Journal of Sociology*, 44, pp. 1–24

Wise R (1859) 'Report from the Select Committee on the condition of the working classes of the metropolis', *New South Wales Parliamentary Papers*, 4

Wissink G A (1980) 'The limits to planning: a comment', *Town Planning Review*, 51, 4, pp. 409–13

Worthington J E (1973) 'Long and short term changes in land prices', *Economic Activity in Western Australia*, January, pp. 13–19

Yearwood R M (1970) 'Land subdivision and development', *American Journal of Economics and Sociology*, 29, pp. 113–26

Yoo B Hee (1978) Maltese settlement in Sydney, unpublished MA thesis, School of Geography, University of New South Wales, Sydney

Young C Y (1976) *Mortality in Australia*, commissioned monograph, National Population Inquiry, Australian Government Publishing Service, Canberra

Young C and Petty M (1980) *Unemployment among Lebanese and Turkish youth*, Australian Government Publishing Service, Canberra

Young E (1981) Socio-economic changes and the 'downzoning' of residential areas in the inner suburbs of Adelaide, 1966–76, unpublished BA Honours thesis in Geography, University of Adelaide

Zill N (1984) *American children: happy, healthy and insecure*, Doubleday, New York

Zubrzycki J (1964) *Settlers of the Latrobe Valley*, Australian National University Press, Canberra

Zukin S (1982a) 'Loft living as historic compromise in the urban core: the New

York experience', *International Journal of Urban and Regional Research*, 6, pp. 256–67

Zukin S (1982b) *Loft living: culture and capital in urban change*, Johns Hopkins University Press, Baltimore

Index